Field Guide to Family Business Research

# Field Guide to Family Business Research

*Edited by*

## Keith H. Brigham

*Professor of Entrepreneurship and Director, Tom Love Division of Entrepreneurship and Economic Development, Price College of Business, University of Oklahoma, USA*

## G. Tyge Payne

*Professor of Entrepreneurship, Stephenson Department of Entrepreneurship & Information Systems, Louisiana State University, USA*

ELGAR FIELD GUIDES

Edward **Elgar**
PUBLISHING

Cheltenham, UK • Northampton, MA, USA

Published by
Edward Elgar Publishing Limited
The Lypiatts
15 Lansdown Road
Cheltenham
Glos GL50 2JA
UK

Edward Elgar Publishing, Inc.
William Pratt House
9 Dewey Court
Northampton
Massachusetts 01060
USA

Paperback edition 2024

A catalogue record for this book
is available from the British Library

Library of Congress Control Number: 2023937413

This book is available electronically in the **Elgar**online
Business subject collection
http://dx.doi.org/10.4337/9781800884144

ISBN 978 1 80088 413 7 (cased)
ISBN 978 1 80088 414 4 (eBook)
ISBN 978 1 0353 4447 5 (paperback)

Printed and bound by CPI Group (UK) Ltd, Croydon, CR0 4YY

# Contents

# Contributors

**Triss Ashton**, Tarleton State University, USA

**Mohamed Mazen M. Batterjee**, IE University, Madrid, Spain

**Danuse Bement**, Texas A&M University, USA

**Isabel C. Botero**, University of Louisville, USA

**Keith H. Brigham**, University of Oklahoma, USA

**Jon C. Carr**, North Carolina State University, USA

**James J. Chrisman**, Mississippi State University, USA and Centre for Entrepreneurship and Family Enterprise, University of Alberta, Canada

**Guido Corbetta**, Bocconi University, Italy

**Justin B. Craig**, Bond University, Australia

**Cristina Cruz**, IE University, Madrid, Spain

**Joshua J. Daspit**, Texas State University, USA

**Sara Davis**, Mississippi State University, USA

**Alfredo De Massis**, Free University of Bozen-Bolzano, Italy and IMD and Lancaster University, UK

**Vanessa Diaz-Moriana**, University of the Balearic Islands (UIB), Majorca

**Clay Dibrell**, University of Mississippi, USA

**Tomasz A. Fediuk**, University of Louisville, USA

**Xin Gao**, Jilin University, China

**Nadine Kammerlander**, WHU – Otto Beisheim School of Management, Germany

**Franz W. Kellermanns**, University of North Carolina at Charlotte, USA and WHU – Otto Beisheim School of Management, Germany

**G. T. Lumpkin**, University of Oklahoma, USA

**Evelyn Micelotta**, University of Ottawa, Canada

**Curt B. Moore**, Oklahoma State University, USA

**Karen Nicholas**, Boise State University, USA

**G. Tyge Payne**, Louisiana State University, USA

**Ludo Peeters**, Hasselt University, Belgium

**Duygu Phillips**, Oklahoma State University, USA

**J. Kirk Ring**, Louisiana Tech University, USA

**Emanuela Rondi**, Università degli Studi di Bergamo, Italy

**Paola Rovelli**, Free University of Bozen-Bolzano, Italy

**Matthew Rutherford**, Oklahoma State University, USA

**Carlo Salvato**, Bocconi University, Italy

**Valeriano Sanchez-Famoso**, University of the Basque Country UPV/EHU, Spain

**Chelsea Sherlock**, Mississippi State University, USA

**Jeremy C. Short**, University of North Texas, USA

**Vitaliy Skorodziyevskiy**, University of Louisville, USA

**Laura Stanley**, University of North Carolina at Charlotte, USA

**Lori Tribble Trudell**, Clemson University, USA

**Alana Vandebeek**, KU Leuven, Belgium

**Wim Voordeckers**, Hasselt University, Belgium

**Theodore Waldron**, Texas Tech University, USA

**James Wetherbe**, Texas Tech University, USA

# 1. Introduction to the *Field Guide to Family Business Research*[1]

## Keith H. Brigham and G. Tyge Payne

## WHY 'FAMILY BUSINESS'?

The family and the business are two of the oldest and most influential organizational entities in the world. When combined as family-led businesses, their importance to the global economy and society is arguably unparalleled. Estimates suggest that, in the United States, family businesses account for as many as 83 million jobs, $7.7 trillion of the gross domestic product, and 87 percent of all tax-paying businesses (Pieper, Kellermanns, & Astrachan, 2021). Presumably, these numbers are representative, and more than likely under-estimated, of the overall impact of family businesses globally.

Given growing recognition of the important and widespread role that family businesses play on the global stage, there has been an exponential expansion in the family business field of study in the recent past. Not only do we see scholarly interest increasing, but also attention is expanding among practitioners, including advisors, consultants, and managers or leaders of family-led organizations. Along with this growth has come major advancements in terms of theories, perspectives, and methodologies that have helped to uncover and broaden the family business domain (Payne, 2018). With roots in entrepreneurship and small business management, but reaching out to other disciplines such as accounting, finance, and marketing, the field of family business is now a multidisciplinary one with the unique organizational unit of 'family' tying the various interests together (Holt, Pearson, Payne, & Sharma, 2018). Families, as we now understand them in the business context, impact the organizations they are involved with in an idiosyncratic, and yet simultaneously diverse, way by influencing how and in what ways business decisions are made. Indeed, family-led businesses commonly market their multi-generational lineage

---

[1] The co-editors contributed equally to the compilation of this book.

because it embodies longevity, cooperativeness, and stability, among other positive characteristics.

The purpose of this book is to help both scholars and practitioners better understand the unique aspects of conducting research in the family business domain. Ultimately, we hope to help improve the quality and quantity of family business research so that knowledge is created and better disseminated. New knowledge that is appropriately and broadly disseminated provides a foundation upon which new and better decisions can be made for businesses, which can promote economic growth and advance society. Our motivation, therefore, is basically to provide a practical guide that can be used by researchers to both produce more and better studies of family businesses (and business families), as well as clarify some of the more technical aspects of family business research for interested practitioners. Overall, we have tried to produce a volume that balances both breadth and depth in terms of topic and coverage so that interested parties—whether they are new to family business research or are long-term veterans in the field—can benefit from the content. Each chapter is presented by some of the very best scholars in the field who have made great efforts to ensure that their work is accessible, concise, and practical.

## WHY A 'FIELD GUIDE'?

Generally, the family business 'field' of study is characterized as an intersection of family and business, which are each interdependent, multifaceted, and constantly changing entities, nested one within the other. Indeed, the study of family business is commonly referred to as one of paradoxes (e.g., Sharma et al., 2012; Zahra & Sharma, 2004), which suggests contradictory yet interconnected perspectives, interests, identities, or practices. Given such interdependent complexities revolving around two already incredibly complex entities, it is easy to see how difficult understanding and studying family businesses can be.

Our interest in producing this guidebook was initially based on our collective experiences as authors, instructors, reviewers, and journal editors. Over the past decade, and more, we have noticed key challenges associated with the complexity of the family business field of study that have limited its expansion and development as a standalone and legitimate discipline. Indeed, despite incredible growth in the number of studies examining family businesses— and, by association, other family-based organizations (e.g., family offices, family-based foundations)—the quality is still often perceived to be lagging other, more established, business domains. We wanted to help change this perspective by providing some answers to fundamental questions regarding research best practices. For without high-quality research being published in high-quality outlets, any new knowledge that is created fails to be recognized and appropriately utilized in both academic- and practitioner-oriented circles. In other words, we are assuming the primary objective of getting published in prestigious journals is to maximize visibility and impact on both the researchers and practitioners of the world, including consultants, advisors, managers, and family business owners. Our desire with this edited book, therefore, is to help overcome some of the ongoing and innate hurdles associated with researching family business.

From both of our experiences, there are three common issues or problems that lead to a paper being rejected at top journals. First, many papers get rejected because they fail to demonstrate a clear and unique contribution to the extant literature. In effect, the reader (often starting with journal editors and reviewers) is unable to perceive what is novel and interesting about the study relative to previous work in the field. For family business research, and due to the interdependent nature of the field, this can be particularly challenging as studies need to make contributions not only to the specific family business context but to the broader field of business as well. Thus, it is generally not sufficient to argue a unique contribution by claiming that a certain phenomenon has not been studied specifically in family businesses. Rather, the reason for studying a phenomenon in family business must often have broader theoretical implications for all types of businesses. Second, reviewers and editors often argue that a research paper fails to properly frame and align the theory and hypotheses. While this problem is often related to the first one mentioned above, it generally has less to do with the research question or topic and more to do with the way the arguments are positioned and the stream of literature within which the study is embedded. For family business research, this challenge is exacerbated by the field's lack of unique and field-specific theories; family business researchers typically draw upon theories from other domains to address family business research questions. As such, it is often difficult to draw clear ties between the theoretical arguments and the more family business-oriented hypotheses being presented.

Finally, the third problem we have commonly noted throughout the years is related to the methodological and empirical approach to a study. Scholars must always be careful to consider the appropriateness of their methodological and empirical approaches, exercising good judgement with regard to the theory, or theories, being evoked and the context (Bettis, Gambardella, Helfat, & Mitchell, 2014; Evert, Martin, McLeod, & Payne, 2016). In particular, issues of measurement and construct validity are often raised by editors and reviewers as serious concerns (e.g., Brigham & Payne, 2019; Pearson & Lumpkin, 2011); this is particularly true for outcomes, which include many nonfinancial constructs that are unique to the family business domain (Yu, Lumpkin, Sorenson, & Brigham, 2012).

## WHY SHOULD YOU READ THIS BOOK?

The *Field Guide to Family Business Research* is built around the core idea of providing a relatively straightforward, concise, and valuable guidebook that addresses the unique challenges associated with conducting high-quality family business research. There are 17 chapters in total, including this short introduction, that cover a wide range of topics. Each topic is written by leading family business scholars, representing many different universities and countries, with the specific goal of providing practical guidance for overcoming the challenges related to conducting and publishing family business research.

The book is laid out in three parts. While there is obviously overlap among the parts, as they are all focused on conducting and publishing high-quality research, each has a broader theme. Part I: General Challenges and Solutions (Chapters 2–7) addresses some of the most common obstacles to publication we often see cited by reviewers for recommending the rejection of a family business research paper. Chapters in this part of the book deal with developing a strong contribution (Chapter 2), incorporating a theoretical perspective (Chapter 3), incorporating implications for practice (Chapter 4), and conducting a thorough and relevant literature review (Chapter 7). In addition, the family business-specific issues of heterogeneity (Chapter 5) and incorporating innovation (Chapter 6) are key components of this first part of the book.

Part II: Qualitative Challenges and Solutions (Chapters 8–11) focuses on approaches to collecting and analyzing non-numerical data to better understand important concepts, relationships, events, and factors associated with family businesses and the people within them. In an effort to gather in-depth insights into problems or generate new ideas or theories about family businesses, we have seen a growing number of qualitative studies over the years. Chapters in this part cover 'best practices' and effectively highlight the most important challenges in this research area. Authors present insights and strategies for both single-case (Chapter 8) and multi-case (Chapter 9) approaches to researching family businesses. Furthermore, a comprehensive look at qualitative approaches (Chapter 10) and the use of computer-aided text analysis (Chapter 11) are offered for the reader.

Finally, Part III: Quantitative Challenges and Solutions (Chapters 12–17) offers strategies for addressing emerging methodological approaches and common issues in numerically-based family business research. These include experimental designs (Chapter 12), measurement of SEW (Chapter 13), non-response bias (Chapter 14), latent profile analysis (Chapter 15), social network analysis (Chapter 16), and endogeneity (Chapter 17).

While many of the chapters that comprise the book deal with topics that are applicable to all social science research, the authors have endeavored to be specific in linking their work to the unique domain and nuances of family business. Depending on the reader's background, goals, and areas of interest, some of the chapters will be more relevant and beneficial than others. However, we feel confident that the body of knowledge included in the *Field Guide to Family Business Research* offers a wealth of expertise and practical information that will be of great benefit to anyone (ranging from a novice to expert) conducting research in Family Business. We wish you the best of luck with your future studies!

## REFERENCES

Bettis, R., Gambardella, A., Helfat, C., & Mitchell, W. (2014). Quantitative Empirical Analysis in Strategic Management. *Strategic Management Journal*, 35, 949–953.

Brigham, K. H., & Payne, G. T. (2019). Socioemotional Wealth (SEW): Questions on Construct Validity. *Family Business Review*, 32(4), 326–329.

Evert, R. E., Martin, J. A., McLeod, M. S., & Payne, G. T. (2016). Empirics in Family Business Research: Progress, Challenges, and the Path Ahead. *Family Business Review*, 29(1), 17–43.

Holt, D. T., Pearson, A. W., Payne, G. T., & Sharma, P. (2018). Family Business Research as a Boundary-spanning Platform. *Family Business Review*, 31(1), 14–31.

Payne, G. T. (2018). Reflections on Family Business Research: Considering Domains and Theory. *Family Business Review*, 31(2), 167–175.

Pearson, A. W., & Lumpkin, G. T. (2011). Measurement in Family Business Research: How do we Measure Up? *Family Business Review*, 24(4), 287–291.

Pieper, T. M., Kellermanns, F. W., & Astrachan, J. H. (2021). Update 2021: Family Businesses' Contribution to the US Economy. *Family Enterprise USA*, 704, 1–29.

Sharma, P., Chrisman, J. J., & Gersick, K. E. (2012). 25 Years of Family Business Review: Reflections on the Past and Perspectives for the Future. *Family Business Review*, 25(1), 5–15.

Yu, A., Lumpkin, G. T., Sorenson, R. L., & Brigham, K. H. (2012). The Landscape of Family Business Outcomes: A Summary and Numerical Taxonomy of Dependent Variables. *Family Business Review*, 25(1), 33–57.

Zahra, S. A., & Sharma, P. (2004). Family Business Research: A Strategic Reflection. *Family Business Review*, 17(4), 331–346.

# PART I

# General challenges and solutions

# 2. Planning your contribution and paths to publication in family business research

**Evelyn Micelotta**

## INTRODUCTION

This chapter offers a practical guide to scholars who ask themselves the following question: how to convince editors and reviewers that my research paper offers a meaningful *theoretical contribution*? Every management journal requires a theoretical contribution for a manuscript to be accepted for publication, so this expectation is very clear from the start of the submission process.[1] And yet, editorial response letters often highlight that this expectation is not fully met. Even the most experienced researchers receive a rejection decision oftentimes and still get high-risk R&Rs! The editorial nudge to authors is often to explain, clarify, and deepen the reasons why the submitted paper contributes to extending current knowledge and to specify what exactly a study adds to the extant literature.

Some authors may be puzzled by editorial comments. They probably think that their paper explains very well what the study does and why it advances knowledge. From their vantage point, they do position the manuscript in the relevant body of literature, explain the motivation for the study (the gap or the puzzle addressed), and extensively discuss methods and findings. In the Introduction and Discussion sections, they clearly state that the study is valuable because 'there is very little research on topic X' (which the study examines) or because 'our findings show X' (the findings are repeated). This is where the problem often lies. Those arguments, generally, do not meet the bar for what editors and reviewers expect a substantive theoretical contribution to be. Contributing to theory means 'to challenge and extend existing knowl-

---

[1]   Family Business Research, although multidisciplinary, has been largely rooted within the Management domain. Hence, I take this into account when discussing expectations of researchers by editors, reviewers, and readers.

edge, not simply to rewrite it' (Whetten, 1989, p. 491). Suggesting that the undertaking of a study is in itself a contribution is an argument that typically leaves editors and reviewers unimpressed. There is often a good reason for the absence or limited research on a certain topic or question. Perhaps the topic has been examined to exhaustion or maybe that research question is not that relevant, after all. Similarly, rewording the findings of a study in more abstract language without telling how these findings extend, enrich, or challenge what we already know is a common misstep. Editors, reviewers, and readers expect a very clear explanation for how and why a research paper is *original* and *useful* (Corley & Gioia, 2011) and to explicitly show the *theoretical feedback loop*. Feeding back to the literature means 'to learn something new about the theory itself as a result of working with it under different conditions. That is, new applications should improve the tool, not merely reaffirm its utility' (Whetten, 1989, p. 493). Several editorials in business journals discuss how to make a theoretical contribution (e.g., Whetten, 1989; Reay & Whetten, 2011; Corley & Gioia, 2011). I encourage researchers to read and study these editorials. They offer clear explanations and useful suggestions to understand how to engage in theory development.

In this chapter, I offer a complementary perspective. Indeed, there may be another reason why making a contribution is confusing for family business scholars. Editors and reviewers in different outlets may just have different expectations about what they want to see. Family business scholars who are planning their research pipeline need to think about *how* to make a contribution to the family business field, but also *to what* conversation (and outlet) their research offers a meaningful contribution. The remainder of the chapter is organized as follows. In the first section, I introduce a matrix framework *to plan your research contribution* by understanding how different papers can be positioned based on your contextual orientation and your target audience. I identify four types of family business papers: *Embedded, Challenger, Integrative*, and *Generalized*. I then draw on examples from published papers to illustrate *what is the contribution* in each of these quadrants.

## PLANNING YOUR CONTRIBUTION: UNDERSTANDING YOUR CONTEXTUAL ORIENTATION AND TARGET AUDIENCE

What does it mean to make a theoretical contribution? It means to add substantial (theoretical) value to a body of existing knowledge. This is seemingly straightforward. For a family business researcher, however, follow-up questions can be relatively trickier to answer. Is it a sufficient contribution to shed new light on a phenomenon that is idiosyncratic in family business organizations (e.g., succession)? Should the paper draw on a theoretical construct that is unique to family firms (e.g., socioemotional wealth)? Can we contribute by showing how the predictions of a general management theory (e.g., behavioral theory of the firm) are modified or challenged in family firms (i.e., by considering the effect of family ownership)? The answer to these questions is: *it depends*. All these ideas have the potential to contribute to the literature, but not all of them are equally acceptable and meet the expectations of reviewers and editors. It depends on the outlet, so the key question is: What kind of publication outlets are friendly and sympathetic to those contributions? Most of this knowledge (especially for Ph.D. students and younger scholars) remains tacit. My goal is to make some of this knowledge explicit.

First, let's take a step back and ask ourselves why we even have this problem. Family business research emerged as a distinctive area of business that has developed in specialized publication outlets (e.g., *Family Business Review* (FBR), *Journal of Family Business Strategy* (JFBS), and *Journal of Family Business Management* (JFBM)). Changes have been brought by two important developments in family business research. First, research focused on family business firms has grown substantially in the past few years, not only in size (i.e., number of published papers) but also in legitimacy and academic status (Bird et al., 2002; Sharma, 2004; Xi et al., 2015; Rovelli et al., 2021). The important implication for scholars with an interest in understanding family firms and their strategies and behaviors is that they can now target a broader array of publication outlets. In addition to specialist journals, there are now generalist business journals interested in publishing theory and insights about family businesses (e.g., *Entrepreneurship Theory and Practice* (ETP), *Academy of Management Journal* (AMJ), *Academy of Management Review* (AMR), *Journal of Management Studies* (JMS), *Organization Studies* (OS), and so on). Studies published in these journals nicely connect family business research with organization theories (Chirico et al., 2021; Salvato et al., 2019) or strategic management (Sasaki et al., 2020). Importantly, generalist journals are very demanding in terms of theoretical contribution to management knowledge (not just family business knowledge). It is therefore important for authors to figure out whether and how the family business component of a study generates knowledge that meets the expectations of those outlets.

Second, scholars from various management fields and theoretical domains have become increasingly interested in family firms as a distinctive type of organization. Not dissimilarly from research at the intersection of organization theory and healthcare organizations (Reay et al., 2021) or professional occupations and organizations (Muzio et al., 2019), there is an increasing appetite for using management lenses to understand family businesses' strategies and behaviors. For example, leveraging family science (Jaskiewicz et al., 2017), adopting an history-informed lens (Suddaby et al., 2020) or digging into the psychological foundations of family business behaviors (De Massis & Foss,

2018) to shed light on the intricate dynamics between family and business. Cross-pollination and integration efforts between fields of study can be very fruitful. What is critical to understand is that discipline-based journals in family business research have strong expectations that published papers will deepen and enrich knowledge in the family business domain. Just overlaying a theoretical framework (e.g., agency theory or institutional theory) on top of an empirical family business setting is not sufficient.

After this brief excursus, let's go back to how these questions can be addressed. A good starting point is to look at two dimensions that define the positioning of a paper into the literature, and therefore impact its potential contribution: (1) the *contextual orientation* of the researcher and (2) the *target audience* to which the research is intended. I present the two dimensions, before considering how their intersection reveals four different types of papers in the family business domain (Figure 2.1).

*Contextual Orientation*: The idea of contextual orientation was developed by Blair and Hunt (1986) to 'get inside the head of management research-ers' (p. 147) and appreciate differences in their 'cognitive styles' (p. 147). Contextual orientation is defined as 'the basic way in which a management researcher thinks about the phenomenon he or she is studying' (p. 148). Seen as a continuum, contextual orientation spans between a 'context-free' orientation and a 'context-specific' orientation. A *context-free orientation* (or theory-specific orientation) is the approach of a researcher whose research interest primarily lies in a theoretical perspective (e.g., institutional theory or agency theory). The research focus is primarily on the key constructs and variables underpinning the theory (e.g., legitimacy in the case of institutional theory, agency costs in the case of agency theory). A contribution is made by advancing the theory through conceptual and empirical research. Relatively less emphasis is placed on the context or setting used to empirically test the predictions of the theory (quantitative research) or to examine its underpinning processes or mechanisms (qualitative research). From the vantage point of the researcher, it is not as relevant whether empirical studies are conducted in a non-profit organization or a large conglomerate, in hospitals or accounting firms. The researcher may develop in-depth knowledge about these settings to collect and interpret data. However, the primary contribution is to the theory itself.

A *context-specific orientation* is the approach of a researcher whose interest lies in developing in-depth knowledge about a specific type of organization, such as family businesses, healthcare firms, professional service firms, or non-profits. The goal of the researcher is to examine a unique type of organ-ization and understand its specific challenges and behaviors. There is less emphasis on advancing one specific theoretical framework, because the array of phenomena involving these organizations is going to be wide and multifaceted. Hence, context-specific research is often theory-agnostic at its inception: a researcher may choose from several theoretical lenses to find the one that is the most useful to address the specific research question at hand. Insights from a specific type of organization are likely to tackle problems that managers care about and which are more easily translatable into 'best practices' that consultants working in organizations can implement. Not surprisingly, this 'practitioner' approach was common in the early stage of family business research when the primary interest was to understand the unique features and challenges of this type of organization (Craig & Lumpkin, Chapter 3 in this book). As the field evolved, the push to develop theory has grown stronger in the family business domain. Ring, Carr, and Kammerlander (Chapter 4 in this book) offer an insightful perspective on how practice and research intersect in the family business domain today.

An interestingly related question is whether researchers can be 'ambidextrous' and move smoothly between context-free and context-specific contextual orientation. An argument can clearly be made for the powerful force of training and socialization at the Ph.D. level. Academic imprint conditions scholars in the development of the set of skills and knowledge that fit either a setting or a theory. However, nowadays scholars engage in multiple collaborations on research projects. A research team is likely to combine different sources of expertise and a dataset can be leveraged to speak to different audiences. Thus, the contextual orientation is conceptualized here not as a fixed attribute of the researcher but as a *parameter* that researchers should consider when thinking about how to strengthen their pipeline of projects.

*Target Audience*: A second element to consider is *to what* exactly a scholar seeks to contribute. A contribution is often associated with the idea of 'joining a conversation' happening in a scholarly community (Huff, 1999). Indeed, research is conducted by drawing on prior work and 'standing on the shoulders of giants.' So, the question becomes: to what conversation is your paper contributing? What audience is being targeted? And what body of knowledge are you going to extend or challenge? To simplify, we can think of two options for family business researchers: a specialist contribution to family business scholarship or a generalist contribution to management (MGMT) scholarship.

First, a scholar may want to pursue research that advances specific knowledge about family firms. The goal is to join a relatively specialized conversation, provide richer insights into organizational mechanisms that are relevant for this type of organizations, or to test hypotheses about variables that impact their behaviors and outcomes. The knowledge generated by these studies is typically field-specific, and generalization to other management areas outside family business is therefore relatively more difficult. These contributions are welcome in journals specialized in family business research (e.g., FBR, JFBS, JFBM) or that are friendly to the family business research field (e.g., ETP).

Overall, journals that are interested in advancing knowledge about family firms. If the contribution to this field of research is clear, you are not likely to be asked how your findings generalize to other types of organizations.

Alternatively, a scholar may also think of contributing to a broader conversation in management studies. For example, contributing to a theoretical debate (e.g., what drives companies to internalize pressures to engage in socially responsible behaviors? – Berrone et al., 2010), advancing a theory by testing moderators or mediators (e.g., how does family ownership affect the prediction of behavioural theory on R&D investments? – Chrisman & Patel, 2012), or enriching a field of study such as networks (e.g., how do actors in a multiplex relationship – one crossing multiple domains – struggle to transition into new roles in one domain without disrupting existing interactions and the role hierarchy in another? – Li & Piezunka, 2020). In this scenario, the family business context provides an excellent way to address calls for *contextualization* of management research. In several disciplines, there has been increasing disquiet over the excessive focus of empirical research on theoretical development at the expense of understanding the context in which theories are being elaborated. For instance, scholars in Organizational Behavior – a large subdiscipline of management – recognize that 'the variety of contexts OB researchers encounter require them to pay special attention when exporting scientific constructs and research methodologies' (Rousseau & Fried, 2001, p. 2). Along the same line, entrepreneurship scholars advocate for more attention to the context of entrepreneurial efforts, to avoid building theories only based on the 'decontextualized "standard model" of entrepreneurship of the Silicon Valley' (Welter et al., 2019, p. 320). Importantly, there is a strong push to create 'indigenous theories', that is research that does not aim to test an existing theory but to derive new theories of the phenomena in their specific contexts (Tsui, 2004, p. 501). For family business scholarship, the push for contextualization brings tremendous opportunities to use the distinctive context of family firms to develop highly contextualized theories, and thereby provide a generalist contribution to management scholarship. Typically, these contributions can be found in generalist management journals (e.g., *Administrative Science Quarterly* (ASQ), AMJ, AMR, OS, etc.). If the contribution is based on a family business setting, you are likely to be asked how your findings generalize to other types of organizations.

When these two dimensions are considered together, four types of family business papers emerge: (1) Embedded; (2) Integrative; (3) Challenger; and (4) Generalized (Figure 2.1).

WHICH CONVERSATION ARE YOU CONTRIBUTING TO?

| | | Specialist contribution to FB audience | Generalist contribution to MGMT audience |
|---|---|---|---|
| | | **EMBEDDED** | **CHALLENGER** |
| **WHAT IS YOUR CONTEXTUAL ORIENTATION?** | Context-specific | • Reveals and explains new strategies and behaviors observed in family firms. <br> • Offers theoretical insights that in the aggregate can help develop theories unique to family businesses. | • Questions the assumptions and predictions of an existing theory in the context of family firms. <br> • Establishes boundary conditions for an existing theory by considering family ownership. <br> • Supports development of unique FB theories (e.g., socioemotional wealth). |
| | | **INTEGRATIVE** | **GENERALIZED** |
| | Context-free or theory-specific | • Applies a theoretical concept or perspective from another field to the family business domain. <br> • Extends the theoretical breadth of existing FB research by connecting with adjacent theories and closing the theoretical loop. | • Addresses questions and extends knowledge in a nonfamily theoretical domain. <br> • Utilizes the "family firm" as an ideal setting to isolate and study a phenomenon. <br> • Offers some implications for family business scholarship. |

*Figure 2.1     Types of family business papers and their contributions*

## FOUR TYPES OF FAMILY BUSINESS PAPERS: WHAT IS THEIR CONTRIBUTION?

Each of these types contributes to scholarship in a different way. In this section, I illustrate such differences drawing on examples from published empirical papers (see Table 2.1).[2]

*Embedded*: This is a type of family business paper where the focus is context-specific – family firms as a specific type of organization – and the goal of the authors is to advance specialist knowledge about family firms. As a starting point, the authors should be aware that the audience is knowledgeable about the domain of family firms and the originality and novelty of the paper needs to reside in expanding the conversation into new domains and providing new insights about the behaviors of family businesses. A good example of this

---

[2]     Illustrative examples are limited to empirical papers. Extending the discussion to conceptual papers is interesting but beyond the scope of this chapter.

*Table 2.1     Types of family business papers and their contributions: illustrative examples*

| | EMBEDDED | INTEGRATIVE | CHALLENGER | GENERALIZED |
|---|---|---|---|---|
| **Title of the paper** | 'Concealing or revealing the family? Corporate brand identity strategies in family firms' (Micelotta & Raynard, 2011, FBR) | 'Succession narratives in family business: The case of Alessi' (Dalpiaz et al., 2014, ETP) | 'Socioemotional wealth and corporate responses to institutional pressures: Do family-controlled firms pollute less?' (Berrone et al., 2010, ASQ) | 'The uniplex third: Enabling single-domain role transitions in multiplex relationships' (Li & Piezunka, 2020, ASQ) |
| **Positioning in the literature** | Marketing and family business studies on how firms can strategically deploy their family identity to gain a competitive advantage. | Key processes and factors that underpin effective and ineffective succession. | The role of sociopolitical factors in how firms respond to institutional pressures. | Opportunities and resistance to change in network conditions of multiplex relationships. |
| **Motivation for the study and RQ** | Paucity of research examining how family firms incorporate and communicate their identities as 'family businesses' in their marketing activities. RQ: How do family firms leverage the familial component of their businesses in communicating their corporate brand identity? | Prior work limited to economics. Neglect of the role of language and meaning in the family business succession processes, in particular narratives. RQ: How do successors use narratives strategically to manage the succession process? | Lacking from prior literatures is attention to the role of diverse principals in enacting varying responses to institutional pressures. RQ: Does the firm's substantive conformity depend on who holds a controlling interest within it? | Prior research on networks has not addressed how actors can overcome inertia and carry out role transitions. RQ: How can actors in a multiplex relationship carry out single-domain role transitions while avoiding disruptions? |

| | EMBEDDED | INTEGRATIVE | CHALLENGER | GENERALIZED |
|---|---|---|---|---|
| **Empirical data and methods** | Qualitative analysis of archival material, i.e., official company websites of 92 of the world's oldest family firms. | Qualitative analysis of the case study of succession at Alessi, a family-owned Italian design and manufacturing firm. | Quantitative analysis of 194 US firms required to report their toxic emissions, of which 101 are family firms. | Qualitative analysis of seven multiple-case studies of father–son leadership successions in China. |
| **Claimed contributions** | • Shows that family firms differ in the extent to which they leverage and communicate both family and corporate heritage in their corporate brand identity strategies.<br>• Highlights a temporal dimension in family-based branding strategies, thus far neglected in the literature.<br>• Reveals potential factors and circumstances that may drive the selection of one strategy or another. | • Extends the application of the concept of narrative within the literature on family business succession.<br>• Identifies specific narrative strategies that family business successors use to legitimate themselves and their actions.<br>• Discusses the connection between succession narratives, the construction of the individual identity of the successor, and the reconstruction of the organizational identity of the family firm. | • Shows that corporate control conditions (i.e., family ownership) can reinforce responses.<br>• Reveals how principals' (owners) motives, preferences, and values influence responses.<br>• Examines ties of executives to control group and financial incentives in enacting policies.<br>• Isolates the unique effect of divergent controlling interests on responses. | • Contributes to the social networks literature by examining the third party in the context of multiplexity.<br>• Extends research on network closure.<br>• Elucidates the network structures that may be most conducive to positive synergies between family and firm. |

type of paper is one of my own (with coauthor Mia Raynard), which examined corporate brand identity strategies in family firms. This paper was published in the 2011 FBR Special Issue on Marketing in Family Firms. As the call for the paper in the Special Issue suggested, the topic was relatively unexplored at the time this research was conducted. The paper is positioned in both the family business and the branding literature; however, it is relatively clear that a family business, and not a marketing audience, is the one targeted. The contribution of the paper resides in (a) the exploration of a topic for which there was not much evidence (i.e., corporate identity branding strategies); (b) the identification of variance between family businesses in the strategies adopted (i.e., preservation, enrichment, subordination), which had not been done before; and (c) potential explanations for why such variance may exist. It should be noted that in this paper there is not much emphasis on a strong theory underpinning the study. Various streams of research provide the theoretical scaffolding to position and interpret the results, but the explanatory use of a theory is limited. In fact, the contribution of the paper is mostly exploratory in nature, meant to identify branding identity strategies in family businesses. It is possible that the accumulation of exploratory studies on one topic will support the elaboration of stronger theoretical frameworks in future research (e.g., a theory of family branding formation and change). This type of paper and its contributions are also promising to unpack the heterogeneity of family businesses (Daspit et al., Chapter 5 in this book).

*Integrative*: This second type of paper is also intended for a specialist family business audience, but the contextual orientation of the author(s) is context-free. What this term means is that the paper is not exclusively oriented towards knowledge about family firms. It seeks to generate novel and original knowledge by integrating theoretical concepts that have not been extensively utilized or applied to family firms into this specialized domain. A good example of this approach is the paper published by Elena Dalpiaz and colleagues in ETP in 2014. This paper draws upon theoretical insights about the key role of narratives in organizational settings. It then integrates this framework into the family business domain by exploring how narrative strategies are used in a family business during succession. The contribution of the paper resides in (a) importing into the succession literature the concept of narratives. This is relatively unexplored and sheds a new light on succession as a cultural and meaning-making process; (b) identifying narrative strategies that enable the successor to acquire legitimacy; and (c) providing a theoretical loop by noting how this case can shed light on the dynamics of identity construction (not just communication) of the successor. Thus, this study opens the way for additional research on identity construction in family firms.

*Challenger*: This type of paper targets a management scholar audience in theoretical domains other than family business. The main goal of this type of paper is to show how the distinctive nature of family firms can alter, extend, and/or modify the well-established predictions and assumptions of existing theories. Authors need to be extremely knowledgeable about the family business domain, but also must have deep expertise in the theoretical domain that is being challenged. Consider, for instance, the paper by Berrone and colleagues published in ASQ in 2010. The paper challenges existing assumptions and findings from institutional theory and strategic management scholars about how controlling interests influence responses to institutional pressures. By looking at the family as a controlling interest, the paper shows that family-controlled firms are particularly responsive to environmental pressures and a firm's strategy mirrors the preferences of dominant shareholders. This work explains why we observe the heterogeneity of responses rather than isomorphic compliance to pressures. Aside from the interesting observation about this distinctive behavior of family firms, the contribution of the paper resides in (a) demonstrating that extant theories have boundary conditions and family ownership may alter their predictions and (b) showing that unique theoretical frameworks may be needed to theorize the behaviors and strategies of family firms (i.e., socioemotional wealth). These arguments leverage insights from the family businesses domain to extend theoretical conversations in the management domain.

*Generalized*: Finally, the fourth type of paper is one where the 'family firm' represents an (often ideal) empirical setting to address theoretical research questions of interest for management scholars. In this type of paper, there are insights to be gained for family business scholars, but the main goal is to examine this setting as an exemplar case of a broader phenomenon. Consider, for instance, the paper by Li and Piezunka about succession in Chinese firms published in ASQ in 2020. This qualitative analysis is primarily meant to fill a gap in network analysis about multiplex relationships and role transitions without disruptions. You will note how the study is not positioned in the family business literature; in fact, the literature review is focused on network theory and the family setting is presented in the Research Setting section of the paper. As the authors note, the family setting is an ideal instance to study role transitions, but the insights generated inductively in the paper could be applied to other multiplex relationships as well (e.g., business partners). The contribution of this paper is (a) to advance a sophisticated stream of research in network theory and (b) offer implications for family business succession. If you note, this second contribution is a relatively less central position (third contribution). This paper shows that family firms may offer distinctive and unique empirical settings to examine phenomena that otherwise may be difficult to isolate in other types of organizations. This is potentially a great opportunity to think about the theoretical advancements that can be yielded when family businesses are used as experimental sites.

# CONCLUSIONS

This chapter offers a practical guide to two audiences: family business scholars, who may have an interest in targeting generalist management journals, and business scholars, who may have an interest in exploring how family businesses provide boundary conditions for well-established theories. Family business scholars have an opportunity to develop knowledge that is intrinsically interesting for the broader field of management. They can also increase their chances of making a theoretical contribution by integrating insights from other theoretical domains or using their in-depth knowledge to challenge established theories. Along the same lines, management scholars can use their expertise in other theoretical domains and apply these concepts in a relatively novel way to a family business domain. They can address questions that are of interest for a family business audience or use the family business as an ideal context. Critically, family business scholars can use the types of paper discussed in this guide to strategically develop multiple paths to publication. These quadrants invite opportunities for new and exciting cross-disciplinary research.

# REFERENCES

Berrone, P., Cruz, C., Gomez-Mejia, L. R., & Larraza-Kintana, M. (2010). Socioemotional wealth and corporate responses to institutional pressures: Do family-controlled firms pollute less? *Administrative Science Quarterly*, 55(1), 82–113.

Bird, B., Welsch, H., Astrachan, J. H., & Pistrui, D. (2002). Family business research: The evolution of an academic field. *Family Business Review*, 15(4), 337–350.

Blair, J. D., & Hunt, J. G. (1986). Getting inside the head of the management researcher one more time: Context-free and context-specific orientations in research. *Journal of Management*, 12(2), 147–166.

Chirico, F., Welsh, D. H., Ireland, R. D., & Sieger, P. (2021). Family versus non-family firm franchisors: Behavioural and performance differences. *Journal of Management Studies*, 58(1), 165–200.

Chrisman, J. J., & Patel, P. C. (2012). Variations in R&D investments of family and nonfamily firms: Behavioral agency and myopic loss aversion perspectives. *Academy of Management Journal*, 55(4), 976–997.

Corley, K. G., & Gioia, D. A. (2011). Building theory about theory building: What constitutes a theoretical contribution? *Academy of Management Review*, 36(1), 12–32.

Dalpiaz, E., Tracey, P., & Phillips, N. (2014). Succession narratives in family business: The case of Alessi. *Entrepreneurship Theory and Practice*, 38(6), 1375–1394.

De Massis, A., & Foss, N. J. (2018). Advancing family business research: The promise of micro foundations. *Family Business Review*, 31(4), 386–396.

Huff, A. S. (1999). *Writing for Scholarly Publication*. Sage.

Jaskiewicz, P., Combs, J. G., Shanine, K. K., & Kacmar, K. M. (2017). Introducing the family: A review of family science with implications for management research. *Academy of Management Annals*, 11(1), 309–341.

Li, J. B., & Piezunka, H. (2020). The Uniplex Third: Enabling single-domain role transitions in multiplex relationships. *Administrative Science Quarterly*, 65(2), 314–358.

Micelotta, E. R., & Raynard, M. (2011). Concealing or revealing the family? Corporate brand identity strategies in family firms. *Family Business Review*, 24(3), 197–216.

Muzio, D., Aulakh, S., & Kirkpatrick, I. (2019). *Professional Occupations and Organizations*. Elements in Organization Theory, Cambridge University Press.

Reay, T., & Whetten, D. A. (2011). What constitutes a theoretical contribution in family business? *Family Business Review*, 24(2) 105–110.

Reay, T., Goodrick, B., & D'Aunno, T. (2021). *Health Care Research and Organization Theory*. Elements in Organization Theory, Cambridge University Press.

Rousseau, D. M., & Fried, Y. (2001). Location, location, location: Contextualizing organizational research. *Journal of Organizational Behavior*, 22(1), 1–13.

Rovelli, P., Ferasso, M., De Massis, A., & Kraus, S. (2021). Thirty years of research in family business journals: Status quo and future directions. *Journal of Family Business Strategy*, 100422.

Salvato, C., Chirico, F., Melin, L., & Seidl, D. (2019). Coupling family business research with organization studies: Interpretations, issues, and insights. *Organization Studies*, 40(6), 775–791.

Sasaki, I., Kotlar, J., Ravasi, D., & Vaara, E. (2020). Dealing with revered past: Historical identity statements and strategic change in Japanese family firms. *Strategic Management Journal*, 41(3), 590–623.

Sharma, P. (2004). An overview of the field of family business studies: Status and directions for the future. *Family Business Review*, 17(1), 1–36.

Suddaby, R., Coraiola, D., Harvey, C., & Foster, W. (2020). History and the micro-foundations of dynamic capabilities. *Strategic Management Journal*, 41(3), 530–556.

Tsui, A. S. (2004). Contributing to global management knowledge: A case for high-quality indigenous research. *Asia Pacific Journal of Management*, 21(4), 491–513.

Welter, F., Baker, T., & Wirsching, K. (2019). Three waves and counting: The rising tide of contextualization in entrepreneurship research. *Small Business Economics*, 52(2), 319–330.

Whetten, D. A. (1989). What constitutes a theoretical contribution? *Academy of Management Review*, 14(4), 490–495.

Xi, J. M., Kraus, S., Filser, M., & Kellermanns, F. W. (2015). Mapping the field of family business research: Past trends and future directions. *International Entrepreneurship and Management Journal*, 11(1), 113–132.

# 3. Unlocking the power of the three-circles paradigm

## Justin B. Craig and G. T. Lumpkin

## INTRODUCTION

The introduction of the three-circle model of family business helped launch family business as a scholarly domain and topic of business school research. It highlighted the complexity and dynamism of family business by drawing attention to three major forces influencing family systems—ownership, management, and the family. It opened the door for research on topics that are both unique to family business and overlap with central issues in management and entrepreneurship—leadership and succession, decision making and strategy, financing and capitalization, and more. As a result, the model can be found in nearly every family business textbook to depict the distinctiveness of family business as a topic. Further, Ken Moores (2009) contends that the community of family business scholars has largely embraced the three-circle model as 'the key *symbolic generalization* of the prevailing family business discipline paradigm' (2009: 168, italics in original) and, as such, it has helped provide the paradigm consensus needed to elevate family business to the level of a standalone scientific discipline (Kuhn, 1970).

Beginning in 1978, Tagiuri and Davis circulated a version of the three-circle model among scholars as a working paper; it was published in Davis's dissertation in 1982 (see johndavis.com). The model was included in two well-cited articles by Tagiuri and Davis published in *Family Business Review* in 1992 and 1996 (Tagiuri & Davis, 1992, 1996) but it was the highly cited 1997 book *Generation to Generation: Life Cycles of the Family Business* where the model was most fully explicated (Gersick, Davis, Hampton, & Lansberg, 1997). Twenty-five years after that book, according to the Cambridge Family Enterprise Group, 'Nothing seems to have the sticking power of the original Three-Circle Model. It is still the widely accepted, organizing framework used worldwide to understand family business systems' (see cfeg.com).

The three-circles Venn diagram is a graphic approach to positioning the groups whose constituents make up the key participants and actors in the field of family enterprise. The three circles provide an important entry-level understanding of the potential complexity of the field. For example, it allows for distinguishing various roles in different combinations—such as being a family member and an owner but having no role in the business. Or, working in the business, but having no role in the family—or other possible combinations. There is also a version of the model in which the intersections of the three circles in the Venn diagram are populated by seven numbers that highlight these various roles. The model enables researchers, as well as other stakeholders, to consider what happens *within* as well as *between*, and *among*, the three circles.

Despite the three-circle model's enduring relevance and appeal, for researchers, it seems to have slipped into the background as a mechanism for understanding family business dynamics. Yet, this iconic depiction incorporates far too many helpful insights to be so readily rebuffed. We suggest a reboot of the three-circle model is needed along with a few upgrades designed to improve its usefulness for analyzing important family enterprise topics such as heterogeneity, dynamism, and temporality. Our discussion endeavors to address any unwarranted undoing of the three-circles paradigm by taking a fresh look at what we believe remains the field's most dominant, yet undervalued, framework. Our revised positioning will consider that a better appreciation for the richness of the framework is gained through (1) distinguishing levels of analysis across the three circles, (2) reinforcing that each circle is independent yet interdependent, (3) highlighting how the circles can inform individual, organizational, and familial life-cycle perspectives, and (4) explaining how the circles provide ways to frame short- and long-term planning strategies and decision making to address and relieve the inevitable tensions that arise as family enterprises evolve. In the remainder of this chapter, therefore, we will draw attention to key features of the three-circle model that highlight its central importance as a fundamental conceptual framework for family business research. We will also discuss how the model addresses the unique challenges that family businesses face, provide guidelines for helping family business researchers meet those challenges, and suggest future directions for moving the family business research field forward.

## LEVELS OF ANALYSIS

A key challenge with the original depiction of the three-circle model revolved around the labels 'family, owners, and business' suggested by Tagiuri and Davis. While the model's key insight that all three of those forces matter still holds, the fact that these labels suggest different levels of analysis has, at times, muddled the message. Despite the tendency by some researchers to claim that the three-circle model provides a depiction of a systems approach to interpreting family businesses, the fact that it is a Venn diagram suggests otherwise. At a more fundamental level, the three-circle model is a way to add family to the dynamics of business ownership. A less complicated way of stating this is to suggest that every business has owners but in family businesses, typically, most of these owners are family members. This simplicity is at the heart of the framework's universal appeal and durability.

To address this concern, Moores (2009) proposed a significant change to the labeling of the circles in the Venn diagram. He argued that a more precise way to consider the three groups is to introduce a consistent level of analysis. Specifically, he contended that since family are people and owners are people, but business are entities, there is a dissonance that impedes the usefulness of the framework. So, to address this, he relabeled the business circle as *managers*. His argument was that managers are people, some of whom will be family, who are charged with managing the various business activities on behalf of owners, many of whom will be family. With this change, the focus of the three-circles model is on people, which aligns with the members of the other two circles.[1]

This modification also draws attention to the owners' circle such that the focus of what is being studied shifts to the people who are owners, not owner-ship vehicles such as trusts and the like (Figure 3.1). Being able to distinguish between those *who* own from *how* that ownership is structured helps address heterogeneity and generalizability issues, which are increasingly being identi-fied as a research concern as the field evolves (Daspit et al., Chapter 5 in this book).

## INDEPENDENT YET INTERDEPENDENT

A quick glance at the three circles may engender the view that all family enterprises are similar. In fact, rather than making all family enterprises appear the same, the people-oriented three-circles model reinforces how heteroge-neous family businesses are. That is so, in part, because it depicts an array

---

[1]    Since its introduction, the label for the 'business' circle in the three-circles model has undergone several changes. At first, Tagiuri and Davis referred to it as 'company', but it quickly became apparent that family enterprises often involve more than one company. In their 1996 article, Tagiuri and Davis mentioned 'managers and employ-ees' but that introduced a multitude of actors, and mixed-in individuals with major and minor roles in the family enterprise. A focus in family business research on the dom-inant coalition as key decision makers (see Chua, Chrisman, Sharma, 1999) shifted attention to the business itself and its management. The change to managers proposed here acknowledges those individuals who have major decision-making roles similar to those of the other key actors in the model—owners and family members.

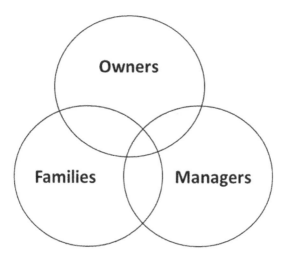

*Figure 3.1*      *Venn diagram with manager replacing business*

of possible interdependencies (Moore & Nicholas, Chapter 16 in this book). Introducing three separate groups of people in a Venn depiction allows each to be examined as (1) a collective of three constituent groups, (2) decoupled groups as dyads, or (3) each group singularly. This highlights the independent yet interdependent nature of the model.

Looking first just at the *owners'* circle provides the opportunity to distinguish one of the fundamental differences between people who own family businesses and those who are owners of publicly traded businesses. In the latter, the utility people gain from ownership is primarily economic. An important implication of this is that the people in the ownership group tend to be homogenous. In the former, among the people who are family enterprise owners, it is more likely that there will be utility heterogeneity. That is, ownership will reflect a wider array of motivations including not only economic gain but also familial support, community benefits, and socioemotional needs. As such, some family enterprise owners will be owners because of the dividend they receive while others will be more inclined to remain as owners because of the attachment they have to their family (Arregle, Hitt, Sirmon, & Very, 2007). In Figure 3.2, this is represented on a continuum anchored by economic and psychological utility.

Sectioning off the people who make up the *family* circle reveals another aspect of heterogeneity. According to most widely accepted definitions, family enterprises are those that have the intent to carry operations forward indefinitely through the involvement of family members. This focus has led some to conclude that the family is, therefore, the most important of the three circles. This can be contentious because, in many cases, it is the owners that ultimately have a greater role in decision making. Given that, remembering that the 'original' family often evolves into a family of families enhances understanding of the potential increased complexity over time, and its implications. This will be further discussed below when we investigate life-cycle influences.

Positioning the third circle as *managers* (rather than business) heightens the opportunity to humanize the framework. As considered earlier, managers are those who are managing on behalf of the owners, most of whom are family members. Nevertheless, depending on the level of professionalization of the family enterprise, when managers—family and non-family—bring unique skills to the managerial role, they can offer a level of independence that is vital for successful operations. Thus, positioning the third circle in terms of managers highlights both their independence and interdependence. Such managers—some who will be family and some who will be management—are responsible for an increasingly diverse portfolio of business activities, which we will now move to discuss.

## LIFE-CYCLE APPRECIATION

Although the three-circles model appears to depict something fixed or static, in fact, each of the three circles is in flux. That is, even though the circles represent relatively stable boundaries, in practice, the scope and types of roles and responsibilities within each of the three circles are ever changing. One way to account for this is to consider each circle from a life-cycle perspective (Moores & Mula, 2000). This nuance is not often appreciated as many give the three circles a cursory glance thinking that it is far less rich than it is. As suggested in the previous section, the people in the managers' circle are often required to manage an ever-changing portfolio of business activities. For successful enterprises, what starts as a small single business over time often morphs into a larger business or even multiple businesses across different sectors as the commercial activities expand. This also typically involves increasing real estate assets, which must be managed. Add to that cash and other liquid assets which also demand attention. At some point, a formalized approach to philanthropy through a foundation or other similar vehicle may also need to be managed. Importantly, this evolving suite of business activities typically requires higher levels of professionalization by increasingly sophisticated managers. These managers need to understand factors such as the idiosyncrasies of various asset classes, the short- versus long-term yield expectations of the owners' group, and other considerations, all of which are also in flux.

Previously, we suggested that the owners' circle was populated by a diverse group of owners characterized by their utility heterogeneity. An implication

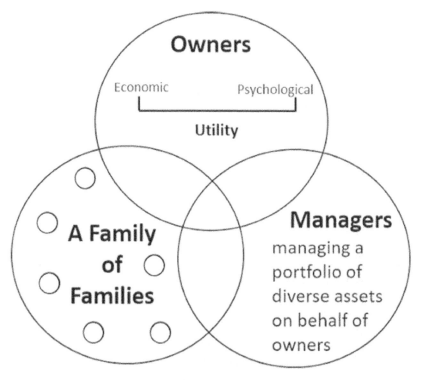

*Figure 3.2      Venn diagram refined*

of this is that the utility that owners expect or receive potentially changes over their individual life stages (Furby, 1978). An owner whose expectations are more centered around economic returns may evolve as s/he matures to appreciate the value of psychological ownership. Add to this that, as ownership moves beyond the second generation, there is increased likelihood that the utility that individual owners receive will potentially differ (López-Vergara & Botero, 2015).

We briefly noted that the family circle often evolves into a family of families. Applying a life-cycle lens to this phenomenon enables a more granular inspection of how such changes influence the way family members perceive their roles and contributions to the family business and related activities, and to their level of involvement. Priorities inevitably change as the offspring of the founder marry and have families of their own (Davis, 1982). But these changes create complications, many of which are exacerbated by the evolution of the family as a social form. Increasingly, families are blended due to divorce and remarriage. Further, views of what was a traditional family unit are increasingly challenged across nearly every culture.

Though in the family system there is often a natural progression that is impacted by extraneous influences, there can also be periods of contraction in the owners and managers systems because of many factors such as changing market or industry conditions, or death and divorce within the family (Brigham & Payne, 2015). Using a life-cycle lens makes it possible to consider that the three circles have temporal and stability limitations and boundaries.

## VIEWING FAMILY BUSINESS THEORIES THROUGH A THREE-CIRCLE LENS

To this point we have suggested that viewing the three-circles from an individual level of analysis and acknowledging the independent, yet interdependent character of the circles addresses the previously overlooked potential of this widely accepted approach to understanding the field. We also considered that there is an opportunity with the model to take a more expansive approach by interpreting the three-circles using a life-cycle lens. Along with these uses, these features of the three-circle model suggest another potential avenue for applying it to family business research—as a basic structure or lens through which to view different theoretical frameworks or perspectives. In other words, the three-circles model can be used to analyze or interpret family business-specific applications of familiar theoretical perspectives.

Stewardship theory provides a useful example (Davis, Schoorman, & Donaldson, 1997). Earlier we suggested that family is what facilitates the need to adopt the Venn diagram, and then further suggested that managers replace the original positioning of business so that each of the audiences can be considered as people. Suggesting each of the groups are stewards adds an additional texture to the original Davis and Tagiuri model. While the theoretical conversation around stewardship has matured in recent years (Neubaum, Thomas, Dibrell, & Craig, 2017), a steward for the purposes we describe here is akin to being a responsible guardian or custodian. Stated simply, if we envision the three circles as populated by people who have an appreciation of their role as owner-stewards (responsible for assets and wealth), family-stewards (responsible for unity and purpose), and/or manager-stewards (responsible for increasing the range of business activities) (Figure 3.3), it provides a richer and more fine-grained approach to using stewardship theory in a family business context.

We posit that the three-circle model could provide similar clarity and precision as a lens for interpreting other theoretical perspectives including agency theory (Schulze, Lubatkin, Dino, & Buchholtz, 2001), the resource-based view (Barney, 1991), long-term orientation (Lumpkin & Brigham, 2011), govern-

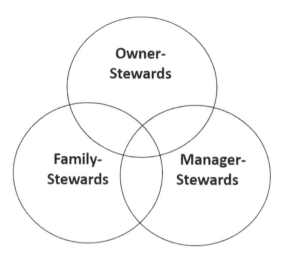

*Figure 3.3*      *Re-imagining the three circles*

ance theory (Tihanyi, Graffin, & George, 2014), resource dependency theory (Drees & Heugens, 2013), and others.

## RELIEVING TENSIONS *BETWEEN* AND *AMONG* THE THREE-CIRCLES THROUGH PLANNING

By highlighting the interdependence of the three circles, clarifying the model's level of analysis, and integrating how the people in each circle are ever changing, we have extended the usefulness of the framework to the researcher community. The intersection between and among the three circles provides researchers with the opportunity to zero-in on the key roles and activities that are associated with each circle and highlight the unique opportunity that family enterprises have to effectively strategize and plan for continuity (Craig, 2021). The overlapping circles adds another frequently overlooked opportunity to appreciate the richness of the Venn diagram, as we now briefly describe.

   Consider first the overlap between the managers and the owners. To address the tension that would occur if managers are not aligned with the owners' expectations, we suggest that *strategic planning* is required (Moores & Craig, 2005). The focus here is on the marketplace realities and operational demands that need to be considered to keep the enterprise viable and sustainable over the long run. Second, it is at the intersection of owners and family where tensions emerge over the business' assets versus the family's assets and how those resources will be distributed, deployed, or reinvested. To address this concern,

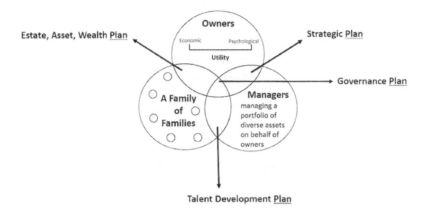

*Figure 3.4      Plans at the intersection of the three circles*

*wealth planning* is needed to reconcile the business' needs and the family's estate (Ward, 1997). Third, the tension between the evolving family of families and the managers' circle shifts attention to the personnel needed to effectively manage the business. Depending on the level of family involvement in the business and the current and potential use of family members as employees, *talent development planning* is needed to engage the family without jeopardizing the business (Carlock & Ward, 2001). Finally, and arguably, most importantly, where all three circles intersect, there is a need to develop *a plan for governing* the family enterprise (Carney, 2005). Research has shown that governance of the forces that influence a family enterprise are central to its effective functioning (Yu, Lumpkin, Sorenson, & Brigham, 2012). Tensions among the three constituent groups is inevitable and yet maintaining a balance among the dynamic forces contributing to a given enterprise requires a well-understood and regularly updated governance plan (Figure 3.4).

## DISCUSSION

We opened our chapter suggesting that, in the family business field, appreciation for the three-circle model of family enterprises is potentially waning and, as a result, the field has tended to undervalue how useful it remains for current research and practice. Thus, we have attempted to bring new attention to this dominant family business paradigm. We have moved the conversation from a static depiction that considered multiple roles to one that suggests that, in fact, the framework is significantly more dynamic. We have suggested that with the Venn diagram, which has paradigm consensus, owners are considered on a continuum anchored by economic and psychological imperatives; family evolves into a family of increasingly complex families; and increasing sophistication is required to manage a growing asset portfolio. Reconceptualizing the model as more complex and ever changing both enriches its usefulness and introduces new challenges.

This repositioning supplies us with a platform to address the questions that are driving this publication.

1.   What are the unique challenges that are posed by the study of family businesses or business families?

The unique challenges also constitute unique opportunities. Dominant among these are those that focus on family as the pivotal constituent. We are reminded of a comment made by a colleague presenting to a group of social entrepreneurship doctoral students. When asked what it is that distinguishes social entrepreneurship from other types of entrepreneurship, his poignant reply was simply, 'well, the adjective must mean something.' This, we argue, can be applied to the family business context—the adjective, in this case, family, must mean something. Given how increasingly different the contemporary family is to previous notions of family, there remains much to learn from those who study families. There is a dearth of research that takes a scientific look at family in these updated contexts, and that is where the opportunity lies.

Moores' (2009) insight to move to a people level of analysis should be taken as an opportunity also. This provides scope to further investigate roles as family, owner, and manager—separately and together. Our suggestion that the three circles are in flux provides impetus for following families across time. The plans that relieve tension also give structure to the role of planning for continuity, as does the depiction of the people as stewards.

2.   What tips, guidelines, rules of thumb, or steps are helpful to other researchers with these or similar challenges? How are these unique to the study of family business?

A clear implication of our discussion is that family enterprises are more complex and have a richer context than is sometimes considered. We have emphasized that in elaborating on the richness of the framework and we see this in the heterogeneity across family enterprises and in the many facets of family business research (Daspit et al., Chapter 5 in this book). In terms of guidelines, this suggests that researchers need to find ways to integrate that complexity into their studies. One way this can be done is by offering more detailed descriptions of data and the implications of using it. For example, specifying (or controlling for) family involvement, family generation (distance from founder), or level of professionalization are all techniques that could provide useful insights for interpreting results. By setting forth key details and underlying assumptions about the family enterprises in a study, researchers enhance their ability to draw conclusions that can be generalized to similar settings.

3.    What future directions or suggestions do you have for how researchers can address the challenges and move the field forward (e.g., new methods, perspectives, techniques)?

We have noted that there is a tendency to view the three-circles model as static when in fact it depicts an ever-changing situation. This suggests that future researchers need to endeavor to capture temporality and the passage of time in their empirical analyses (e.g., Craig, Cassar, & Moores, 2006). This, of course, also adds to the complexity of family enterprise research but it is vital for achieving a more fine-grained understanding of the dynamics underlying success and failure. Indeed, an overarching research question that business families are clamoring to know more about is, 'how are the changes in the family changing the business?' The three-circles model provides the ideal starting point to answer that question—by highlighting the evolving nature of the family, the temporal dimensions of ownership, and, for managers, the ever-changing dynamics of family involvement. By drawing on the three-circles model, future researchers can gain insights that contribute to a deeper understanding of the challenges and move the field forward (also see, Lumpkin & Bacq, 2021; Zahra, 2021).

Finally, we must emphasize that data often dictates publication decisions. Researchers who build close relationships with business-owning families and commit to smaller more focused samples that are tracked over time will likely have a stronger chance of convincing editorial decision makers that they have a rich story worth telling (Trudell, Waldron, & Wetherbe, Chapter 8 in this book; Ring, Carr, & Kammerlander, Chapter 4 in this book).

## CONCLUSION

Our conceptual reset of the three-circles paradigm highlights that, not only are there many entrances into understanding family enterprises, but also that, once inside, there are also many rooms, hallways, and corners to explore. Equally important to remember is that, by definition, the enterprising family is constantly being updated and refurbished, creating even more opportunities for new research.

# REFERENCES

Arregle, J. L., Hitt, M. A., Sirmon, D. G., & Very, P. (2007). The development of organizational social capital: Attributes of family firms. *Journal of Management Studies*, *44*, 73–95.

Barney, J. B. (1991). Firm resources and sustained competitive advantage. *Journal of Management*, *17*, 99–120.

Brigham, K. H., & Payne, G. T. (2015). Article commentary: The transitional nature of the multifamily business. *Entrepreneurship Theory and Practice*, *39*(6), 1339–1347.

Carlock, R. S., & Ward, J. L. (2001). *Strategic Planning for the Family Business: Parallel Planning to Unify the Family and Business*. New York: Palgrave Macmillan.

Carney, M. (2005). Corporate governance and competitive advantage in family-controlled firms. *Entrepreneurship Theory and Practice*, *29*, 249–265.

Chua, J. H., Chrisman, J. J., & Sharma, P. (1999). Defining the family business by behavior. *Entrepreneurship Theory and Practice*, *23*(4), 19–39.

Craig, J. B. (2021). *Continuity Model Generation*. New York: John Wiley & Sons Publishing.

Craig, J. B., Cassar, G., & Moores, K. J. (2006). A ten-year investigation of strategy, systems and environment upon innovation in family firms. *Family Business Review*, *19*, 1–10.

Davis, J. A. (1982). *The Influence of Life Stage on Father–son Work Relation in Family Companies*. Ann Arbor, MI: University Microfilms Inc.

Davis, J. H., Schoorman, F. D., & Donaldson, L. (1997). Toward a stewardship theory of management. *Academy of Management Review*, *22*(1), 20–47.

Drees, J. M., & Heugens, P. P. (2013). Synthesizing and extending resource dependence theory: A meta-analysis. *Journal of Management*, *39*(6), 1666–1698.

Furby, L. (1978). Possessions: Toward a theory of their meaning and function throughout the life cycle. In P. B. Baltes (Ed.), *Life Span Development and Behavior* (pp. 297–336). New York: Academic Press.

Gersick, K. E., Davis, J. A., Hampton, M. M., & Lansberg, I. (1997). *Generation to Generation: Life Cycles of the Family Business*. Boston: Harvard University Press.

Kuhn, T. S. (1970). *The Structure of Scientific Revolutions*. Chicago: Chicago University Press.

López-Vergara, M. P., & Botero, I. C. (2015). The role of non-economic goals for psychological ownership in family firms. *European Journal of International Management*, *9*(2), 201–220.

Lumpkin, G. T., & Bacq, S. (2021). Family business, community embeddedness, and civic wealth creation. *Journal of Family Business Strategy*. https://doi.org/10.1016/j.jfbs.2021.100469

Lumpkin, G. T., & Brigham, K. H. (2011). Long-term orientation and intertemporal choice in family firms. *Entrepreneurship Theory & Practice*, *35*(6), 1147–1167.

Moores, K. (2009). Paradigms and theory building in the domain of business families. *Family Business Review*, *22*(2), 167–180.

Moores, K. J., and Craig, J. B. (2005). Balanced scorecards to drive the strategic planning of family firms. *Family Business Review*, *18*(2), 105–122.

Moores, K., & Mula, J. (2000). The salience of market, bureaucratic, and clan controls in the management of family firm transitions: Some tentative Australian evidence. *Family Business Review*, *13*(2), 91–106.

Neubaum, D. O., Thomas, C. H., Dibrell, C., & Craig, J. B. (2017). Stewardship climate scale: An assessment of reliability and validity. *Family Business Review, 30*(1), 37–60.

Schulze, W. S., Lubatkin, M. H., Dino, R. N., and Buchholtz, A. K. (2001). Agency relationships in family firms: Theory and evidence. *Organization Science, 12*(2), 99–116.

Tagiuri, R., & Davis, J. A. (1992). On the goals of successful family companies. *Family Business Review, 5*(1), 43–62.

Tagiuri, R., & Davis, J. (1996). Bivalent attitudes of the family firm. *Family Business Review, 9*(2), 47–74.

Tihanyi, L., Graffin, S., & George, G. (2014). Rethinking governance in management research. *Academy of Management Journal, 57*(6), 1535–1543.

Ward, J. L. (1997). Growing the family business: Special challenges and best practices. *Family Business Review, 10*(4), 323–337.

Yu, A., Lumpkin, G. T., Sorenson, R. L., & Brigham, K. H. (2012). The landscape of family business outcomes: A summary and numerical taxonomy of dependent variables. *Family Business Review, 25*(1), 33–57.

Zahra, S. (2021). International entrepreneurship by family firms post-Covid. *Journal of Family Business Strategy.* https://doi.org/10.1016/j.jfbs.2021.100482

# 4. The important role of family business practice and its influence on family business research

**J. Kirk Ring, Jon C. Carr, and Nadine Kammerlander**

## INTRODUCTION

Scholars commonly express concerns that their academically focused research efforts result in little, if any, impact on business practice. Many journal articles and editorials have been published in recent years that point to a significant gap between research and practice (e.g., Simsek, Bansal, Shaw, Heugens, & Smith, 2018) and this theory/practice gap has the potential to widen greatly in the future because of an intensified academic focus on intricate, new methodological approaches and sophisticated theories that are increasingly difficult to relate back to real-world problems. If business research is indeed supposed to impact the way practitioners think and act, then look no further than the field of family business for an ideal topic area within the management discipline to fully illustrate why this is so important (Sharma, Chrisman, & Gersick, 2012).

Family firms refer to businesses where multiple family members actively participate in its operations and family members possess a significant ownership stake (Chua, Chrisman, & Sharma, 1999); involvement and ownership gives the family the ability to shape the current and long-term direction of the firm. These firms are also typified by a desire to pass on the business to the next generation of family members and thereby building a legacy that impacts their families and communities. Importantly though, a key feature of the family business that makes it a unique type of organization is the interaction of the family unit and the business unit as independent, yet highly connected, systems (Craig & Lumpkin, Chapter 3 in this book; Gersick, Davis, Hampton, & Lansberg, 1997). Thus, family business scholars must be able to develop academic studies that are theoretically interesting and practically relevant for (a) business operations, (b) issues specific to the family unit, and (c) issues specific to the way the family and business interact simultaneously. These practically relevant conclusions are often associated with a specific section within the study, and are in fact even labeled as such – 'Practical Implications of The Study'.

Not surprisingly, academic research and institutions like the Family Firm Institute and the Family Business Network also encourage better understanding of the connections between family business academic scholarship and family business practice (Astrachan, Astrachan, Kotlar, & Michiels, 2021). More importantly, an extensive network of family business advisors and consultants offer consulting services to address the practical needs of such businesses. This network overwhelmingly offers these services for profit, and are thus likely to be highly in tune with what these family businesses are focused on from a practice standpoint.

Thus, a set of important questions to consider are – Can we characterize what practicality means in academic studies? Is there a way to compare practical implication sections associated with family business research with what is currently offered by the consulting network most responsive to actual practice? And, if so, what areas of current family business research are underexplored, and what future research opportunities exist, based upon this comparison?

Thus, our work seeks to accomplish two objectives: (1) to provide a brief overview and characterization of what is meant by 'practical implications' within studies, and (2) to provide a unique way for scholars to identify the topics that are the most critical to family business practitioners for future study using this characterization as a guide.

Our chapter unfolds as follows. We introduce the different characteristics associated with practicality (i.e., Booker, Bontis, & Serenko, 2008) and provide a table that outlines these characteristics (Table 4.1). We then briefly review the key areas of research within the field of family business and what types of problems these areas of research have already attempted to solve for family firms. This provides a general review of what has thus far been focused upon in the field of family business research.

We then offer the preliminary results from a novel empirical approach to determine the most critical issues *currently occurring* within family firms, based upon what consultants and advisors are providing to these firms. Specifically, we identified 390 consulting firms across the United States and 78 consulting firms across Germany that in some way identify their firms as focused upon services which assist family firms in their business and family operations. Through these firms' websites, we then content analyzed and categorized all of their consulting services. We argue that this data highlights the most frequent, critical issues for which family business owners are willing to devote time and financial capital. Indeed, if family firms are opting to pay outside consulting services for assistance with pressing family and business issues, then scholars should find ways to theoretically understand these issues through the development of rigorous analysis that subsequently offers insight to practitioners that is practically relevant.

By reviewing the characteristics of practical implications and the past/current areas of focus in family business research, and then identifying the current hot button problems in family firms, we are able to see where our research may need to be focused in the future. In other words, we will identify where there may be only some or no overlap between family business research and problems family firms are facing in the real world. Armed with a better understanding of how to communicate the findings of academic research in a practical way, family business scholars have the opportunity to bridge the gap between research and practice in a pragmatic and problem-focused approach.

## PRACTICALITY OF FAMILY BUSINESS RESEARCH

Creating practically relevant research that is also theoretically sound is a challenge that the entirety of the social science research community grapples with because, in some ways, these two endeavors can be diametrically opposed. The operational demands of practicality, which requires the ability to apply what has been learned to context-specific issues or settings, is sometimes in direct conflict with the philosophical demands of academic research whereby scholars seek a global-level understanding of phenomena through theoretical and empirical analyses that can be generalized to various contexts. It is often difficult to successfully conduct one activity without affecting the success of the other (Bansal, Bertels, Ewart, MacConnachie, & O'Brien, 2012). Within the business disciplines, academics are trained extensively to derive theoretical insights from current literature and from issues they perceive to be present in business practice. They are also trained extensively to subsequently develop testable hypotheses related to their theoretical work. Interestingly, in our experience these same academics are not often trained to develop practical advice stemming from their research. Indeed, developing practical implications is not often an emphasis within PhD training programs. Likewise, we have only rarely noticed conference sessions or professional developmental workshops dedicated to this important topic. Instead, practical applications of research are frequently an afterthought in the journal publication process.

Some of the most impactful, practically relevant research begins with research questions and/or problems that are derived directly from observations in the business world (Drnevich, Mahoney, & Schendel, 2020). These research questions are then rigorously studied within the context of a variety of academic theories. If the results of research projects are meant to influence the ways practitioners think and act (Hideg, DeCelles, & Tihanyi, 2020; Nicolai & Seidl, 2010), then simply providing summaries of these results or restatements of academic implications in practical terms will be woefully inadequate. Thus, it is important to know what constitutes practicality for a practitioner, and how to convey the results of a study to practitioners in an effective way. In family business research, practicality takes on additional importance owing to the duality of possessing a family system and a business system within the organization. Hence, practical implications might refer to each of the two systems – as well as their interface. Properly conveying the practicality of the results can greatly affect the long-term health of both the family and the business.

There are several characteristics associated with practical implications as they relate to academic research, and these characteristics have been explored in differing ways (e.g., Baldridge, Floyd, & Markóczy, 2004; Booker et al., 2008; Vermeulen, 2007). To help understand these characteristics, we conducted a literature review of such studies to determine whether there are some commonalities associated with them. While there are some widely diverse characterizations of practicality, there are some frequently mentioned commonalities that have been identified as most important.

In general, the characteristics of practicality vary based upon a number of justifiable reasons. Not surprisingly, academics tend to use language that is somewhat precise in nature to describe study results (Booker et al., 2008). This precision therefore can lead to both positive (specific, measurable) or negative (not practical) characterizations of pragmatic implications associated with study results and insights. Conversely, family business practitioners need results and interpretations that can be easy to read, interpret, and use (generalizable to their circumstances), and such results and practical interpretations that can be used quickly and effectively (immediacy). Based upon our literature review of studies that identify practical implications as a source of insight, the most common characteristics of practicality include: *relevance* – which suggests that the insights obtained from the study can be readily used by practitioners within their own firms (Vermeulen, 2007); *novelty* – which implies that the practical implications may challenge existing approaches, or reveal conclusions that are counterintuitive in nature (Booker et al., 2008); *specificity* – which reflects the degree to which the practical conclusion is unambiguous and could be applied specifically to a particular problem (Beyer & Trice, 1982); *managerial knowledge extension* – which suggests that the implication clarifies existing practical knowledge to some insight that is beyond what is currently done (Baldridge et al., 2004; Booker et al., 2008); *understandability* – which means that the implication does not contain academic jargon and is thus easy for practitioners to understand (Booker et al., 2008); *controllability* – which implies that the implication can actually be something that the practitioner can exert control over (Vermeulen, 2007); *actionability* – which means the degree to which a practitioner can use the implication to help make actionable decisions (Booker et al., 2008); and *measurability* – which is the

*Table 4.1*    *Practical implications (PI) characteristics*

| PI Characteristic | Description | Reference |
|---|---|---|
| Relevance | The generation of insights that practitioners can utilize in their own organization | (Booker et al., 2008; Vermeulen, 2007) |
| Novelty | The degree to which the implication challenges existing practice and could lead to counterintuitive conclusions | (Booker et al., 2008) |
| Specificity | The degree to which the implication unambiguously defines an application to a particular problem | (Beyer & Trice, 1982) |
| Managerial Knowledge Extension | The degree to which the implication is clarifying knowledge through application beyond what is currently done | |
| Understandability | The degree to which the implication lacks jargon and is written so that practitioners will understand it | (Booker et al., 2008; Vermeulen, 2007) |
| Controllability | The degree to which practitioners are actually able to control the phenomena of study and its variables | (Vermeulen, 2007) |
| Actionability | Practitioners can use what is stated rather easily in making a number of decisions; operational validity | (Booker et al., 2008; Vermeulen, 2007) |
| Measurability | The degree to which practitioners will know that the changes in their actions toward particular phenomena have been effective | (Booker et al., 2008) |

degree to which practitioners will know that the changes in their actions toward particular phenomena have been effective (Booker et al., 2008).

Each of these characteristics can be found in different ways, and to varying degrees, within academic research studies. In some circumstances, an academic article on family business displays no practical implications, based upon the criteria discussed above. Therefore, it is important to link both the major academic research domains associated with family business with the actual family business 'practices' that are called for by family business founders/owners themselves. We assume (and we feel that this assumption is valid) that success in family business advising is a function of offering services that family businesses are requesting. If so, then the alignment of practice-based activities with family business research is a novel and powerful opportunity to advance both research and practice as well. A review of major themes in family business, and its alignment (or misalignment) with advising practice is presented below.

## CURRENT THEMES IN FAMILY FIRM RESEARCH

Academic research has long been interested in family businesses and enterprises. This interest has been inspired by the particular idiosyncrasies that are associated with families, their relationships among themselves and with others, and what this means to their family and/or business. Most notably, several somewhat-unique aspects of family enterprises are often explored as research topics. These unique aspects include succession processes that are by definition a hallmark of family enterprises, the roles and relationships of family members to their family firms, the strategies designed to manage both family and business growth and wealth, and how external actors support such businesses through coaching or advising. Each of these broad areas have developed theory and empirical evidence that has helped inform other family business scholars and interested practitioners.

Family business succession is, not surprisingly, a core research area of interest to family business scholars. Business succession is, in fact, a core part of the definition of what constitutes a family firm (De Massis, Chua, & Chrisman, 2008). The planning, identification, and acculturation process of potential successors seen in family businesses is often driven by the desire of the family founder(s) to maintain family ownership and leadership into the next generation. Research on succession has explored how internal family members assume family business leadership, how their experiences and existing family relationships affect their acceptability to family business founders, and how this process is seen as a success or failure (De Massis et al., 2008). This line of research has extended across generations (Jaskiewicz, Combs, & Rau, 2015), and across cultural components (Feldman, Lukes, & Uhlaner, 2020). Not surprisingly, the long history of academic research on succession has been informed by qualitative and quantitative methodologies, and through the historical narratives seen in popular media.

An additional area of scholarly research that touches on the practice of family business is the interconnected nature (and potential for synergies or conflicts) associated with family firms. Research in this broad area has examined the relationships between the family members themselves, the family, and the business (Michael-Tsabari, Houshmand, Strike, & Treister, 2020), and the family and non-family members of family firms (Tabor, Chrisman, Madison, & Vardaman, 2018). This rich area of research has explored topics at the micro-level of analysis, to include the psychological nature of individual relationships between family members and the conflict and compromise that can result at the family and business interface (i.e., Frank, Kessler, Nose, & Suchy, 2011). Yet this literature stream has also noted the potential for the development of familiness (Habbershon & Williams, 1999), which denotes the unique and valuable resources that families bring to their businesses, and how it can ultimately result in competitive advantage. At a broader level, the 'interconnectedness' associated with family business research can be seen in the relationships between multi-family firms (Duran & Ortiz, 2020) as well.

Likewise, these micro and macro areas of family business research influence the oftentimes unique organizational-level strategies, to include the tactics and processes of growth and wealth creation, associated with family firms. Family business research has highlighted the application of different theoretical frameworks (such as agency and stakeholder theories), as well as the application of mainstream strategic management theories (such as the resource-based view and dynamic capabilities), as a means to describe the common and disparate characteristics between family and non-family businesses regarding strategic decision-making (i.e., Chrisman, Chua, & Sharma, 2005). These same strategic management perspectives have been examined solely within the family business domain, as a mechanism to explore the heterogeneity seen among family firms themselves (Chua, Chrisman, Steier, & Rau, 2012; Daspit et al., Chapter 5 in this book).

Finally, it is important to note that the field of family business research has explored the important role of coaching and advising as it relates to family firms (Gersick, 2015). This broad area of research is somewhat unique to academic scholarship in this domain, since the ownership and management of family businesses touches on both sides of the equation – the family side and the business side. Researchers have explored the roles and relationships between families and their advising contacts (Strike, Michel, & Kammerlander, 2018), to include the role of family offices (Welsh, Memili, Rosplock, Roure, & Segurado, 2013) and peer-advising engagements (Caspersz & Thomas, 2015). Mentorship, coaching, and the importance these advising activities have on the relationships between and among family business members is also a prominent area of research within the advising arena (Dhaenens, Marler, Vardaman, & Chrisman, 2018).

Each of these broad areas of family business research have connections between the practitioner and the academic scholar. However, a central question that remains is: To what degree do the actual needs of family business owners/founders match up with the academic scholarship we have seen over the last several decades? Our novel approach to broadly address this question is provided below.

## PRACTICE THEMES ASSOCIATED WITH FAMILY FIRM CONSULTING

Family business scholars often begin their research efforts by focusing on theoretical contributions, drawing upon prior academic work (Micelotta, Chapter

2 in this book). Likewise, a strong focus on new methods to test the theory are also prominent. We see examples of this, such as the use of multi-level modeling techniques and the use of structural equation modeling (SEM) tools that can capture latent constructs and causal linkages. This focus has the potential to remove family business scholars from the phenomenon of interest (Whetten, 1989) making it difficult to even identify the practical problems that should be addressed. What can come from this situation is scholars consistently focusing on the same problems with increasingly incremental contributions to the existing body of knowledge. We believe that this type of academic research can be important, but it is also very important to try to solve new problems and/or the most painful problems as identified by practitioners themselves.

With this in mind, we identified 390 consulting firms across the United States and 78 consulting firms across Germany that in some way claim they focus their consulting work on family-owned business problems. We contend that consulting firms address the most pressing needs/problems of their clients, as evidenced by the willingness of clients to pay to have their problems solved. Indeed, firms would not spend money or time on a particular issue unless it was important.

Consulting firms act much like any entrepreneurial business venture in that they interact with the customer and provide services to solve the needs of customers as problems present themselves. If the customer need is strong enough, then the consulting firm will figure out a way to solve the need. Therefore, family business consulting firm services are a reflection of family firm practical problems 'in the field'. Consequently, to identify the most significant problems within family firms, we content analyzed the services offered by our sample of family business consulting firms via an analysis of their public websites. The result was an extensive list of services that ranged from numerous types of different estate planning activities to family meetings and family constitutions, to conflict resolution and children/sibling rivalry. We then grouped these activities into 15 categories. In each category, we are able to state what percentage of firms – within the sample of 390 US firms and 78 German firms – offer certain types of services. Finally, we then numerically ordered the 15 categories to show how many consulting firms offer similar services and this provides us with what we believe are the most pressing issues facing family firms in the United States and in Germany (see Table 4.2).

Overall, our comparison shows that succession still seems to be the most pressing issue among countries.[1] Other topics seem to be more country spe-

---

[1]    German family business consulting firms seem to be more focused on specific topic areas, instead of offering a broad array of services. This results in an overall lower percentage of numbers as compared to the US firms.

*Table 4.2     Family business consulting firm service offerings*

| Services Offered | US | | GERMANY | |
| --- | --- | --- | --- | --- |
| | Number of Firms | Percent of Firms | Number of Firms | Percent of Firms |
| Succession | 278 | 81.76% | 56 | 71.79% |
| Non-HR Business Issues | 218 | 64.12% | 23 | 29.49% |
| Strategic Planning | 201 | 59.12% | 21 | 26.92% |
| Estate Planning | 177 | 52.06% | 2 | 2.56% |
| Boards of Directors | 166 | 48.82% | 14 | 17.95% |
| Family Issues (Not Conflict) | 162 | 47.65% | 16 | 20.51% |
| Family Conflict | 150 | 44.12% | 25 | 32.05% |
| Leadership | 135 | 39.71% | 15 | 19.23% |
| Next Generation Issues | 125 | 36.76% | 5 | 6.41% |
| Family Office/Family Planning | 122 | 35.88% | 3 | 3.85% |
| Wealth Management | 97 | 28.53% | 9 | 11.54% |
| Human Resources | 94 | 27.65% | 19 | 24.36% |
| Business Growth | 76 | 22.35% | 6 | 7.69% |
| Cash Flow | 75 | 22.06% | N/A | N/A |
| Compensation | 49 | 14.41% | N/A | N/A |

*Note*:     Family business consulting firms often offer numerous services. Therefore, the percentage of firms do not add up to 100 percent.

cific. For instance, the focus on cash flow and compensation is much less salient in Germany as compared to the US. Yet, family strategy and family governance-focused issues, such as family charters, are more prevalent among German consulting firms. Interestingly, the next generation consulting of US firms covers a broad range of education topics, while the German firms focus more on owner qualification in general, potentially addressing somewhat older family members compared to the US.

## LINKING THEORY WITH PRACTICE IN FAMILY FIRMS

Our contention is that the examination of what family firm consultants and advisors offer to family businesses is a prime opportunity to link current family business research themes to possible future research opportunities. Using our approach to identify topics of research as a guide, several intriguing opportunities can be leveraged. Some examples of this approach, and the implications associated with our framework are provided below.

A key theme that is of constant interest in family business research is focused on the structuring characteristics, and why they are used, within family businesses. For example, how might business restructuring and corporate turn-arounds differ in the family business context considering that many restructuring processes include the firing of key employees, the sell-off of potentially unrelated business entities, or the re-organization of units or subunits? Would socio-emotional wealth (SEW) needs result in less effective restructuring for family firms versus non-family firms? What are the best ways to study these differences other than through a SEW theoretical lens?

Moreover, a detailed look at the German data shows that a relatively large number of consulting firms (9 out of 78) offer support in *implementing*, rather than drafting, strategies. This indicates that family firms serve specific needs when incorporating changes into their business operations. While academic research has touched upon these differences – e.g., relating to different decision-making structures and available resources – we lack knowledge about the pitfalls and best practices on how to *implement* change in long-standing, tradition-laden family firms with potentially long-tenured employees.

Some recent academic research has been done on advisors in the family business literature (Strike et al. 2018 comes to mind) and on the overall advising process associated with family business consulting. Since consultants are often tasked with helping family businesses build their advisory boards, to what extent are family businesses encouraged to include individuals who also own family businesses on the board, and have some connection to the advisors as well? This question can get at the heart of the agency challenges that can occur in the establishment of advisor boards, and the interconnected relationships that can often form. Likewise, we need more information about which competences family firm board members need, and where these competencies are best developed or obtained. The analysis of German consulting firms revealed an increasing focus (10 out of 78 consulting firms) on digitalization, indicating that technological change is one of the most pressing, contemporary challenges of family firms. While research on digitalization in family firms is expanding (Soluk & Kammerlander, 2021; Soluk, Miroshnychenko, Kammerlander, & De Massis, 2021) we still do not know how those trends affect the optimal board composition of family firms. Moreover, bridging the research-teaching domains, researchers might take a more active role in designing and running programs which can help new board members to understand the family and business issues associated with their firms.

Examining the activities conducted by consultants, we see an emphasis on personal and family-related aspects that are at times critical but understudied. For example, advising services that concern alcohol or drug addiction amongst family members is an open area of study, as is the mechanisms associated with new spouses and stepfamily accommodations. Likewise, how does personal coaching influence family business success? Family governance was a topic offered by more than 20 percent of all German family firm consultants – in research, we observe much less attention paid to these issues. In particular, practice assumes that governance structures such as charters help families become more effective. But more research about what these structures are, how they can be best decided upon and implemented, and under which conditions they are more or less efficient are critical consulting activities that family business scholars are just now exploring.

Finally, while significant research efforts have been dedicated to the study of the processes and outcomes of succession, there are still critical areas of consulting practice that are unexplored with family business scholarship. For example, a detailed analysis of the consultancy services offered reveals that a substantial number of German consulting firms (21%) offer specialized services on selling the family firm. While entrepreneurial exit literature (e.g., Wennberg, Wiklund, DeTienne, & Cardon, 2010) has studied this subject, we still don't know enough about the family side of selling the business. For instance – How can the family agree on sales in general and the buyer and sales price of the business in particular? How should the next generation be involved in this process, if at all? And how does the entrepreneurial family act (together as one family) after the sale of the firm? To address the latter issue, dedicated consultancies offer families advice on how to set up and run a family office subsequent to the sale of the business. In order to help those practitioners, more research is needed, as family office research is still in its infancy (see Schickinger, Bierl, Leitterstorf, & Kammerlander, 2021).

These and other opportunities showcase how linking what family business advisors and consultants do more concretely to existing family business research literature streams can serve to inspire future family business scholarship going forward. We believe that this effort can serve as a model framework for connecting family business research and practice in the future.

## CONCLUSIONS

Family business research has, since its inception, required a great deal of effort to capture the internal and external characteristics of both the firms and the families to generate insights on how these structures interact within the business and family domain. As a result, these efforts are often informed and supported by those advisors and consultants that help connect researchers to these often-private business organizations. It is our belief that there are other ways that insights can be gained from what advisors and consultants do. By examining the services they provide, family business scholars are able to determine how well or poorly these services align with existing family business literature streams. Our efforts with this chapter are designed to provide one useful approach to expanding these insights. By capturing 'what the consultants actually do for family businesses,' we as family business scholars can see 'what research is needed,' and in that way more tightly connect the practice of family business with the research that is designed to understand and inform it.

# REFERENCES

Astrachan, C. B., Astrachan, J. H., Kotlar, J., & Michiels, A. (2021). Addressing the theory–practice divide in family business research: The case of shareholder agreements. *Journal of Family Business Strategy, 12*(1), 100395.

Baldridge, D. C., Floyd, S. W., & Markóczy, L. (2004). Are managers from Mars and academicians from Venus? Toward an understanding of the relationship between academic quality and practical relevance. *Strategic Management Journal, 25*(11), 1063–1074.

Bansal, P., Bertels, S., Ewart, T., MacConnachie, P., & O'Brien, J. (2012). Bridging the research–practice gap. *Academy of Management Perspectives, 26*(1), 73–92.

Beyer, J. M., & Trice, H. M. (1982). The utilization process: A conceptual framework and synthesis of empirical findings. *Administrative Science Quarterly, 27*(4), 591–622.

Booker, L. D., Bontis, N., & Serenko, A. (2008). The relevance of knowledge management and intellectual capital research. *Knowledge and Process Management, 15*(4), 235–246.

Caspersz, D., & Thomas, J. (2015). Developing positivity in family business leaders. *Family Business Review, 28*, 60–75.

Chrisman, J., Chua, J., & Sharma, P. (2005). Trends and directions in the development of a strategic management theory of the family firm. *Entrepreneurship Theory and Practice, 29*, 555–576.

Chua, J. H., Chrisman, J. J., & Sharma, P. (1999). Defining the family business by behavior. *Entrepreneurship Theory and Practice, 23*(4), 19–39.

Chua, J., Chrisman, J., Steier, L., & Rau, S. (2012). Sources of heterogeneity in family firms: An introduction. *Entrepreneurship Theory and Practice, 36*, 1103–1113.

De Massis, A., Chua, J., & Chrisman, J. (2008). Factors preventing intrafamily succession: An investigation of its antecedents. *Family Business Review, 29*, 278–300.

Dhaenens, A., Marler, L., Vardaman, J., & Chrisman, J. (2018). Mentoring in family businesses: Toward an understanding of commitment outcomes. *Human Resource Management Review, 28*, 46–55.

Drnevich, P., Mahoney, J., & Schendel, D. (2020). Has strategic management research lost its way? *Strategic Management Review, 1*(1), 35–73.

Duran, P., & Ortiz, M. (2020). When more is better: Multifamily firms and firm performance. *Entrepreneurship Theory and Practice, 44*, 761–783.

Feldman, M., Lukes, M., & Uhlaner, L. (2020). Disentangling succession and entrepreneurship gender gaps: Gender norms, culture, & family. *Small Business Economics*, 1–17.

Frank, H., Kessler, A., Nose, L., & Suchy, D. (2011). Conflicts in family firms: State of the art and perspectives for future research. *Journal of Family Business Management, 1*, 130–153.

Gersick, K. (2015). Essay on practice: Advising family enterprise in the fourth decade. *Entrepreneurship Theory and Practice, 39*, 1433–1450.

Gersick, K. E., Davis, J. A., Hampton, M. M., & Lansberg, I. (1997). *Generation to Generation: Life Cycles of the Family Business*. Cambridge, MA: Harvard Business Press.

Habbershon, T. G., & Williams, M. L. (1999). A resource-based framework for assessing the strategic advantages of family firms. *Family Business Review, 12*(1), 1–25.

Hideg, I., DeCelles, K. A., & Tihanyi, L. (2020). Publishing practical and responsible research in AMJ. *The Academy of Management Journal, 63*(6), 1681–1686.

Jaskiewicz, P., Combs, J., & Rau, S. (2015). Entrepreneurial legacy: Toward a theory of how some family firms nurture transgenerational entrepreneurship. *Journal of Business Venturing, 30*, 29–49.

Michael-Tsabari, N., Houshmand, M., Strike, V. M., & Treister, D. E. (2020). Uncovering implicit assumptions: Reviewing the work–family interface in family business and offering opportunities for future research. *Family Business Review, 33*, 64–89.

Nicolai, A., & Seidl, D. (2010). That's relevant! Different forms of practical relevance in management science. *Organization Studies, 31*(9–10), 1257–1285.

Schickinger, A., Bierl, P. A., Leitterstorf, M. P., & Kammerlander, N. (2021). Family-related goals, entrepreneurial investment behavior, and governance mechanisms of single family offices: An exploratory study. *Journal of Family Business Strategy*. https://doi.org/10.1016/j.jfbs.2020.100393.

Sharma, P., Chrisman, J. J., & Gersick, K. E. (2012). 25 Years of *Family Business Review*: Reflections on the past and perspectives for the future. *Family Business Review, 25*(1), 5–15.

Simsek, Z., Bansal, P., Shaw, J. D., Heugens, P., & Smith, W. K. (2018). From the editors: Seeing practice impact in new ways. *Academy of Management Journal, 61*(6), 2021–2025.

Soluk, J., & Kammerlander, N. (2021). Digital transformation in family-owned Mittelstand firms: A dynamic capabilities perspective. *European Journal of Information Systems, 30*(6), 676–711.

Soluk, J., Miroshnychenko, I., Kammerlander, N., & De Massis, A. (2021). Better equipped for digital business models: How does the owning family influence how businesses develop digital business model innovation? *Entrepreneurship Theory and Practice, 45*(4), 867–905.

Strike, V., Michel, A., & Kammerlander, N. (2018). Unpacking the black box of family business advising: Insights from psychology. *Family Business Review, 31*, 80–124.

Tabor, W., Chrisman, J., Madison, K., & Vardaman, J. (2018). Nonfamily members in family firms: A review and future agenda. *Family Business Review, 31*, 54–79.

Vermeulen, F. (2007). 'I shall not remain insignificant': Adding a second loop to matter more. *Academy of Management Journal, 50*(4), 754–761.

Welsh, D., Memili, E., Rosplock, K., Roure, J., & Segurado, J. (2013). Perceptions of entrepreneurship across generations in family offices: A stewardship theory perspective. *Journal of Family Business Strategy, 4*, 213–226.

Wennberg, K., Wiklund, J., DeTienne, D., & Cardon, M. (2010). Reconceptualizing entrepreneurial exit: Divergent exit routes and their drivers. *Journal of Business Venturing, 25*(4), 361–375.

Whetten, D. A. (1989). What constitutes a theoretical contribution? *Academy of Management Review, 14*(4), 490–495.

# 5. Researching family firm heterogeneity: a guide to identifying firm-level categorical and variational differences

**Joshua J. Daspit, James J. Chrisman, Vitaliy Skorodziyevskiy, Sara Davis, and Triss Ashton**

Family business research has evolved considerably in recent decades. In addition to a substantial increase in the number of studies published (Zhang, Fang, Dou, & Chrisman, 2022), the field has gained more attention and its boundary-spanning reach has grown (Holt, Pearson, Payne, & Sharma, 2018). As a result of the field's reach, rigor, and relevance (Sharma, 2015), studies of family businesses have gained more legitimacy in top-tier outlets (Brinkerink, 2023). With the field's evolution, studies have progressed from primarily examining differences between family and nonfamily firms toward an increased focus on understanding the differences among family firms.[1] The family's involvement in the firm creates unique complexities that are not observed in other organizational contexts, leading to potentially greater differences among family firms than the differences observed among nonfamily firms (Bennedsen, Pérez-González, & Wolfenzon, 2010).

Despite the growth of the field and the increased focus on understanding family firm heterogeneity (i.e., the differences among family firms), researchers continue to face challenges identifying and articulating such differences across family firms. These challenges originate from inconsistent and vague conceptualizations of heterogeneity and a lack of clarity related to how and why such differences exist. The inability to articulate differences among family firms has the potential to result in the imprecise development of theory, empirical inaccuracies, a mistaken understanding of family firms, and mis-

---

[1] We define the family firm as a firm in which ownership and/or management are controlled by a family or small number of families who possess the ability, and usually the intention, for transgenerational succession (Chua, Chrisman, & Sharma, 1999).

guided recommendations for firm leaders (Chua, Chrisman, Steier, & Rau, 2012).

Therefore, this chapter offers a practical guide to support researchers and their studies of family firm heterogeneity. Specifically, a description of family firm heterogeneity is offered that highlights two key types of differences among family firms: categorical and variational differences. Examples are offered to describe categorical and variational differences within the goals, governance factors, and resources of family firms. Furthermore, promising opportunities are presented for researchers interested in investigating family firm heterogeneity.

## FAMILY FIRM HETEROGENEITY

The scope of differences among family firms is vast. Studies note family firms differ in many ways, including in their values (Rau, Schneider-Siebke, & Gunther, 2019), socioemotional wealth (SEW) endowments (Gómez-Mejía, Haynes, Núñez-Nickel, Jacobson, & Moyano-Fuentes, 2007), the pursuit of noneconomic goals (Chrisman, Chua, Pearson, & Barnett, 2012), governance configurations (Chrisman, Chua, & Litz, 2004), resources (Sirmon & Hitt, 2003), and long-term orientation (Chrisman & Patel, 2012). While researchers acknowledge the multitude of differences, in family firm scholarship, 'heterogeneity' has become *omnia omnibus*: a phrase meaning 'many things to many people.' As a result, studies have taken numerous approaches to conceptualize and measure the differences among family firms.

In a recent review of over 700 articles on family firm heterogeneity, Daspit, Chrisman, Ashton, and Evangelopoulos (2021) integrated insights from the field of ecology—a field that has experienced similar challenges regarding heterogeneity—to define family firm heterogeneity as 'the range of categorical and/or variational difference(s) between or among family firms at a given time or across time' (p. 298). This definition notes a distinction between categorical and variational differences among family firms. Following this, we recognize the challenges researchers face when articulating such distinctions in family firm heterogeneity studies.

To date, researchers have historically faced a lack of definitional consistency, which has led to inconsistent descriptions of differences. However, even though a definition of family firm heterogeneity is now available, precisely identifying and clearly describing the differences among family firms may remain a challenge. Thus, to help scholars overcome potential hurdles, we offer descriptions and examples of categorical and variational differences among family firms. Following the work of Chrisman, Sharma, Steier, and Chua (2013), we examine heterogeneity at the firm level and share examples of categorical and variational differences within family firm goals, governance factors, and resources.[2]

## EXAMPLES OF CATEGORICAL AND VARIATIONAL DIFFERENCES IN FAMILY FIRM GOALS, GOVERNANCE, AND RESOURCES

### Goals

Family firms are comprised of two separate, yet interrelated, systems: the firm and the family (Habbershon, Williams, & MacMillan, 2003). Family firms pursue both economic and noneconomic goals, and studies indicate that non-economic goals, at times, are of greater importance to the controlling family (e.g., Chrisman & Patel, 2012). Thus, given the differing types of goals in the family firm, and their importance, examples of categorical differences among family firm goals are offered. To structure these examples, we adapt the model of family firm outcomes by Holt, Pearson, Carr, and Barnett (2017).[3] As seen in Figure 5.1, goals may be categorized as relating primarily to the firm or family. Both categorizations can be further deconstructed into sub-categorical classifications, which include economic goals, noneconomic (internal) goals, and noneconomic (external) goals.

### Economic goals

Firm-specific, economic goals generally set the boundary for the expected financial well-being and survivability of the business. As such, the firm-oriented, economic goals of family firms include aspirations for profitability, growth, and profit margin (e.g., ROI, ROE, ROA). Further, the firm's economic goals may also include market-specific variables (e.g., Tobin's Q, P/E ratio, market share, sales growth). Like their nonfamily counterparts, family firms differ in which of the categorically unique economic goals are pursued. Of the goals pursued, the extent to which an economic goal is pursued varies across family firms, affecting the goal's outcome.

Additionally, family firms are distinct from nonfamily firms given the pursuit of family-specific goals. Family-oriented, economic goals include

---

[2]    Family firms pursue economic and noneconomic goals (Gómez-Mejía et al., 2007), are known for governance structures that accentuate parsimony and unilateral decision making (Carney, 2005), and possess unique resources (Sirmon & Hitt, 2003). Thus, we rely on a broad, firm-level classification that recognizes goal, governance, and resource differences among family firms (Chrisman et al., 2013).

[3]    We recognize that the family firm's goal pursuit is the means through which 'stocks' of outcomes are achieved (Chua, Chrisman, & De Massis, 2015).

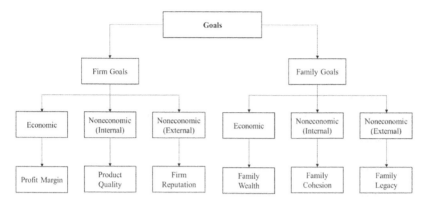

*Note*: With respect to family firm goals, examples of categorical differences are offered following the family firm outcomes model by Holt et al. (2017). Variation may be observed within the respective (sub)categorical elements noted. This is not an exhaustive representation of all potential (sub)categorical differences that exist related to family firm goals.

*Figure 5.1     Heterogeneity of goals*

creating wealth, assets, and market returns that benefit the controlling family. Similarly, this unique aspect varies across family firms: some family firms place greater importance on such goals. Thus, studies of family firm heterogeneity may examine, for example, differing categories of economic goals (e.g., firm- versus family-oriented economic goals) and/or the extent to which each type of goal is pursued.

**Noneconomic goals**
Family firms are widely acknowledged for the potential emphasis they place on noneconomic goals. Given that numerous types of noneconomic goals exist, we offer examples of noneconomic goals related to both firm goals and family goals. Within each of these categories, noneconomic goals are categorized as being internal or external. For instance, noneconomic goals that are internal to the firm include product/service quality and employee job satisfaction. The categorizations of firm-specific, internal noneconomic goals differ depending on numerous factors that include the strategy pursued, industry, location, and culture. Much like nonfamily firms, family firms pursue firm-specific, noneconomic goals that are external to the firm, which include firm reputation, customer satisfaction, and customer loyalty. While the categories of firm-level (internal and external) noneconomic goals are also common to nonfamily firms, the categories of firm-level noneconomic goals—along

with the extent to which the goals are pursued—are not necessarily consistent across family firms.

Additionally, the firm's controlling family may use the business to pursue noneconomic goals that specifically benefit them. Noneconomic goals that benefit the internal welfare of the family include the family's intention for succession, the desire to behave altruistically toward family members, as well as the cohesion, commitment, and social status of the family (Schulze, Lubatkin, Dino, & Buchholtz, 2001). Also, family firms may strive to achieve noneconomic goals that benefit the family in external ways (e.g., the family being highly regarded by external stakeholders and/or the family having a multigenerational legacy). With respect to goals, family firms exhibit categorical differences, which are observed by the distinct types of goals that exist. Further, the extent to which any goal is pursued creates variational differences across family firms (i.e., some family firms pursue a given goal more than others). Thus, accounting for the type of goal (category) and the extent to which the goal is viewed as important and ultimately pursued (variation) elucidates categorical and variational differences, providing refined insight into the heterogeneity of family firm goals.

## Governance

Family firms have unique governance structures given the involvement of family members in owning, managing, and/or controlling the firm (Chua et al., 1999). To offer examples of heterogeneity that is specific to family firm governance, we follow the work of Hambrick and Mason (1984) to highlight observable and psychological differences in the categorical types of family firm governance, and we note examples of variation within each type (see Figure 5.2).

### Family ownership

Observable differences include characteristics that are tangible and easily detectable (e.g., demographics). The familial status of owners is an observable characteristic that offers insight into the type of governance structure used by the family firm. Family ownership configurations differ across several dimensions including the number of owners, the family's share of ownership and its dispersion among family members, the relationships among family owners, the characteristics of family owners, and the extent to which family owners are involved in the firm's management and/or board of directors (Daspit, Chrisman, Sharma, Pearson, & Mahto, 2018). For example, the family firm may be classified as a sibling partnership or a cousin consortium depending on the type of familial relationship among the owners (Gersick, Davis, McCollom-Hampton, & Lansberg, 1997). As another categorical

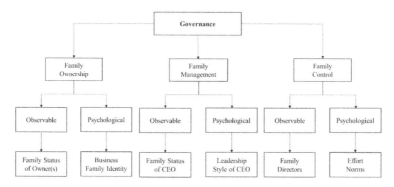

*Note*:     With respect to family firm governance, examples of categorical differences (e.g., family ownership, management, and control) are offered following the work of Chua et al. (1999) with sub-categorical differences noted based on upper echelons theory (Hambrick & Mason, 1984). Variation may be observed within the respective (sub)categorical elements noted. This is not an exhaustive representation of all potential (sub)categorical differences that exist related to family firm governance.

*Figure 5.2     Heterogeneity of governance*

example of family ownership, multi-family firms—firms in which ownership is shared among several families—face additional complexities inherent to this governance form that are noted to impact their behaviors and outcomes (Chrisman, Madison, & Kim, 2021). Accordingly, the variation of ownership can be a metric used (in part) to determine whether the family's involvement reaches a given threshold, allowing for the firm to be considered a family firm (e.g., >50% family ownership). For examples of other criteria, see Chapter 9 in this book by Kammerlander and Diaz-Moriana.

Numerous psychological factors, which are less-easily observed, are relevant to understanding differences among family ownership. Owners may, for example, obtain utility from their psychological ownership of the firm (Craig & Lumpkin, Chapter 3 in this book), or they may experience a unique type of business-family identity, which exists when family owners closely identify with the firm (Berrone, Cruz, & Gómez-Mejía, 2012). Business-family identity influences the principal–principal dynamics among owners. In fact, a high level of this identity enhances the family firm's growth depending on the size of the ownership group. One study finds that having approximately ten owners is ideal for controlling principal–principal issues (Calabrò, Campopiano, & Basco, 2017). Of course, if one family member owns 100 percent of the firm, principal–principal conflict is irrelevant. Nonetheless, psychological factors can have both categorical and variational differences.

**Family management**

The CEO—or top manager—of the family firm may be categorized using numerous factors. Concerning observable factors, family firms led by a family member CEO are shown to outperform those with a nonfamily (professional) CEO (Jaskiewicz & Luchak, 2013) while Bennedsen and colleagues (2007) find that second-generation family firms with nonfamily CEOs outperform those with family successors. These findings suggest that the interaction of these two aspects, relational and generational, may yield opposite outcomes. Moreover, the extent of formal education, 'growing up' in the family firm, and working outside the firm are additional observable factors that vary across family firm CEOs. In some cases, the differences have major performance implications (Pérez-González, 2006).

From a psychological perspective, differences among family firms can manifest from the CEO's leadership style. For instance, family firm CEOs classified as Machiavellian (i.e., highly manipulative in their leadership style) tend to engage in strategic alliances that are not necessarily sustainable (Chandler, Petrenko, Hill, & Hayes, 2021). As a further example, for top management team (TMT) members who are kin, psychological ownership of the firm is highly correlated with their psychological ownership of the job, yet this is not the case for nonfamily TMT members (Lee, Makri, & Scandura, 2019). Nonetheless, a CEO's leadership style, personality trait, or psychological ownership is likely to vary in comparison to others. As demonstrated, family firms exhibit both categorical and variational differences when kin are involved in management roles.

**Family control**

Family members may exert control of the family firm through their involvement in the board of directors. The family's involvement in the board is an observable characteristic, and when making observations across family firms, board classifications may include those with or without family involvement. Also, the extent of family involvement in the board varies widely. Studies note that some family firms are reluctant to appoint professional (nonfamily) directors and, hence, appoint family members with potentially lower levels of knowledge and capabilities (Dunn, 1995). The extent to which the family is involved in the board—alongside the extent of knowledge, capabilities, and other factors—creates variational differences among family firms.

Psychological differences also exist with respect to family management. For instance, outside (nonfamily) members on the board are noted to have influential effects that are both positive and negative. Interestingly, in her study of family firm boards, Bettinelli (2011) finds that when outside directors are involved, effort-related norms and cohesiveness of the board are altered. On the other hand, variation in the board's composition can create faultlines that negatively impact performance (Vandebeek, Voordeckers, Lambrechts, & Huybrechts, 2016). Thus, in addition to observable characteristics, psychological differences contribute to categorical and variational differences among family firms.

## Resources

Like goals and governance structures, resources also differ across family firms. Family involvement generates unique resources and capabilities that impact the behaviors and outcomes of the firm (Habbershon et al., 2003). While acknowledging that numerous resources exist within any firm, we follow the work of Danes, Stafford, Haynes, and Amarapurkar (2009) to offer examples of categorical and variational differences related to the social, human, and financial resources of family firms. These are displayed in Figure 5.3.

### Social capital

Social capital is 'the sum of the actual and potential resources embedded within, available through, and derived from the network of relationships possessed by an individual or social unit' (Nahapiet & Ghoshal, 1998, p. 243). To illustrate the heterogeneity of social capital among family firms, we highlight two distinct categorizations of social capital: bonding and bridging. Bonding social capital is developed from the tight bonds of trust found in a group of relatively homogeneous individuals (Putnam, 2000). Based on the unique trust,

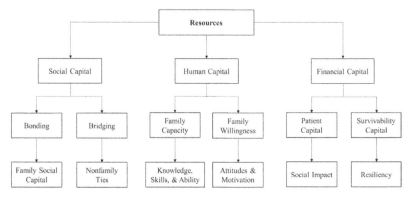

*Note*: With respect to family firm resources, examples of categorical differences (e.g., social, human, and financial) are offered following the work of Danes et al. (2009). Variation may be observed within the respective (sub)categorical elements noted. This is not an exhaustive representation of all potential (sub)categorical differences that exist related to family firm resources.

*Figure 5.3    Heterogeneity of resources*

stability, interdependence, and closure present in the family, the social capital formed among kin creates a unique type of social capital, known as family social capital, which is '… one of the most enduring and powerful forms of social capital' (Arregle, Hitt, Sirmon, & Very, 2007, p. 77). Family social capital exists in family firms, yet it is not necessarily ubiquitous. In fact, family social capital varies among family firms due, in part, to structural, cognitive, and relational differences (Sanchez-Ruiz, Daspit, Holt, & Rutherford, 2019).

While the social capital among family members is an example of bonding social capital, bridging social capital consists of (external) ties with less-similar individuals and/or collectives where relationships are comparatively weaker and less-frequently leveraged (Adler & Kwon, 2002; Putnam, 2000). Employing nonfamily members—individuals with whom the family may not have strong ties—is typically necessary for the professionalization and growth of the family firm (Stewart & Hitt, 2012). On the other hand, the lack of trust with nonfamily 'outsiders' is known to create faultlines, impede progress, and lead to the bifurcated treatment of family and nonfamily employees (Verbeke & Kano, 2012).

The bridging social capital that manifests between the dominant coalition of kin and nonfamily employees results from weaker ties, fewer common experiences, and ultimately, less trust. Accordingly, as Tabor and colleagues (2018) note, the strength of ties with nonfamily members varies. For example, some family firms leverage their social networks to hire nonfamily members with whom they have (at least some level of) trust. In contrast, other family firms are less willing to invest in cultivating stronger ties with nonfamily members. Despite the type of social capital, family firms vary in the extent to which each exists.

## Human capital

Leonard (2004) notes that, according to some theorists, social capital can 'pave the way' for acquiring human and financial capital. Human capital—the combined knowledge, skills, and capabilities of individuals involved in the firm (Sirmon & Hitt, 2003)—takes many forms. Herein, we offer an example of the categorical distinctions made by Dawson (2012) in her conceptualization of family firm human capital that includes the family's (1) knowledge, skills, and abilities (KSAs) and (2) attitudes and motivation. Concerning KSAs, family members tend to possess deep tacit knowledge given their early exposure to and involvement in the family firm (Sirmon & Hitt, 2003). However, family firms suffer from labor-related capacity constraints when the pool of human capital is limited to kin (Carney, 2005). Nevertheless, the KSAs of family members can be enhanced through formal education, employment experience outside of the family firm, and additional training, creating variation in the KSAs of family members.

In her conceptualization of family human capital, Dawson (2012) also argues that family firms uniquely benefit from the willingness of family members. The willingness of family members to contribute to the family firm—given their alignment of personal and firm-level goals—underscores an idiosyncratic behavioral dimension of family human capital with the potential to create a sustainable competitive advantage. Despite the presence of such willingness, though, notable variation exists among family firms due to the array of factors contributing to the attitudes and motivations that create this alignment.

**Financial capital**

Financial capital can be categorized in numerous ways. As an example of categorical distinctions, though, we highlight patient capital and survivability capital given their uniqueness to the family firm (Sirmon & Hitt, 2003). Family firms are often more consistent in their 'business-building efforts' given their long-term orientation and desire to create transgenerational success (Ward, 1997). Because of this expanded temporal horizon, they benefit from patient financial capital, which is financial capital invested over an extended period with no immediate expectation of repayment (Sirmon & Hitt, 2003). Sharma and Sharma (2019) note that among the common characteristics of family firms, leveraging patient capital is a willingness to forego short-term financial returns to achieve long-term economic, social, and/or environmental returns. Given the costs and benefits associated with patient capital, the extent to which it exists across family firms, and the reasons for why it exists, certainly vary.

Another type of capital that is more salient in family (versus nonfamily) firms is survivability capital. Survivability capital includes the collective resources kin are willing to offer or loan the family business to secure its welfare (Sirmon & Hitt, 2003). When faced with an economic crisis, for example, family members may reduce their pay to avoid reducing the firm's labor force (Su & Carney, 2013). This type of capital provides a safety net for the business during difficult times. Of course, not all family firms have access to the same types or levels of survivability capital because of the ability and/or willingness of family members to provide it. As a result, not all family firms are similar in their resilience to turbulent conditions.

## DISCUSSION, FUTURE DIRECTIONS, AND LIMITATIONS

Despite the increased research attention focused on understanding family firm heterogeneity, researchers studying this topic continue to face challenges with consistently identifying and articulating differences across family firms. In this chapter, we attempt to enhance clarity by unpacking the definition of family firm heterogeneity and offering researchers a practical guide with examples of categorical and variational differences related to the goals, governance components, and resources of family firms. Provided that much remains to be understood, modern scholars have abundant opportunities to contribute to the growing body of knowledge on family firm heterogeneity.

First, this chapter focuses on heterogeneity at the firm level by noting differences in family firm goals, governance, and resources. This is not intended to be an all-encompassing description of differences among family firms. Rather, we use this as a framework to offer examples of categorical and variational differences across family firms. Accordingly, other broad categories may exist at the firm level, and indeed, many sub-categorical conceptualizations remain to be articulated. Furthermore, the firm-level categorical differences are likely to be distinct from those at other levels of analysis (e.g., Bement & Short, Chapter 11 in this book). Understanding the scope of categorical and variational differences at other levels of analysis will offer more robust insight into the broader array of categories across which family firms differ and the magnitude of difference that exists in each category.

Second, understanding differences at the family (group) level remains an area ripe for further explanation. Early studies of family firms focused on explaining the differences between family and nonfamily firms. However, as the field evolved, a consensus emerged: family firms are fundamentally different from nonfamily firms. Moreover, in addition to having distinct differences with nonfamily firms (e.g., Skorodziyevskiy, Fang, Memili, & Chrisman, 2022), the scope of differences among family firms is potentially greater than the differences observed among nonfamily firms (Bennedsen et al., 2010). As research has focused on investigating family firm heterogeneity, the potential remains to improve upon our understanding of the within-group differences among family firms. One means for further development is an enhanced focus on the differences among families. Given the notion that the family resides at the core of the family business, understanding family-specific differences will help clarify a primary source from which firm-level differences emerge. Investigations along this path—especially those generating in-depth insights into the family (see Salvato & Corbetta, Chapter 10 in this book)—will propel our knowledge of how family heterogeneity drives family firm heterogeneity.

Third, we look forward to studies that examine functional heterogeneity, or the relationships among categories and across levels (Kolasa & Rollo, 1991). For example, numerous insights are sure to be gained from studying how family firms with a family CEO pursue the noneconomic goal of family prestige compared to those led by a nonfamily CEO. Abstractly, researchers can offer value by examining combinations of categorical and variational differences to extend our understanding of how the relationships among such factors create further differences across family firms. Specifically, using the goals, governance, and resources framework presents opportunities to develop configurations—or even a classification system of family firms—that can help understand the effects of heterogenous attributes on family firm behavior and performance. Techniques, such as latent profile analysis, may be particularly useful for such endeavors (Gao, Stanley, & Kellermanns, Chapter 15 in this book).

There are also several limitations that, if addressed, provide additional research opportunities. We offer examples of a limited number of categories to highlight differences among family firms, but more categories certainly exist (e.g., Craig & Lumpkin, Chapter 3 in this book). While we offer the example that CEOs categorically differ based on their status (i.e., family versus non-family CEO), it should be recognized that the CEOs can also be categorized by age, gender, experience, education, etc. Different combinations of these categories are likely to impact the behaviors and outcomes of family firms in distinct ways. Additionally, while we offer examples of categorical and variational heterogeneity in this guide, we note that the definition of family firm heterogeneity referenced also mentions spatial and temporal differences. Along this line, examining the spatial differences among categories (i.e., examining functional heterogeneity) and how the differences among categorical elements change over time (i.e., examining dynamic heterogeneity) are other promising approaches to advance our collective understanding of family firm heterogeneity.

## CONCLUSION

This chapter aims to help researchers overcome (at least some of) the challenges faced when studying family firm heterogeneity. Thus, we follow the definition of family firm heterogeneity and provide examples of categorical and variational differences that can manifest at the family firm level. By offering examples of categorical and variational differences, we aim to help researchers develop more precise, consistent descriptions of the differences among family firms in order to further knowledge on family firm heterogeneity. In turn, we hope to minimize the potential for theoretical inaccuracies, empirical indeterminacies, and imprecise recommendations to practitioners. With this, we look forward to future studies that advance our understanding of family firm heterogeneity, which is an area of study with abundant potential that has yet to be fully realized.

## REFERENCES

Adler, P. S., & Kwon, S. W. (2002). Social capital: Prospects for a new concept. *Academy of Management Review, 27*(1), 17–40.

Arregle, J-L., Hitt, M. A., Sirmon, D. G., & Very, P. (2007). The development of organizational social capital: Attributes of family firms. *Journal of Management Studies, 44*(1), 73–95.

Bennedsen, M., Nielsen, K. M., Perez-Gonzales, F., & Wolfenzon, D. (2007). Inside the family firm: The role of families in succession decisions and performance. *Quarterly Journal of Economics, 122*(2), 647–691.

Bennedsen, M., Pérez-González, F., & Wolfenzon, D. (2010). The governance of family firms. In Baker, H. K., & Anderson, R. (Eds.), *Corporate Governance: A Synthesis of Theory, Research, and Practice* (pp. 371–390). John Wiley & Sons, Inc.

Berrone, P., Cruz, C., & Gómez-Mejía, L. R. (2012). Socioemotional wealth in family firms: Theoretical dimensions, assessment approaches, and agenda for future research. *Family Business Review, 25*(3), 258–279.

Bettinelli, C. (2011). Boards of directors in family firms: An exploratory study of structure and group process. *Family Business Review, 24*(2), 151–169.

Brinkerink, J. (2023). When shooting for the stars becomes aiming for asterisks: *P*-hacking in family business research. *Entrepreneurship Theory and Practice, 47*(2), 304–343.

Calabrò, A., Campopiano, G., & Basco, R. (2017). Principal–principal conflicts and family firm growth: The moderating role of business family identity. *Journal of Family Business Management, 7*(3), 291–308.

Carney, M. (2005). Corporate governance and competitive advantage in family-controlled firms. *Entrepreneurship Theory and Practice, 29*(3), 249–265.

Chandler, J. A., Petrenko, O. V., Hill, A. D., & Hayes, N. (2021). CEO Machiavellianism and strategic alliances in family firms. *Family Business Review, 34*(1), 93–115.

Chrisman, J. J., & Patel, P. C. (2012). Variations in R&D investments of family and nonfamily firms: Behavioral agency and myopic loss aversion perspectives. *Academy of Management Journal, 55*(4), 976–997.

Chrisman, J. J., Chua, J. H., & Litz, R. A. (2004). Comparing the agency costs of family and non–family firms: Conceptual issues and exploratory evidence. *Entrepreneurship Theory and Practice, 28*(4), 335–354.

Chrisman, J. J., Chua, J. H., Pearson, A. W., & Barnett, T. (2012). Family involvement, family influence, and family-centered non-economic goals in small firms. *Entrepreneurship Theory and Practice, 36*(2), 267–293.

Chrisman, J. J., Madison, K., & Kim, T. (2021). A dynamic framework of noneconomic goals and inter-family agency complexities in multi-family firms. *Entrepreneurship Theory and Practice, 45*(4), 906–930.

Chrisman, J. J., Sharma, P., Steier, L. P., & Chua, J. H. (2013). The influence of family goals, governance, and resources on firm outcomes. *Entrepreneurship Theory and Practice, 37*(6), 1249–1261.

Chua, J. H., Chrisman, J. J., & De Massis, A. (2015). A closer look at socioemotional wealth: Its flows, stocks, and prospects for moving forward. *Entrepreneurship Theory and Practice, 39*(2), 173–182.

Chua, J. H., Chrisman, J. J., & Sharma, P. (1999). Defining the family business by behavior. *Entrepreneurship Theory and Practice, 23*(4), 19–39.

Chua, J. H., Chrisman, J. J., Steier, L. P., & Rau, S. B. (2012). Sources of heterogeneity in family firms: An introduction. *Entrepreneurship Theory and Practice, 36*(6), 1103–1113.

Danes, S. M., Stafford, K., Haynes, G., & Amarapurkar, S. S. (2009). Family capital of family firms: Bridging human, social, and financial capital. *Family Business Review, 22*(3), 199–215.

Daspit, J. J., Chrisman, J. J., Ashton, T., & Evangelopoulos, N. (2021). Family firm heterogeneity: A definition, common themes, scholarly progress, and directions forward. *Family Business Review, 34*(3), 296–322.

Daspit, J. J., Chrisman, J. J., Sharma, P., Pearson, A. W., & Mahto, R. V. (2018). Governance as a source of family firm heterogeneity. *Journal of Business Research, 84*, 293–300.

Dawson, A. (2012). Human capital in family businesses: Focusing on the individual level. *Journal of Family Business Strategy, 3*(1), 3–11.

Dunn, B. (1995). Success themes in Scottish family enterprises: Philosophies and practices through generations. *Family Business Review, 8*(1), 17–28.

Gersick, K. E., Davis, J. A., McCollom-Hampton, M., & Lansberg, I. (1997). *Generation to Generation: Life Cycles of the Family Business.* Harvard Business School Press.

Gómez-Mejía, L. R., Haynes, K. T., Núñez-Nickel, M., Jacobson, K. J., & Moyano-Fuentes, J. (2007). Socioemotional wealth and business risks in family-controlled firms: Evidence from Spanish olive oil mills. *Administrative Science Quarterly, 52*(1), 106–137.

Habbershon, T. G., Williams, M., & MacMillan, I. C. (2003). A unified systems perspective of family firm performance. *Journal of Business Venturing, 18*(4), 451–465.

Hambrick, D. C., & Mason, P. A. (1984). Upper echelons: The organization as a reflection of its top managers. *Academy of Management Review, 9*(2), 193–206.

Holt, D. T., Pearson, A. W., Carr, J. C., & Barnett, T. (2017). Family firm(s) outcomes model: Structuring financial and nonfinancial outcomes across the family and firm. *Family Business Review, 30*(2), 182–202.

Holt, D. T., Pearson, A. W., Payne, G. T., & Sharma, P. (2018). Family business research as a boundary-spanning platform. *Family Business Review, 31*(1), 14–31.

Jaskiewicz, P., & Luchak, A. A. (2013). Explaining performance differences between family firms with family and nonfamily CEOs: It's the nature of the tie to the family that counts! *Entrepreneurship Theory and Practice, 37*(6), 1361–1367.

Kolasa, J., & Rollo, C. D. (1991). Introduction: The heterogeneity of heterogeneity: A glossary. In Kolasa, J., & Pickett, S. T. A. (Eds.), *Ecological Heterogeneity* (Vol. 86, pp. 1–23). Springer.

Lee, K., Makri, M., & Scandura, T. (2019). The effect of psychological ownership on corporate entrepreneurship: Comparisons between family and nonfamily top management team members. *Family Business Review, 32*(1), 10–30.

Leonard, M. (2004). Bonding and bridging social capital: Reflections from Belfast. *Sociology, 38*(5), 927–944.

Nahapiet, J., & Ghoshal, S. (1998). Social capital, intellectual capital, and the organizational advantage. *Academy of Management Review, 23*(2), 242–266.

Pérez-González, F. (2006). Inherited control and firm performance. *American Economic Review, 96*(5), 1559–1588.

Putnam, R. D. (2000). *Bowling Alone: The Collapse and Revival of American Community.* Simon and Schuster.

Rau, S. B., Schneider-Siebke, V., & Gunther, C. (2019). Family firm values explaining family firm heterogeneity. *Family Business Review, 32*(2), 195–215.

Sanchez-Ruiz, P., Daspit, J. J., Holt, D. T., & Rutherford, M. W. (2019). Family social capital in the family firm: A taxonomic classification, relationships with outcomes, and directions for advancement. *Family Business Review, 32*(2), 131–153.

Schulze, W. S., Lubatkin, M. H., Dino, R. N., & Buchholtz, A. K. (2001). Agency relationships in family firms: Theory and evidence. *Organization Science, 12*(2), 99–116.

Sharma, P. (2015). Editor's Notes: 2014—A year in review. *Family Business Review, 28*(1), 4–9.

Sharma, S., & Sharma, P. (2019). *Patient Capital: The Role of Family Firms in Sustainable Business*. Cambridge University Press.

Sirmon, D. G., & Hitt, M. A. (2003). Managing resources: Linking unique resources, management and wealth creation in family firms. *Entrepreneurship Theory and Practice, 27*(4), 339–358.

Skorodziyevskiy, V., Fang, H., Memili, E., & Chrisman, J. J. (2022). The impact of governance structure on the performance of small family and nonfamily firms: the moderating role of firm age. *Review of Corporate Finance, 2*(4), 721–743.

Stewart, A., & Hitt, M. A. (2012). Why can't a family business be more like a non-family business? Modes of professionalization in family firms. *Family Business Review, 25*(1), 58–86.

Su, E., & Carney, M. (2013). Can China's family firms create intellectual capital? *Asia Pacific Journal of Management, 30*, 657–675.

Tabor, W., Chrisman, J. J., Madison, K., & Vardaman, J. M. (2018). Nonfamily members in family firms: A review and future research agenda. *Family Business Review, 31*(1), 54–79.

Vandebeek, A., Voordeckers, W., Lambrechts, F., & Huybrechts, J. (2016). Board role performance and faultlines in family firms: The moderating role of formal board evaluation. *Journal of Family Business Strategy, 7*(4), 249–259.

Verbeke, A., & Kano, L. (2012). The transaction cost economics theory of the family firm: Family-based human asset specificity and the bifurcation bias. *Entrepreneurship Theory and Practice, 36*(6), 1183–1205.

Ward, J. L. (1997). Growing the family business: Special challenges and best practices. *Family Business Review, 10*(4), 323–337.

Zhang, X., Fang, H., Dou, J., & Chrisman, J. J. (2022). Endogeneity issues in family business research: Current status and future recommendations. *Family Business Review, 35*(1), 91–116.

# 6. A methodological guide to advance family business innovation research

**Alfredo De Massis, Emanuela Rondi, and Paola Rovelli**

## 1. INTRODUCTION

Innovation – the set of activities through which a firm conceives, designs, produces, and introduces to the market a new product, technology, system, or technique (Freeman, 1976) – is a key strategic means to ensure economic prosperity (Porter, 1980) and business survival (Schumpeter, 1934). Research on innovation in family firms has grown in recent years (Calabrò et al., 2019), being interested in capturing the specificities of these firms. In fact, theoretical and empirical evidence shows that innovation management differs in family and nonfamily firms (Chrisman et al., 2015; De Massis et al., 2013). Among other strategic phenomena, innovation is key to family firms as their intergenerational essence intertwines family and organizational past roots with current initiatives and the future of next generations (Dalpiaz et al., 2014). This in turn places the owning family in the struggle to manage the need and reluctance to change, a distinctive and challenging relation that is worth further investigation. However, in recent examinations of the literature, a fragmented picture of the understanding of and approaches adopted in innovation management in family firms emerges (Rondi & Rovelli, 2021b; Rovelli et al., 2021).

Scholars interested in family firm innovation management have examined the antecedents, activities, and outcomes, identifying elements of distinctions from nonfamily firms. Antecedents relate to resources attributed to innovation, such as R&D expenditures and personnel dedicated to innovation, but also the governance characteristics and goals. Innovation activities include the orchestration of the family and firm's resources that lead to value creation, such as strategy, leadership, organizational culture, and R&D. Innovation outcomes describe the level of transformation – radical or incremental – and the object of the innovation – product, service, process, or business model. Knowledge regarding the antecedents, activities, and outcomes of innovation specific to family firms is still limited (Calabrò et al., 2019; Urbinati et al., 2017) and focused primarily on the firm perspective rather than grasping aspects at the family, individual, and ecosystem level (e.g., Chrisman et al., 2015; Kraus et al., 2012). In addition, most studies compare family firms to nonfamily firms – with the former typically considered less innovative than the latter. Few studies focus on family firm heterogeneity in relation to innovation, while very little consideration has been given to the context in which family firms operate and its impact on innovation decisions and management (Brinkerink & Rondi, 2020).

While studies examining innovation in the context of family firms have bloomed in the last decade (Rovelli et al., 2021), they have converged toward only a handful of routinized methods. With a brief synthesis of the empirical research on family business innovation, we present what scholars have studied so far and the methodological approaches adopted. Qualitative inquiry has mostly adopted multiple case studies (Eisenhardt, 1989; Yin, 2012), deductively approaching this topic by theoretically sampling family vs nonfamily firms or heterogeneous types of family firms based on either innovation type or performance. Such an attitude has allowed to build knowledge about configurations and types of family business innovation management but has yet to embrace an in-depth inductive analysis that fully grasps the process of innovating in family firms and how it unfolds. On the other hand, quantitative inquiry has mostly relied on secondary data sources and survey data collections, and adopted regression analysis; only a limited number of studies used other approaches (e.g., econometric models, structural equation modeling). These approaches allowed investigating both the differences between family and nonfamily firms in terms of innovation and the moderation/mediation effects pertaining to innovation in family business.

Our synthesis highlights the necessity to address such a lack of methodological pluralism to develop a more nuanced understanding of family business innovation. The convergence on few methods is detrimental for the development of research on family firm innovation as the selection of methodological approaches should depend on the questions being pursued (Lamont & Swidler, 2014). Therefore, the adoption of a limited set of methods is symptomatic of a limited variety of the questions addressed and consequently of the limited depth and breadth of current understanding. We see the need for enhancing methodological pluralism in this area of research by adopting novel research methods as a means to address research questions that can advance the dialogue among the plurality of viewpoints. Such an endeavor not only offers the opportunity to observe the phenomenon of interest from different perspectives that might underline the peculiarities of family firms' innovation, but also has the potential to transform research tools and how they are used in this context, thereby also innovating those research methods (Lê & Schmid, 2020). Therefore, in this chapter we suggest two methodological approaches, one in the qualitative and the other in the quantitative inquiry realm. As per qualitative research, we highlight the potential of adopting narrative analysis in naturalistic approaches (ethnographies and grounded theory). In terms of quantitative research, we examine the potential of social network analysis (SNA). Moreover, we develop sets of research questions that are relevant to enhance the current understanding on the phenomenon and are suitable to be addressed with the methods presented. By following our recommendations, we hope to encourage and inspire scholars to further advance this research domain.

## 2.    QUALITATIVE RESEARCH

Only 15 percent of the articles reviewed in the recent reconciling study by Calabrò et al. (2019) adopted qualitative methods to investigate phenomena related to family business innovation. This limited portion is even graver recognizing the lack of pluralism in the methodologies and units of analysis adopted. Indeed, qualitative studies in this area tend to adopt the firm as the unit of analysis and consider the organizational and family's characteristics as the drivers of innovation outcomes or processes. Moreover, these studies mostly rely on multiple case studies (Eisenhardt, 1989; Yin, 2012), with the goal of identifying, comparing, and contrasting innovation patterns and mechanisms across firms and/or families (e.g., Kammerlander & Ganter, 2015). This approach emerges as embedded in a positivistic epistemology and founds the recommendations of Eisenhardt (1989) as the beacon light for the research design. This predominance identified in the innovation area mirrors the observation by Fletcher et al. (2016) conducted in the broader qualitative family business literature.

Multiple case studies have strongly contributed to the development of family business innovation as an area of research by identifying sources of distinctiveness in family vs nonfamily firms' innovation attitudes, goals, and behaviors (see also Kammerlander & Diaz-Moriana, Chapter 9 in this book). Only recently scholars have started addressing the elements of heterogeneity in terms of innovation among family firms. By theoretically sampling comparable cases, these studies are intended to isolate alternative sources of divergence to identify the relevant drivers of innovation. For instance, by exploring new product development across four Italian family firms, Cassia et al. (2011) illustrate the role of family involvement in terms of communication in the family combined with shared family values and the desire to promote the family name and reputation.

Temporal orientation has been deeply investigated in qualitative studies on family firm innovation, in relation to constructs such as long-term orientation and long-term view but also tradition and generational transition. For instance, by digging into the paradox between the past-oriented tradition and the future-oriented innovation, Erdogan et al. (2020) examined eight Turkish family firms that showed diverse strategies to reconcile such tension by innovating through tradition as well as adopting innovation as the engine that allows the family to keep tradition alive. Other articles adopting a case-based approach have illustrated the tendency of family firms to pursue an open innovation strategy (Lambrechts et al., 2017) and innovate across generations (Woodfield & Husted, 2017).

The widely adopted positivistic philosophical tradition in family business innovation studies drives toward multiple case study as a fertile method for cross-case comparative purposes, able to show the distinctiveness of family vs nonfamily firms. However, such tendency adopts an internal perspective within the organizations that decontextualizes them from their environment and the temporal frame in which they are embedded. The increasing interest in the heterogeneity in family firms' innovation processes (see also Daspit et al., Chapter 5 in this book) raises the need for deeper examinations aimed at grasping the holistic nature of the phenomenon (Fletcher et al., 2016). Given the trade-off between the number of cases examined in a study and the richness and depth of the investigation, single case study seems to be more suitable to achieve an in-depth understanding of the processes as they occur in practice within the socio-cultural-political context (see also Trudell et al., Chapter 8 in this book). Indeed, the attention devoted by family business scholars to the single case study to examine innovation is still little but increasing. The reason for embracing this turn stems from the need for a more socially constructed approach to the topic, not intended to identify 'what' aspects of the family, the firm, and the environment influence innovation but more centered around the 'hows' and 'whys' of the daily life of family business actors dealing with innovation, through a process of empathetic understanding. According to this view, recent studies such as those conducted for instance by Raitis et al. (2021) and Rondi et al. (2021) rely on the longitudinal investigation of a single-family firm by collecting data through complementary techniques such as interviews and participatory and nonparticipatory observations.

Beside multiple and single case studies, a third use of cases in family business innovation research is illustrative (Siggelkow, 2007). A range of cases is adopted to corroborate a conceptually developed typology or process model in order to provide evidence of real family firms that have adopted specific strategies as a means to show how reality can be framed according to the pre-theorized framework. Examples of studies that adopt this research design examine innovation through tradition strategy (De Massis et al., 2016) and the ambivalence of socioemotional preferences on family business approaches to innovation (Miller et al., 2015).

# 3. QUANTITATIVE RESEARCH

Quantitative research on family business innovation has so far relied on secondary data sources[1] (e.g., Kotlar et al., 2014; Matzler et al., 2015) and survey data collections (e.g., Beck et al., 2011; De Massis et al., 2020). Scholars analyzed these data mainly using regressions; only a limited number of studies adopted other quantitative approaches, such as principal component analyses (e.g., Llach & Nordqvist, 2010), econometric models (e.g., Wagner, 2010), and structural equation modeling (e.g., Brinkerink & Bammens, 2018; Kraus et al., 2012).

These quantitative approaches allowed scholars to investigate two types of issues related to family business innovation. On the one hand, the effect of having a family owning and/or managing the firm on innovation, or, in other words, the differences in term of innovation between family and nonfamily firms. On the other hand, the moderating role played by family firm-related characteristics in the relation between innovation and performance in the family business context (e.g., Diéguez-Soto et al., 2016), or the moderating role of innovation in the relation between family firms' characteristics and performance (e.g., Kellermanns et al., 2012), or the mediators in the relation between family firms and innovation (e.g., Filser et al., 2018; Hsu & Chang, 2011).[2]

The first stream of research implies studying the direct relationship between an independent variable that points to the family nature of the firm, or a family firm's defining characteristics, and a dependent variable measuring innovation or aspects pertaining to innovation. For instance, studies investigated the effect of family involvement in the ownership of the firm on innovation decisions (e.g., Lopez-Fernandez et al., 2016), R&D investments (e.g., De Massis et al., 2018), innovation productivity (e.g., Lodh et al., 2014), number of patents (e.g., Decker & Günther, 2017), or technological innovation (e.g., Ashwin et al., 2015). Other studies focused instead on the involvement of the family in the management or governance of the firm (e.g., Sciascia et al., 2015). In these cases, family management has been related to, for instance, innovation capabilities (e.g., Craig & Dibrell, 2006), R&D investments (e.g., Kotlar et

---

[1]  Some examples are databases by Bureau Van Dijk, the ESEE Survey on Business Strategies by the Spanish Ministry of Industry (e.g., Kotlar et al., 2014), the PATSTAT database provided by the European Patent Office (e.g., Matzler et al., 2015), the Patentscope database maintained by WIPO (e.g., Ashwin et al., 2015), and the DEPATISnet by the German Patent and Trade Mark Office (e.g., Decker & Günther, 2017).

[2]  For a full understanding of these mediating and moderating relationships, see Calabrò et al. (2019, p. 328).

al., 2014), the acquisition of external technology (Classen et al., 2012), or the number of patents (e.g., Matzler et al., 2015). Finally, scholars looked at the effect of some family firms' peculiar characteristics, such as generational involvement and stage (Beck et al., 2011) or resource endowments and risk aversion (e.g., Nieto et al., 2015).

The second stream of research goes further in exploring what elements affect and/or explain the relationship between family firms and innovation; for instance considering socioemotional wealth (e.g., Brinkerink & Bammens, 2018; Filser et al., 2018), social capital (e.g., Sanchez-Famoso et al., 2015), behavioral strategic control (e.g., Hsu & Chang, 2011), knowledge exchange (e.g., Rondi & Rovelli, 2021a), and organizational design (e.g., De Massis et al., 2020). Other studies investigate instead moderating factors of the relationship between family influence in the firm and family firm characteristics or performance, such as innovativeness (e.g., Kellermanns et al., 2012) and R&D intensity (e.g., Fang et al., 2018). Finally, other scholars looked at the relation between innovation and performance in the family business context and investigated the moderating role of the family-related characteristics; for instance, family governance (e.g., Bughin & Colot, 2010), family management (e.g., Diéguez-Soto et al., 2016), family commitment (e.g., Hatak et al., 2016), and generational involvement (e.g., Kraiczy et al., 2014).

## 4.     ADDRESSING THE LACK OF PLURALISM IN THE METHODOLOGIES FOR INVESTIGATING FAMILY BUSINESS INNOVATION

The qualitative and quantitative methods that scholars have used to investigate family business innovation have created a sort of methodological tradition that compromises pluralism, thereby hampering the possibility to holistically grasp the peculiarities of this phenomenon. For this reason, in the following we propose two promising yet scantly pursued methodological avenues which might be explored by family business scholars interested in innovation: on the qualitative side, narratives in naturalistic approaches (grounded theory and ethnographies); on the quantitative one, SNA. With the intent of stimulating and guiding future research endeavors, we also propose intriguing research questions suitable to be addressed with the introduced methods.

### 4.1     Narratives in Naturalistic Approaches

Our reflection on the past and current methodological underpinnings of qualitative research in family business innovation reveals an overreliance on case-based methods rooted in traditional approaches to data collection and analysis – e.g., semi-structured interviews (see also Salvato & Corbetta,

Chapter 10 in this book). Therefore, we echo Fletcher et al. (2016) arguing that the full potential of qualitative research in family business is not yet being fully realized. We see this need especially in the area of innovation, where the adoption of case study methods has allowed to scratch its surface, but a wider range of approaches to research design, data collection, and analysis is needed to grasp the complexity, discursivity, contextualization, and relationality. Indeed, if we keep relying on the same restricted range of methods, we miss the opportunity to really recognize how family business actors frame, experience, make sense of, and act in relation to innovation processes, thereby seriously constraining the possibility to theorize about them (Fletcher et al., 2016). With this goal in mind, we call for further adoption of naturalistic approaches such as grounded theory and ethnographies to especially examine narratives in the family business innovation.

The value of grounded theory and ethnographic research consists in the possibility to attend the centrality of discourse, language, and socially constructed meanings and interpretations (Chia, 2000). We thus see a great potential in narratives to examine family business innovation processes. According to Reay and Zhang (2014, p. 582), ethnographies allow to 'have the groundwork in place to push forward with developing new and important theoretical contributions to the field of family business and perhaps the organizational literature more broadly'. Unfortunately, as shown in the recent review by Fletcher and Adiguna (2020), ethnographic research in family business settings is rarely published and is missing innovation studies. While narrative approaches can be adopted in analyzing data such as semi-structured interview transcripts in case studies (e.g., Kammerlander et al., 2015), we argue that grounded theory and ethnographies enable scholars to collect richer data and better interpret the diverse meanings attributed to narratives (Short & Payne, 2020).

Family businesses are especially suitable for adopting narrative approaches because of their longevity, values, heritage, and traditions that often imbue family stories that are passed down through generations in the family dynasty (Dodd et al., 2013), formalized into family documents and/or custodied in museums and foundations. Family business stories and myths that intertwine past, present, and future (Dalpiaz et al., 2014) become intrinsic forces that influence the family business strategy and decisions (Rae, 2004). Indeed, narratives address multifaceted social constructs performed by different actors in diverse contexts (Dawson & Hjorth, 2012). Family and business systems forge two contrasting yet complimentary discursive narratives that help them to reciprocally make sense of themselves (Smith, 2018). Such nature stimulates negotiated, polyphonic, and synchronic narratives (Cunliffe et al., 2004), meanings, and behaviors that might encourage emulation, especially when incorporating the hero-journey stories across generations (Miller, 1999). As such, next generations may feel the duty to perpetuate family heritage and

identity (Smith, 2018). Interestingly, narratives can also be fictional and pur-
posefully developed to justify specific strategies or decisions. Therefore, the
ambivalence and complexity of narratives clearly emerges as drivers of family
business innovation by being sources of innovative inspiration or impressing
rigidity into the family business strategy by setting next generations in a cage
of the inescapable past (Labaki et al., 2019).

Due to the ambiguous role of narratives in family business innovation,
grounded theory and ethnographies are essential to make sense of how such
stories are told, interpreted, enacted, and impressed in future perspectives and
goals. According to Dawson and Hjorth (2012, p. 341), narrative methods
'make it possible to study processes in a way that does not squeeze the processual aspect out of our empirical material'. Since narratives are especially able
to embed the temporality and the context of the research setting, it is therefore
important for the researcher to interpret such narratives by developing an
embedded, in-depth but also critical perspective, ideally grasped through
grounded theory and ethnographies. By embarking on naturalistic approaches,
researchers can complement the mimetic content of narratives (what the stories
say) typical of case studies with diegetic content (how the story is told, who
tells it, comparison of different narratives) (Cunliffe et al., 2004) to develop
a deeper understanding of family business innovation.

In the examination of family business innovation, narratives – concerned
with *how* questions and processes – offer a great opportunity to overcome the
input–output perspective to finally address the process of *innovating* in family
firms (Röd, 2016). In terms of data collection and analysis, researchers should
carefully understand the context, ensure a deep level of engagement with and
access to the family businesses for collecting both primary data, but also have
access to secondary data (e.g., letters, diaries, corporate documents, meeting
minutes) through which they can implement longitudinal narrative analysis.
With the aim to address this lack of investigation under such promising
premises, we offer relevant future research directions and questions that are
especially suitable to be addressed through the suggested methods (see Table
6.1). It is worth noting that, due to the level of engagement and openness
required for the collection of narrative data, it is crucial to develop a deep
understanding of the context as well as relational trust between the family
leaders/members and the researcher. To fulfill these conditions, researchers
need to not only master the methodologies but also be endowed with relational
skills, time, and patience to empathize with the research field. For exemplary
studies implementing naturalistic approaches see Logemann et al. (2019) and
Sonenshein (2010).

*Table 6.1*     *Research questions and methodological suggestions in the*
                *light of naturalistic approaches*

| Potential Research Questions | Methodological suggestions |
|---|---|
| **RQ1.** *How does the interpretation of founders' narratives shape the innovation attitude of the second generation?* | Gather founders' autobiographical data from archives and retrospective accounts about the stories told by founders. Ethnographically explore how such narratives currently shape innovation attitudes in the sensemaking and framing of family members about innovation opportunities and initiatives. |
| **RQ2.** *How can next generation family members learn from the narratives of past failures to better innovate?* | Understand the meaning of 'failure' and the episodes of past failures that are still in the memory of current leaders and examine when and how those episodes are currently recalled in relation to innovation management. |
| **RQ3.** *How does the interpretation of family myths evolve according to contextual and situational changes, and how does such evolution affect innovation?* | Identify family myths through narrative retrospective accounts, gather data from current leaders to understand their rational understanding of key myths and then analyze how such myths shape their current behavior (for example in heuristics). |
| **RQ4.** *Do family and nonfamily firms frame innovation differently when collaborating in innovation ecosystems?* | Examine the inter-organizational collaborations of innovation ecosystems and explore in a open innovation project the language and sense giving that firms adopt when communicating about innovation. Compare/contrast the language used by family and non-family firms. |
| **RQ5.** *How do polyphony and silence about the family's past affect family business innovation? What rhetorical strategies allow family businesses to alter the meaning of their narratives to detach from continuity toward change and innovation?* | Identify an emblematic case with important scandal(s) in its past. Then, ethnographically collect narratives and through a functional approach to narrative analysis, try to understand how silence and diverse storytelling about the same event are balanced in the family firm context when making decisions about and managing innovation. |
| **RQ6** . *How do different family members make sense of the tension between innovation and tradition? What happens when the interpretations of such tension do not converge?* | Within an innovation project, collect data on the different perspectives about the challenges that such change requires to the status quo and the family tradition. Then, examine whether and how family leaders coordinate to make decisions about how to pursue the innovation project. |

| Potential Research Questions | Methodological suggestions |
|---|---|
| *RQ7 . How do family leaders shape the language they use to refer to traditional products in the process of innovation? Do the languages of senior and junior family leaders differ?* | By ethnographically exploring product innovation projects, explore the language that managers (either belonging to the family or not) use to give sense to the past products they are innovating and examine whether family members have different attitudes toward such change that is reflected in the language they use to refer to the traditional products. |
| *RQ8 . Do fictional stories about the past developed by family businesses for external stakeholders harm the possibility to innovate through tradition?* | Examine a family firm that has developed monographs in the past and gives access to old archival documents destinated to external stakeholders. In these documents, detect how the organization framed its past and tradition. Then engage with the firm to ethnographically understand how that former communication is currently framed internally when making innovation decisions. |

## 4.2    Social Network Analysis

A network is generally defined as 'a specific type of relation linking a defined set of persons, objects, or events' (Knoke & Kuklinski, 1991, p. 175). Over the years, the study of networks of individuals and firms became increasingly important to understand connectivity and attachment within and between organizations (Thorelli, 1986). Among the approaches available to study networks, the most diffused one from a quantitative point of view is SNA. SNA is indeed concerned with 'understanding the linkages among social entities and the implications of these linkages' (Wasserman & Faust, 1994, p. 17).

SNA is implemented by using databases covering information about firms or individuals and 'events' through which they are related. These databases are typically constructed using data retrieved from historical records (such as email exchanges), survey data, or a combination of these. Once a network is built, different dimensions can be computed, which characterize the network itself and the relationships among the individuals or firms involved (for further details see Moore & Nicholas, Chapter 16 in this book).

Network studies allow to investigate the 'density, diversity, range, composition, strength, transactional content and properties of relationships within (intra) and between (inter) organizations' (Fletcher, 2002, p. 401). These relationships (i.e., network linkages) and their characteristics might in turn affect the ability of firms to face competition, start up a new business, grow their business, or access resources and market opportunities (e.g., Tichy et al., 1979). Accordingly, network-based research has already been conducted in the fields of strategic management (e.g., Tsai & Ghoshal, 1998), entrepreneurship (e.g., Greve & Salaff, 2003), small business (e.g., Donckels & Lambrecht, 1995), and innovation (e.g., Martínez-Torres, 2014). Only a few initial steps have instead been made in the family business field.

Nevertheless, SNA can play an important role in the family firm context. Specifically, it has the potential of explaining how networks of individuals and firms affect family business dynamics. Indeed, relationships between family and nonfamily members, as well as those with external stakeholders, have been proved to be of key importance for family firms (e.g., Habbershon & Williams, 1999). Similarly, the importance of ties is highlighted by the socioemotional wealth perspective (Gomez-Mejia et al., 2007), which is at the core of family business research and practice.

Few studies have so far adopted a network approach to study family business. Distelberg and Blow (2011) employed a mixed-method approach, including SNA, to categorize the strength of boundaries around the family system. Zamudio et al. (2014) made an attempt to introduce this method in the field by providing a brief review of network-related concepts and its potential to advance family business research. More recently, Baggio and Valeri (2022) proposed network science as a suitable instrument to support the sustainable performance of family business in tourism. Finally, Burt et al. (2021) used SNA to portray what it means for a firm to be embedded within a family, and then to understand whether different types of family firms have different network advantages.

We suggest that SNA might help scholars to better understand how the configuration and characteristics of the networks of individuals within the family firm (or within its R&D unit) and of the network in which the firm is embedded shape and influence its innovation processes and performance. For instance, SNA would allow to understand how (new) information and knowledge are acquired and disseminated within the family firm. Drawing on the network of the individuals involved in the family firm might allow to better understand diversity – in terms of family vs nonfamily status, backgrounds, gender, age, tenure, etc. – and who are the key actors in the innovation decision-making and processes. Building and analyzing the network of email communications among individuals employed in the R&D department would allow to understand the dynamics in their interactions and communications and identify who plays the main role in innovation (e.g., whether innovation is driven by family or nonfamily individuals). Similarly, clusters of individuals might be identified, then investigating if and how their composition matters for innovation. For instance, the centrality of family or nonfamily members in these clusters might in turn influence the implementation of decisions pertaining to innovation and innovation performance. Of course, also the networks in which the firm is embedded can be examined, thus considering external stakeholders and the wider ecosystem. This would allow to understand how family firms, and their members, connect with external individuals, and how external knowledge is brought into the firm (e.g., through which individuals, also considering their characteristics and roles). In so doing, the distribution of the knowledge within the family firm could be analyzed in combination with the external network of knowledge in which the firm is embedded. In Table 6.2 we propose some research questions and suggestions to explore them through the use of SNA, which complement the examination by Moore and Nicholas (Chapter 16 in this book) who provided practical suggestions on how to use SNA in family business research.

*Table 6.2      Research questions and SNA methodological suggestions*

| Potential Research Questions | Methodological suggestions |
| --- | --- |
| **RQ1.** *How is the network of top management team members in family firms structured? Do family and nonfamily individuals cluster in different groups? How do these individuals communicate and interact in the network? What are the implications in terms of strategic decision-making pertaining to innovation?* | Gather data on the composition of family firms' top management team, including names, surnames, family status, and family relations, as well as information on how communications take place among them (e.g., email exchanges). Analyze the network of communication exchanges to understand whether clusters of individuals emerge, whether there are managers that are more 'central' to discussions, and whether these aspects have implications on innovation decision-making. |
| **RQ2.** *How is the network of individuals involved in the R&D department of family firms structured? Which type of individuals play the key role in the innovation process of family firms? Do clusters of individuals exist in this network? What are the implications in terms of the innovation process?* | Analyze email exchanges among employees working in the R&D department of family firms. Analyze the network of individuals involved in the email exchange to identify the 'leaders of innovation' – that is, individuals who are most frequently involved in the innovation projects and decisions of the R&D department. |
| **RQ3.** *Do family ties play a central role in the network of individuals involved in the family firm's innovation process? Do family ties overlap with those where the main exchanges of information and knowledge take place? What are the implications in terms of innovation?* | Within the network of individuals involved in the innovation process, collect information on the family relationships in place among them. Analyze family relationships in the network to understand the role that the family plays in innovation – that is, whether and how frequently family members are involved when decisions pertaining to innovation have to be made. |
| **RQ4.** *How does a business family make sure to convey its values and role in communications with the family firm employees, especially those involved in innovation processes? Does the structure of the organization's network of individuals and the centrality of some of its members favor the perpetuation of family firm traditions in innovation?* | Analyze the content of the family members' communications to employees involved in innovation processes using text mining and content analysis techniques. Pair this analysis with the degree of centrality of the family members in the network of employees and information about the perpetuation of family firm tradition in innovations. |

| Potential Research Questions | Methodological suggestions |
|---|---|
| *RQ5. What role do different generations play in the network of the family firm, especially considering the actors involved in the innovation process? Do old and new generation members play different roles (e.g., with respect to centrality)? What are the implications for innovation of having new versus old generation individuals in the key nodes of the network?* | Analyze the network of individuals involved in innovation processes with particular focus on family membership and generation. Observe whether old and new generation family members cover different roles in the network – with specific reference to the degree of centrality – and whether different configurations of old and new generation family members in the network associate with different innovation performance. |
| *RQ6 . Does the composition, structure, and dynamics of the network of individuals involved in innovation decisions and processes affect family firm performance?* | Identify individuals involved in innovation decision-making by analyzing attendance at meetings and email exchanges. Analyze the network of individuals – composition, structure, and evolution over time – and relate its characteristics to the performance of the family firm. |
| *RQ7. How does knowledge flow within the family firm and throughout its boundaries? Who plays the gatekeeper role in connecting the family firm with the external network of knowledge? What are the activities through which such knowledge transfer dynamics unfold?* | Analyze the flow of information between the family firm and external sources of knowledge (e.g., university, research centers, R&D department of parent or subsidiaries). Analyze the composition of the research team mentioned in the family firm's patents to understand whether researchers working for external institutions are involved. |
| *RQ8. How do family firms build their network with external stakeholders? Who are the gatekeepers that allow building sustainable relationships? Are the relationships with family and nonfamily firms managed differently? How does this affect their ability to innovate?* | By leveraging email exchanges with external stakeholders (e.g., clients), draw the network of individuals including the family firm's employees and externals. Analyze the networks to identify the organizational role and individual characteristics (e.g., family membership) of the individuals serving as gatekeepers in the relationship of the firm with the external side of the network. Examine whether the nature of the gatekeeper relates to innovation performance. |

## 5. CONCLUSIONS

Innovation is crucial to maintain a sustainable competitive advantage and prosperity in the long run. Yet, innovation is particularly challenging for family firms, where the family involved in the business typically exerts a strong influence on innovation decisions though its distinctive values, goals, discretion, and abilities. As highlighted in the first part of this chapter, family business scholars have so far mainly adopted 'traditional' qualitative and quantitative methods. By calling for more methodological pluralism, we have thus proposed two promising yet scantly adopted methods that can contribute to better grasp the peculiarities of innovation in family firms, namely, from a qualitative viewpoint, narratives in naturalistic approaches, and from a quantitative one, SNA. To this aim, we have offered a selected list of future research questions that, if explored in light of the methodological suggestions offered, hold the potential to enrich our understanding of family business innovation.

## REFERENCES

Ashwin, A. S., Krishnan, R. T., & George, R. (2015). Family firms in India: Family involvement, innovation and agency and stewardship behaviors. *Journal of Management*, *32*(4), 869–900.

Baggio, R., & Valeri, M. (2022). Network science and sustainable performance of family businesses in tourism. *Journal of Family Business Management*, *12*(2), 200–213.

Beck, L., Janssens, W., Debruyne, M., & Lommelen, T. (2011). A study of the relationships between generation, market orientation, and innovation in family firms. *Family Business Review*, *24*(3), 252–272.

Brinkerink, J., & Bammens, Y. (2018). Family influence and R&D spending in Dutch manufacturing SMEs: The role of identity and socioemotional decision considerations. *Journal of Product Innovation Management*, *35*(4), 588–608.

Brinkerink, J., & Rondi, E. (2020). When can families fill voids? Firms' reliance on formal and informal institutions in R&D decisions. *Entrepreneurship Theory and Practice*. https://doi.org/https://doi.org/10.1177/1042258719899423

Bughin, C., & Colot, O. (2010). Does family governance encourage innovation. *Journal of Business & Economics*, *2*(2), 199–218.

Burt, R. S., Opper, S., & Zou, N. (2021). Social network and family business: Uncovering hybrid family firms. *Social Networks*, *65*, 141–156.

Calabrò, A., Vecchiarini, M., Gast, J., Campopiano, G., De Massis, A., & Kraus, S. (2019). Innovation in family firms: A systematic literature review and guidance for future research. *International Journal of Management Reviews*, *21*(3), 317–355.

Cassia, L., De Massis, A., & Pizzurno, E. (2011). An exploratory investigation on NPD in small family businesses from Northern Italy. *International Journal of Business, Management and Social Sciences*, *2*(2), 1–14.

Chia, R. (2000). Discourse analysis organizational analysis. *Organization*, *7*(3), 513–518.

Chrisman, J. J., Chua, J. H., De Massis, A., Frattini, F., & Wright, M. (2015). The ability and willingness paradox in family firm innovation. *Journal of Product Innovation Management*, *32*(3), 310–318.

Classen, N., Van Gils, A., Bammens, Y., & Carree, M. (2012). Accessing resources from innovation partners: The search breadth of family SMEs. *Journal of Small Business Management*, *50*(2), 191–215.

Craig, J., & Dibrell, C. (2006). The natural environment, innovation, and firm performance: A comparative study. *Family Business Review*, *19*(4), 275–288.

Cunliffe, A. L., Luhman, J. T., & Boje, D. M. (2004). Narrative temporality: Implications for organizational research. *Organization Studies*, *25*(2), 261–286.

Dalpiaz, E., Tracey, P., & Phillips, N. (2014). Succession narratives in family business: The case of Alessi. *Entrepreneurship Theory and Practice*, *38*(6), 1375–1394.

Dawson, A., & Hjorth, D. (2012). Advancing family business research through narrative analysis. *Family Business Review, 25*(3), 339–355.

De Massis, A., Ding, S., Kotlar, J., & Wu, Z. (2018). Family involvement and R&D expenses in the context of weak property rights protection: An examination of non-state-owned listed companies in China. *European Journal of Finance, 24*(16), 1506–1527.

De Massis, A., Eddleston, K. A., & Rovelli, P. (2020). Entrepreneurial by design: How organizational design affects family and nonfamily firms' opportunity exploitation. *Journal of Management Studies, 58*(1), 27–62.

De Massis, A., Frattini, F., Kotlar, J., Petruzzelli, A. M., & Wright, M. (2016). Innovation through tradition: Lessons from innovative family businesses and directions for future research. *Academy of Management Perspectives, 30*(1), 93–116.

De Massis, A., Frattini, F., & Lichtenthaler, U. (2013). Research on technological innovation in family firms: Present debates and future directions. *Family Business Review, 26*(1), 10–31.

Decker, C., & Günther, C. (2017). The impact of family ownership on innovation: Evidence from the German machine tool industry. *Small Business Economics, 48*(1), 199–212.

Diéguez-Soto, J., Manzaneque, M., & Rojo-Ramírez, A. A. (2016). Technological innovation inputs, outputs, and performance: The moderating role of family involvement in management. *Family Business Review, 29*(3), 327–346.

Distelberg, B. J., & Blow, A. (2011). Variations in family system boundaries. *Family Business Review, 24*(1), 28–46.

Dodd, S. D., Anderson, A., & Jack, S. (2013). Being in time and the family owned firm. *Scandinavian Journal of Management, 29*(1), 35–47.

Donckels, R., & Lambrecht, J. (1995). Networks and small business growth: An explanatory model. *Small Business Economics, 7*(4), 279–289.

Eisenhardt, K. M. (1989). Building theories from case study research. *Academy of Management Review, 14*(4), 532–550.

Erdogan, I., Rondi, E., & De Massis, A. (2020). Managing the tradition and innovation paradox in family firms: A family imprinting perspective. *Entrepreneurship Theory and Practice, 44*(1), 20–54.

Fang, H., Kotlar, J., Memili, E., Chrisman, J. J., & De Massis, A. (2018). The pursuit of international opportunities in family firms: Generational differences and the role of knowledge-based resources. *Global Strategy Journal, 8*(1), 136–157.

Filser, M., De Massis, A., Gast, J., Kraus, S., & Niemand, T. (2018). Tracing the roots of innovativeness in family SMEs: The effect of family functionality and socioemotional wealth. *Journal of Product Innovation Management, 35*(4), 609–628.

Fletcher, D. (2002). A network perspective of cultural organising and 'professional management' in the small, family business. *Journal of Small Business and Enterprise Development, 9*(4), 400–415.

Fletcher, D., & Adiguna, R. (2020). Ethnography: A much-advocated but underused qualitative methodology in published accounts of family business research. In A. De Massis & N. Kammerlander (Eds.). *Handbook of Qualitative Research Methods for Family Business* (pp. 72–97). Cheltenham, UK and Northampton, MA, USA: Edward Elgar Publishing.

Fletcher, D., De Massis, A., & Nordqvist, M. (2016). Qualitative research practices and family business scholarship: A review and future research agenda. *Journal of Family Business Strategy, 7*(1), 8–25.

Freeman, C. (1976). *Economics of Industrial Innovation.* Pinter.

Gomez-Mejia, L. R., Haynes, K. T., Núñez-Nickel, M., Jacobson, K. J., & Moyano-Fuentes, J. (2007). Socioemotional wealth and business risks in family-controlled firms: Evidence from Spanish olive oil mills. *Administrative Science Quarterly*, *52*(1), 106–137.

Greve, A., & Salaff, J. W. (2003). Social networks and entrepreneurship. *Entrepreneurship Theory and Practice*, *28*(1), 1–22.

Habbershon, T. G., & Williams, M. L. (1999). A resource-based framework for assessing the strategic advantages of family firms. *Family Business Review*, *12*(1), 1–25.

Hatak, I., Kautonen, T., Fink, M., & Kansikas, J. (2016). Innovativeness and family-firm performance: The moderating effect of family commitment. *Technological Forecasting and Social Change*, *102*(4), 120–131.

Hsu, L. C., & Chang, H. C. (2011). The role of behavioral strategic controls in family firm innovation. *Industry and Innovation*, *18*(7), 709–727.

Kammerlander, N., & Ganter, M. (2015). An attention-based view of family firm adaptation to discontinuous technological change: Exploring the role of family CEOs' noneconomic goals. *Journal of Product Innovation Management*, *32*(3), 361–383.

Kammerlander, N., Dessi, C., Bird, M., Floris, M., & Murru, A. (2015). The impact of shared stories on family firm innovation: A multicase study. *Family Business Review*, *28*(4), 332–354.

Kellermanns, F. W., Eddleston, K. A., Sarathy, R., & Murphy, F. (2012). Innovativeness in family firms: A family influence perspective. *Small Business Economics*, *38*(1), 85–101.

Knoke, D., & Kuklinski, J. H. (1991). Network analysis: Basic concepts. In G. Thompson, J. Frances, R. Levacic, & J. Mitchell (Eds.), *Markets, Hierarchies and Networks: The Coordination of Social Life* (pp. 173–182). Sage Publications.

Kotlar, J., Fang, H., De Massis, A., & Frattini, F. (2014). Profitability goals, control goals, and the R&D investment decisions of family and nonfamily firms. *Journal of Product Innovation Management*, *31*(6), 1128–1145.

Kraiczy, N. D., Hack, A., & Kellermanns, F. W. (2014). New product portfolio performance in family firms. *Journal of Business Research*, *67*(6), 1065–1073.

Kraus, S., Pohjola, M., & Koponen, A. (2012). Innovation in family firms: An empirical analysis linking organizational and managerial innovation to corporate success. *Review of Managerial Science*, *6*(3), 265–286.

Labaki, R., Bernhard, F., & Cailluet, L. (2019). The strategic use of historical narratives in the family business. In E. Memili & C. Dibrell (Eds.), *The Palgrave Handbook of Heterogeneity Among Family Firms* (pp. 531–553). Springer.

Lambrechts, F., Voordeckers, W., Roijakkers, N., & Vanhaverbeke, W. (2017). Exploring open innovation in entrepreneurial private family firms in low- and medium-technology industries. *Organizational Dynamics*, *46*(4), 244–261.

Lamont, M., & Swidler, A. (2014). Methodological pluralism and the possibilities and limits of interviewing. *Qualitative Sociology*, *37*(2), 153–171.

Lê, J. K., & Schmid, T. (2020). The practice of innovating research methods. *Organizational Research Methods*, 1094428120935498.

Llach, J., & Nordqvist, M. (2010). Innovation in family and non-family businesses: A resource perspective. *International Journal of Entrepreneurial Venturing*, *2*(3–4), 381–399.

Lodh, S., Nandy, M., & Chen, J. (2014). Innovation and family ownership: Empirical evidence from India. *Corporate Governance: An International Review*, *22*(1), 4–23.

Logemann, M., Piekkari, R., & Cornelissen, J. (2019). The sense of it all: Framing and narratives in sensegiving about a strategic change. *Long Range Planning, 52*(5), 101852.

Lopez-Fernandez, M. C., Serrano-Bedia, A. M., & Gómez-López, R. (2016). Determinants of innovation decision in small and medium-sized family enterprises. *Journal of Small Business and Enterprise Development, 23*(2), 408–427.

Martínez-Torres, M. R. (2014). Analysis of open innovation communities from the perspective of social network analysis. *Technology Analysis & Strategic Management, 26*(4), 435–451.

Matzler, K., Veider, V., Hautz, J., & Stadler, C. (2015). The impact of family ownership, management, and governance on innovation. *Journal of Product Innovation Management, 32*(3), 319–333.

Miller, D., Wright, M., Breton-Miller, I. L., & Scholes, L. (2015). Resources and innovation in family businesses: The Janus-face of socioemotional preferences. *California Management Review, 58*(1), 20–40.

Miller, R. L. (1999). *Researching Life Stories and Family Histories.* Sage.

Nieto, M. J., Santamaria, L., & Fernandez, Z. (2015). Understanding the innovation behavior of family firms. *Journal of Small Business Management, 53*(2), 382–399.

Porter, M. E. (1980). *Competitive Strategy: Techniques for Analyzing Industries and Competitors.* New York: Free Press.

Rae, D. (2004). Practical theories from entrepreneurs' stories: Discursive approaches to entrepreneurial learning. *Journal of Small Business and Enterprise Development.*

Raitis, J., Sasaki, I., & Kotlar, J. (2021). System-spanning values work and entrepreneurial growth in family firms. *Journal of Management Studies, 11*(2), 195–202.

Reay, T., & Zhang, Z. (2014). Qualitative methods in family business research. In L. Melin, M. Nordqvist, & P. Sharma (Eds.), *The SAGE Handbook of Family Business* (pp. 573–593). Sage Publications.

Röd, I. (2016). Disentangling the family firm's innovation process: A systematic review. *Journal of Family Business Strategy, 7*(3), 185–201.

Rondi, E., & Rovelli, P. (2021a). Exchanging knowledge in the TMT to realize more innovation opportunities: What can family firms do? *Journal of Knowledge Management.* https://doi.org/10.1108/JKM-08-2020-0645

Rondi, E., & Rovelli, P. (2021b). *La Gestione Dell'Innovazione Nelle Imprese Familiari.* Eurilink University Press.

Rondi, E., Überbacher, R., von Schlenk-Barnsdorf, L., De Massis, A., & Hülsbeck, M. (2021). One for all, all for one: A mutual gains perspective on HRM and innovation management practices in family firms. *Journal of Family Business Strategy,* 100394.

Rovelli, P., Ferasso, M., De Massis, A., & Kraus, S. (2021). Thirty years of research in family business journals: Status quo and future directions. *Journal of Family Business Strategy, 13*(3), 100422.

Sanchez-Famoso, V., Iturralde, T., & Maseda, A. (2015). The influence of family and non-family social capital on firm innovation: Exploring the role of family ownership. *European Journal of International Management, 9*(2), 240–262.

Schumpeter, J. (1934). *The Theory of Economic Development.* Harvard University Press.

Sciascia, S., Nordqvist, M., Mazzola, P., & De Massis, A. (2015). Family ownership and R&D intensity in small- and medium-sized firms. *Journal of Product Innovation Management, 32*(3), 349–360.

Short, J. C., & Payne, G. T. (2020). In their own words: A call for increased use of organizational narratives in family business research. *Family Business Review, 33*(4), 342–350.

Siggelkow, N. (2007). Persuasion with case studies. *Academy of Management Journal, 50*(1), 20–24.

Smith, R. (2018). Reading liminal and temporal dimensionality in the Baxter family 'public-narrative'. *International Small Business Journal, 36*(1), 41–59.

Sonenshein, S. (2010). We're changing – Or are we? Untangling the role of progressive, regressive, and stability narratives during strategic change implementation. *Academy of Management Journal, 53*(3), 477–512.

Thorelli, H. B. (1986). Networks: Between markets and hierarchies. *Strategic Management Journal, 7*(1), 37–51.

Tichy, N. M., Tushman, M. L., & Fombrun, C. (1979). Social network analysis for organizations. *Academy of Management Review, 4*(4), 507–519.

Tsai, W., & Ghoshal, S. (1998). Social capital and value creation: The role of intrafirm networks. *Academy of Management Journal, 41*(4), 464–476.

Urbinati, A., Franzò, S., De Massis, A., & Frattini, F. (2017). Innovation in family firms: A review of prior studies and a framework for future research. In A. Brem & E. Viardot (Eds.) *Revolution of innovation management* (pp. 213–246). Springer.

Wagner, M. (2010). Corporate social performance and innovation with high social benefits: A quantitative analysis. *Journal of Business Ethics, 94*(4), 581–594.

Wasserman, S., & Faust, K. (1994). *Social Network Analysis: Methods and Applications.* Cambridge University Press.

Woodfield, P., & Husted, K. (2017). Intergenerational knowledge sharing in family firms: Case-based evidence from the New Zealand wine industry. *Journal of Family Business Strategy, 8*(1), 57–69.

Yin, R. K. (2012). Case study methods. In H. Cooper, P. Camic, D. Long, A. Panter, D. Rindskopf, & K. Sher (Eds.), *APA Handbook of Research Methods in Psychology, Vol. 2: Research Designs: Quantitative, Qualitative, Neuropsychological and Biological* (pp. 141–155). American Psychological Association.

Zamudio, C., Anokhin, S., & Kellermanns, F. W. (2014). Network analysis: A concise review and suggestions for family business research. *Journal of Family Business Strategy, 5*(1), 63–71.

# 7. What does the literature say? Performing a systematic literature review in family business research

**Chelsea Sherlock and Clay Dibrell**

## INTRODUCTION

Providing a complete evaluation of a prominent area of research is critical to summarize the evolution of the literature over time and to understand its influence across multiple disciplines. A systematic review approach offers an opportunity to assess the delineation of knowledge within a domain and to identify changes and trends across multiple publication outlets using an approach that can be replicated by other scholars, often providing a stronger degree of objectivity than individual studies, which may suffer from subjective bias (e.g., Xiao & Watson, 2019). Systematic reviews have a long tradition of being used to critically analyze many areas of literature from medical scholarship to the family business domain (Denyer & Tranfield, 2009; Swab, Sherlock, Markin, & Dibrell, 2020). Specifically, in family business research, reviews have been leveraged to consolidate information on particular topics such as conflict and cohesion (e.g., Bettinelli, Mismetti, De Massis, & Del Bosco, 2021), socioemotional wealth (e.g., Swab et al., 2020), nonfamily members in family firms (e.g., Tabor, Chrisman, Madison, & Vardaman, 2018), internationalization strategies (e.g., Arregle, Chirico, Kano, Kundu, Majocchi, & Schulze, 2021), and family business restructuring (e.g., King, Meglio, Gómez-Mejía, Bauer, & De Massis, 2021) to name a few. Further, systematic reviews also aid in revealing gaps in our knowledge and identifying avenues for future research (De Massis, Sharma, Chua, & Chrisman, 2012; Debicki, Matherne, Kellermanns, & Chrisman, 2009; Gedajlovic, Carney, Chrisman, & Kellermanns, 2012; Rovelli, Ferasso, De Massis, & Kraus, 2021).

What we know about family businesses stems from a broad variety of domains and across a number of unique journal outlets (Payne, 2018), and thus, it becomes difficult for scholars to identify the phenomena and theoretical boundaries of the field.

> Although historically tied to entrepreneurship due to its roots in small business, [family business] is not built on a singular discipline. It instead represents a large set of interrelated subfields that are bound together by the recognition that families, as owners and operators, can have a unique influence on a wide variety of business activities and outcomes. (Payne, 2018, p. 167)

With this challenge, it becomes difficult to discern the boundaries of the field and gain an understanding of the phenomena studied across so many subfields. As a consequence, it becomes increasingly difficult for scholars to concisely and cohesively address the breadth of topics covered in family business research.

Accordingly, the purpose of this chapter is to provide guidelines and rules of thumb on conducting family business systematic literature reviews, using family firm diversification as an exemplar, to maximize contributions to the family business field. We offer a systematic review of this literature from different disciplines (entrepreneurship, family business, finance, and management) to synthesize extant knowledge, uncover relevant gaps in the literature, and further to promote growth in the field (Short, 2009). We also highlight some of the specific challenges and issues that researchers should be cognizant of when conducting a literature review on the topic of family business research, and how reviews in this area differ from those conducted in the broader management literature.

## A BASIC REVIEW FRAMEWORK

The systematic literature review is derived from the medical field (e.g., Greenhalgh, 1997) and allows for a more rigorous analysis and greater dissemination of findings than from a single study. Going beyond traditional meta-analyses, which look to statistically analyze empirical findings from other peer-reviewed studies (Khan, Kunz, Kleijnen, & Antes, 2003), a systematic literature review may include conceptual and/or empirical articles to provide a broader, more robust understanding of the topic of interest (Kembro, Selviaridis, & Näslund, 2014). A systematic literature review is one that provides 'an overview of primary studies which contains an explicit statement of objectives, materials, and methods and has been conducted according to explicit and reproducible methodology' (Greenhalgh, 1997, p. 672).

Drawing from the work of Thorpe, Holt, Macpherson, and Pittaway (2005), there are several broad foundational steps necessary for a systematic literature review: defining the objectives, preparing the proposal, developing the protocol, conducting the review, and reporting the review. This systematic methodology for conducting a literature review centers on conducting the review, where authors search, evaluate, refine, and analyze peer-reviewed articles relevant to the previously defined objectives. A summary of this basic process is presented in Figure 7.1 and serves as the framework for the remainder of this chapter.

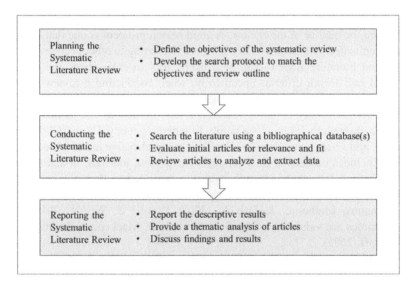

*Figure 7.1      Guidelines for a systematic literature review process*

**Planning the Systematic Literature Review**

**Define the objectives of the systematic review**
It is necessary for researchers to identify the research question and the gap the review will fill. The entirety of the review should be positioned toward answering the research question(s). The lack of a clear research question may result in a disjointed review that fails to tell a compelling story of the literature to date. As Short (2009) argues, a review that is too broad, or one that fails to capture a topic offers little value. In contrast, a review that depicts an interesting research topic can contribute to the literature by providing an insightful synthesis of a particular research stream. Given the broad nature of disciplines that family business draws upon, this first step is of critical significance. For instance, in a recent review of socioemotional wealth (SEW), Swab et al. (2020) pose three distinct research questions to guide their review.

Through the process of answering the research questions, the contributions of the review become clearer.

**Develop the search protocol to match the objectives**
The search protocol used in systematic reviews is similar to a study design that is operationalized in primary data research studies. The goal is to outline the steps of the search criteria to ensure that they match the objectives and research question(s) of the review. The search protocol outlined in this step will directly influence the quality of the review. A good search protocol is one that can be easily replicated by others to verify the work. Referring to other peer-reviewed published literature reviews can be a useful tool to cross-check the search protocol and search criteria. Specifically, when conducting a review in the family business domain, it may be necessary to consider a cross-discipline journal list as family business research is not limited to one domain. For instance, through their review on family firm heterogeneity, Daspit, Chrisman, Ashton, and Evangelopoulos (2021) offer a comprehensive list of 33 journals, which includes economic, finance, and management journals, in addition to family business journals. Overall, it is recommended to limit the search to leading peer-reviewed journals across multiple domains (Chrisman, Chua, Kellermanns, Matherne, & Debicki, 2008; Fayolle & Wright, 2014), as such articles are validated by the field (Podsakoff, Mackenzie, Bachrach, & Podsakoff, 2005).

It is also necessary to identify the electronic databases (e.g., Elsevier's Scopus or EBSCOhost (ABI/Inform ProQuest and Business Source Complete)) available to search to arrive at a group of relevant research articles. Specific to family business literature reviews, it is important to consider the journals and data that each database offers. For example, at the time of this printing, Business Source Complete does not include *Journal of Family Business Strategy* or *Journal of Family Business Management*, both of which are strong contributors to family business research. Therefore, a systematic protocol that covers multiple databases ensures a more comprehensive search of extant family business literature. The best practice for a systematic review would be to include as many relevant sources as possible to ensure that the search is all-inclusive and adequately captures previous research. Similarly, the timeframe used to search for articles is necessary and should be justified by past literature or follow other similar best practices. In our diversification example (see Appendix A), the timeframe of 1999–2019 was identified because 1999 coincides with a seminal piece of family business research (Chua, Chrisman, & Sharma, 1999) and offers a comprehensive 20-year view of the research conducted in this area.

The keywords used for the search protocol should align with the research question(s). Researchers should carefully consider the list of keywords to ensure that the list is exhaustive but not restrictive (Xiao & Watson, 2019). At this stage, it is imperative that the search is broad enough to capture *all* work related to the topic. To do so, the use of an asterisk (*) following a keyword is a wildcard operator and allows for variations in the root of the keyword and thus, ensures a more exhaustive search. For example, using the keyword '*family involve**', the search results yield variations of the keyword such as family involvement and family involved.

## Conducting the Systematic Literature Review

### Search the literature using a bibliographical database(s)

The next step in the literature review process is to use bibliographical databases (e.g., Scopus) to search for articles that match the search protocol developed in the planning phase. The search keywords should encompass a wide range of terms to adequately capture the breadth of the topic, phenomenon, or theory of interest. Drawing from our diversification exemplar, we searched for the following terms: *diversif**, *merge**, *acquisition*, *acquire*, *mergers and acquisitions*, and *divest**, published between 1999–2019. The search criteria should include 'or' statements to separate each keyword to allow for multiple topics, in this example of diversification strategies, to be covered in the search (see Appendix A).

Given the objective of a systematic family business literature review is to examine research relating to various strategies, topics, and theories in family firms, incorporating keywords that are specific to family firms should also be included. For example, in our exemplar on diversification strategies, the following terms relevant to family firm literature were also included: *family firm, family business, family enterprise, family control*, family-control*, family influence, family involve**, and *family own**. The family firm-specific keywords were used in conjunction with other relevant keywords, such that an 'and' statement was included in the search. For example, '(*acquisition* OR *divest**) AND (*family firm* OR *family own**)' (see Appendix A). It is vital for family business scholars to include the '*family firm*' search phrase to narrow the search, which would not need to be done if the researchers were exclusively focusing on a more established domain, such as the management domain.

### Evaluate/selection of initial articles for relevance and fit

Following the bibliometric search of the literature it is necessary to review the initial articles yielded for both relevance and fit by evaluating each article independently. This initial search is often executed by reviewing the abstracts of each article (Xiao & Watson, 2019). This evaluation should match the objectives of the review to ensure that the main context of each article aligns with the goals of the systematic review. Within this step, it is crucial to keep a record of the number of articles that were excluded from the sample and justification for *why* these articles were removed. Referring to our diversification example, some articles were removed due to their focus on knowledge acquisition (e.g., Duarte Alonso & Kok, 2018) or resource acquisitions (e.g., Blanco-Mazagatos, de Quevedo-Puente, & Castrillo, 2007), because these articles did not evaluate diversification strategies, which was the objective of the review. Additionally, when conducting systematic literature reviews on family firm topics, it is necessary that researchers review each article to ensure that *family firms* are the main context of the study and not simply listed as an avenue for future research or referring to family members in nonfamily firm contexts.

Next, based on the objective of the review, it may be necessary to remove items listed as corrigenda, errata, editorials, or commentaries. Typically, corrigenda and errata are excluded from the final sample because they are often duplicate entries that only indicate a correction to an error in a previous publication, therefore, these types of work do not offer additional insights to the review topic of interest. Similarly, the decision to cut other article types may be necessary if they do not align the stated focus of the review or aid in answering the research question(s). Lastly, best practices suggest that at least two researchers should work independently to analyze each article based on the inclusion criteria, then the researchers should compare results and resolve any discrepancies (Xiao & Watson, 2019). This process ensures that there is strong interrater reliability across reviewers. Again, each researcher should keep a record of the number of articles that were excluded from the sample and justification for *why* these articles were removed, to ensure that the systematic review is replicable.

### Review articles to analyze and extract data

From the initial search of the articles, researchers should further analyze the full text of each article along multiple dimensions related to topic, theory, or phenomena of interest. This step is useful to assess the quality and content of each article and can aid in revealing gaps in the literature, conflicting findings, or discrepancies in the research. There are several means through which researchers can analyze extant research, but generally it is best to code each article along multiple dimensions. For example, it may be useful to code for the type of article (e.g., empirical, conceptual, case study, review, meta-analysis), topic area (e.g., M&A, divestment, diversification, etc.), type of family firm (e.g., founder, transgenerational), country of sample, theory(s) used, as well as independent, dependent, and mediating/moderating variables. The specific assessment of each article will vary based on the objective of the review and the research question(s) researchers are seeking to answer (see Jiang, Kellermanns, Munyon, & Morris, 2018, p. 137; Strike, Michel, &

Kammerlander, 2018, p. 87; Tabor et al., 2018, p. 57, for examples of different coding dimensions within a family business context[1]). In this step, it is better to over-analyze each article and capture a wide variety of information from each article because this information will aid in identifying themes and generating conclusions from the literature. Specific to family business reviews, it may be useful to analyze and code for the criteria used in extant work to define the family firm because 'different definitions can lead to completely different outcomes, although the same sample and research design are used' (Schmid, Ampenberger, Kaserer, & Achleitner, 2015, p. 298), which can be very problematic and is fairly unique to family business research. In other words, discrepancies across extant findings may be in part due to the varying definitions used in the family business field, and thus, it is imperative to examine the criteria/definitions used to classify family firms from their nonfamily counterparts.

**Reporting the Systematic Literature Review**

**Data synthesis and reporting the descriptive results**
Reporting the descriptive results of a systematic literature review can provide an opportunity for scholars to justify their review efforts by demonstrating the importance of the topic, theory, or phenomenon by displaying the growth or popularity within the extant literature. Tables and figures are useful tools to provide descriptive information in a concise format. For instance, to understand how research surrounding the topic of interest has evolved over the time period studied, it may be useful to plot the published studies included in the final sample by the year of publication. Such a plot can clearly illustrate the trends in publishing over several years and provide a visual representation of the ebbs and flows of interest of the topic.

Additionally, it can be useful to report a table of the outlets publishing the work of interest. Specifically, in family business research, there are a breadth of areas that may publish work related to the review. A table of the specific journal outlets may shed light on whether work in a particular area is derived more from a specific single field (i.e., management, psychology, family sciences, entrepreneurship, finance, family business). While descriptive results from the systematic search are useful for demonstrating the breadth of a topic, these results do not provide an in-depth analysis or synthesize the themes from the literature. Thus, the most useful reviews are those that go beyond the breadth of the topic to examine the depth of the topic and provide a thematic analysis of the extant work.

---

[1]    In Appendix B, a generic summary of a systematic literature review procedure is provided.

### Provide a thematic analysis of articles

As a result of the coding scheme, a thematic analysis of the literature may result in a framework to report the findings produced over the time period. For example, Tabor et al. (2018) in their review on nonfamily members in family firms provide a thorough summary of the nonfamily member literature by organizing extant work into a figure (Tabor et al., 2018, p. 56) to categorize the aggregate dimensions of employment. Alternatively, based on the scope of the systematic review, it may be best to summarize the articles using a 2x2 figure based on the themes identified through the coding and analysis stage. For instance, Gedajlovic et al. (2012, p. 1013) develop a 2x2 figure to catalog family business research based on the joint effects of effort intensity and ability to produce four distinct scenarios of family firm performance. Similarly, in their review on family firms and institutional contexts, Soleimanof, Rutherford, and Webb (2018, p. 36) develop a 2x2 framework to synthesize prior research and provide avenues for future research.

### Discuss findings and results

A good systematic literature review should go beyond the surface-level data and instead summarize a research stream by providing broad themes (Short, 2009) to provide the 'so what' moment for scholars (e.g., Fuetsch & Suess-Reyes, 2017). It is in the discussion of the findings and results that researchers can share new insights into the theoretical perspectives, boundary conditions, themes, or resolve equivocal findings based on their analysis of the articles in the review. The discussion should also reveal unique insights into a particular literature stream that is not readily apparent to scholars in the field. By reporting novel findings as a non-intuitive result suggests a *theoretical blind spot* may exist amongst family business scholars, suggesting future research is warranted. Additionally, scholars can use the systematic literature review results to identify various future research areas, which may not be intuitive to domain scholars. This is of vital importance for all systematic literature reviews, as scholars are looking for a revelation to guide their own future scholarship, as they read through this section.

## DISCUSSION

Researchers in the family business field should often take stock of the literature, and the steps and suggestions provided in this chapter offer a model for future work to develop systematic literature reviews. The purpose of this chapter is to create guidelines and rules of thumb on conducting family business systematic literature reviews. Systematic reviews on family business research differ from reviews of topics in the general management field on a number of dimensions (see Table 7.1). First, because family business research has the

*Table 7.1*     *Comparisons of family business research and general*
                *management reviews*

|  |  | Family Business Literature Reviews | General Management Literature Reviews |
|---|---|---|---|
| **Planning the Systematic Literature Review** | **Define the objectives of the systematic review** | Breadth of topics – family business has a lack of breadth | Breadth of topics – general management is very broad and encompasses a wide variety of topics |
|  | **Preparation of the review and search protocol** | Different domains – highly fragmented across a variety of disciplines (e.g., entrepreneurship, management, finance, family sciences, etc.) | Within the management domain – more consolidated within the field of management |
| **Conducting the Systematic Literature Review** | **Search the literature using a bibliographical database(s)** | Broad set of family-specific keywords to capture the family influence. High potential for false positives | Availability of more precise keywords because the field is more well defined and topical areas have distinct boundaries |
|  | **Selection of articles – evaluate for relevance and fit** | Boundary spanning – extremely broad | Boundary spanning – more narrowly focused |
|  | **Data extraction** | Similar approaches | Similar approaches |
| **Reporting the Systematic Literature Review** | **Data synthesis** | Similar approaches | Similar approaches |
|  | **Report the descriptive results, provide a thematic analysis of articles, discuss findings and provide recommendations** | It is necessary to define the audience – there is the option to appeal to a broad array of disciplines with the findings and recommendations | It is necessary to define the audience – findings and recommendations are often focused to a narrow selection of management scholars |

capacity to serve as a boundary-spanning platform for management research (Holt, Pearson, Payne, & Sharma, 2018), research extends across a variety of disciplines, and thus the preparation for a family business review may be more encompassing than a general management review. For instance, in a recent FBR review publication, Kubíček and Machek (2020) explore intrafamily conflict in family businesses and expand their systematic search to include interdisciplinary journals such as *Family Relations and Journal of Family and Economic Issues* as these outlets have studies relevant to their topic. Therefore, when outlining the initial search criteria, it is generally advantageous to look outside the family business domain when conducting a literature search.

Second, a broad set of family specific keywords exist to capture the family influence thus, there is potential for false positive results when searching the literature. Family business scholars must be cognizant of such issues when searching and reviewing extant literature. Further, due to the inconsistent criteria used to define family firms, the ability to draw conclusions across heterogenous family firms becomes challenging (Daspit, Chrisman, Skorodziyevskiy, Davis, & Ashton, Chapter 5 in this book). Indeed, as Daspit et al. (2021, p. 297) lament, 'the continued inability to precisely articulate differences among family firms has the potential to result in theoretical inaccuracies, empirical indeterminacies, and a fallacious understanding'. This challenge presents an opportunity for systematic reviews to contribute to family business research by exposing such inconsistencies and reconciling findings.

Lastly, it is necessary to define the audience when reporting the findings and providing recommendations for future family business research topics. In contrast to general management research, systematic reviews on family business research have the option to appeal to a broad array of disciplines in part due to the boundary-spanning nature of the family business field and how the field has progressed in the last decade (Payne, 2018). Therefore, family business scholars are tasked with outlining contributions that appeal to a specific audience (Micelotta, Chapter 2 in this book). As Short (2009) suggests, reviews that offer strong contributions should address *why does this matter?* while also outlining explicit insights to a specific stream of research. The contributions of the systematic review should move beyond descriptive results of the literature search and offer an extensive examination of the depth of the topic and provide a thematic analysis of previous work that would not be apparent by simply reading articles related to the topic.

## CONCLUSION

The purpose of our chapter is to create guidelines and rules of thumb for family business scholars conducting systematic literature reviews. We provide a review framework to help guide future systematic literature reviews. We also discuss how literature reviews in family business research differ from those in the broader management literature. Specifically, we highlight how the distinctive features of family firms (e.g., ownership, legacy, transgenerational aspirations, etc.) can lead to inconsistencies across extant work and therefore, scholars should consider such idiosyncrasies when conducting their own systematic literature reviews in the family business domain. Through our example of a systematic literature review of the family firm diversification literature, we provide an outline for the multiple structured steps necessary to produce a replicable selection of the literature for future scholars to conduct systematic reviews in other areas of family business research.

# REFERENCES

Arregle, J. L., Chirico, F., Kano, L., Kundu, S. K., Majocchi, A., & Schulze, W. S. (2021). Family firm internationalization: Past research and an agenda for the future. *Journal of International Business Studies*, *52*(6), 1159–1198.

Bettinelli, C., Mismetti, M., De Massis, A., & Del Bosco, B. (2021). A review of conflict and cohesion in social relationships in family firms. *Entrepreneurship Theory and Practice*. https://doi.org/10.1177/10422587211000339.

Blanco-Mazagatos, V., de Quevedo-Puente, E., & Castrillo, L. A. (2007). The trade-off between financial resources and agency costs in the family business: An exploratory study. *Family Business Review*, *20*(3), 199–213.

Chrisman, J. J., Chua, J. H., Kellermanns, F. W., Matherne III, C. F., & Debicki, B. J. (2008). Management journals as venues for publication of family business research. *Entrepreneurship Theory and Practice*, *32*(5), 927–934.

Chua, J. H., Chrisman, J. J., & Sharma, P. (1999). Defining the family business by behavior. *Entrepreneurship Theory and Practice*, *23*(4), 19–39.

Daspit, J. J., Chrisman, J. J., Ashton, T., & Evangelopoulos, N. (2021). Family firm heterogeneity: A definition, common themes, scholarly progress, and directions forward. *Family Business Review*. https://doi.org/10.1177/08944865211008350.

De Massis, A., Sharma, P., Chua, J. H., & Chrisman, J. J. (2012). *Family Business Studies: An Annotated Bibliography*. Edward Elgar Publishing.

Debicki, B. J., Matherne III, C. F., Kellermanns, F. W., & Chrisman, J. J. (2009). Family business research in the new millennium: An overview of the who, the where, the what, and the why. *Family Business Review*, *22*(2), 151–166.

Denyer, D., & Tranfield, D. (2009). Producing a systematic review. In D. A. Buchanan & A. Bryman (Eds.), *The Sage Handbook of Organizational Research Methods* (pp. 671–689). Sage Publications.

Duarte Alonso, A., & Kok, S. (2018). Adapting through learning and knowledge acquisition: The cases of four global family firms. *Journal of Family Business Management*, *8*(3), 274–292.

Fayolle, A., & Wright, M. (Eds.). (2014). *How to Get Published in the Best Entrepreneurship Journals: A Guide to Steer your Academic Career*. Edward Elgar Publishing.

Fuetsch, E., & Suess-Reyes, J. (2017). Research on innovation in family businesses: Are we building an ivory tower? *Journal of Family Business Management*, *7*(1), 44–92.

Gedajlovic, E., Carney, M., Chrisman, J. J., & Kellermanns, F. W. (2012). The adolescence of family firm research: Taking stock and planning for the future. *Journal of Management*, *38*(4), 1010–1037.

Greenhalgh, T. (1997). How to read a paper: Papers that summarise other papers (systematic reviews and meta-analyses). *British Medical Journal*, 315, 672–675.

Holt, D. T., Pearson, A. W., Payne, G. T., & Sharma, P. (2018). Family business research as a boundary-spanning platform. *Family Business Review*, *31*(1), 14–31.

Jiang, D. S., Kellermanns, F. W., Munyon, T. P., & Morris, M. L. (2018). More than meets the eye: A review and future directions for the social psychology of socioemotional wealth. *Family Business Review*, *31*(1), 125–157.

Kembro, J., Selviaridis, K., & Näslund, D. (2014). Theoretical perspectives on information sharing in supply chains: A systematic literature review and conceptual framework. *Supply Chain Management: An International Journal*, *19*(5–6), 609–625.

Khan, K. S., Kunz, R., Kleijnen, J., & Antes, G. (2003). Five steps to conducting a systematic review. *Journal of the Royal Society of Medicine, 96*(3), 118–121.

King, D. R., Meglio, O., Gómez-Mejía, L. R.., Bauer, F., & De Massis, A. (2021). Family business restructuring: A review and research agenda. *Journal of Management Studies.* https://doi.org/10.1111/joms.12717.

Kubíček, A., & Machek, O. (2020). Intrafamily conflicts in family businesses: A systematic review of the literature and agenda for future research. *Family Business Review, 33*(2), 194–227.

Payne, G. T. (2018). Reflections on family business research: Considering domains and theory. *Family Business Review, 31*(2), 167–175.

Podsakoff, P. M., MacKenzie, S. B., Bachrach, D. G., & Podsakoff, N. P. (2005). The influence of management journals in the 1980s and 1990s. *Strategic Management Journal, 26*(5), 473–488.

Rovelli, P., Ferasso, M., De Massis, A., & Kraus, S. (2021). Thirty years of research in family business journals: Status quo and future directions. *Journal of Family Business Strategy,* 100422.

Schmid, T., Ampenberger, M., Kaserer, C., & Achleitner, A. K. (2015). Family firm heterogeneity and corporate policy: Evidence from diversification decisions. *Corporate Governance: An International Review, 23*(3), 285–302.

Short, J. (2009). The art of writing a review article. *Journal of Management, 35*(6), 1312–1317.

Soleimanof, S., Rutherford, M. W., & Webb, J. W. (2018). The intersection of family firms and institutional contexts: A review and agenda for future research. *Family Business Review, 31*(1), 32–53.

Strike, V. M., Michel, A., & Kammerlander, N. (2018). Unpacking the black box of family business advising: Insights from psychology. *Family Business Review, 31*(1), 80–124.

Swab, R. G., Sherlock, C., Markin, E., & Dibrell, C. (2020). 'SEW' what do we know and where do we go? A review of socioemotional wealth and a way forward. *Family Business Review, 33*(4), 424–445.

Tabor, W., Chrisman, J. J., Madison, K., & Vardaman, J. M. (2018). Nonfamily members in family firms: A review and future research agenda. *Family Business Review, 31*(1), 54–79.

Thorpe, R., Holt, R., Macpherson, A., & Pittaway, L. (2005). Using knowledge within small and medium-sized firms: A systematic review of the evidence. *International Journal of Management Reviews, 7*(4), 257–281.

Xiao, Y., & Watson, M. (2019). Guidance on conducting a systematic literature review. *Journal of Planning Education and Research, 39*(1), 93–112.

# APPENDIX A: FAMILY FIRM DIVERSIFICATION SYSTEMATIC LITERATURE REVIEW PROCEDURE

1. Source of information
   a. The Scopus bibliographical database was used to search for peer-reviewed journal articles.
2. Search method
   a. Articles published between January 1999 and December 2019.
      i. **Search Criteria:** (pubyear >1998 AND pubyear <2020).
   b. Articles published in 23 management, entrepreneurship, family business, and finance journals.
      i. **Search Criteria:** (srctitle ('Academy of Management Journal' OR 'Academy of Management Review' OR 'Administrative Science Quarterly' OR 'Corporate Governance' OR 'Entrepreneurship: Theory and Practice' OR 'Family Business Review' OR 'International Small Business Journal' OR 'Journal of Banking and Finance' OR 'Journal of Business Research' OR 'Journal of Business Venturing' OR 'Journal of Corporate Finance' OR 'Journal of Family Business Management' OR 'Journal of Family Business Strategy' OR 'Journal of Finance' OR 'Journal of Financial Economics' OR 'Journal of Management' OR 'Journal of Management Studies' OR 'Journal of Small Business Management' OR 'Management Science' OR 'Organization Science' OR 'Small Business Economics' OR 'Strategic Entrepreneurship Journal' OR 'Strategic Management Journal')).
   c. Articles pertaining to corporate diversification in family firms by searching the title, abstract, and keywords.
      i. **Search Criteria:** ((title-abs-key ('diversif*' OR 'merge*' OR 'acquisition' OR 'acquire' OR 'mergers and acquisitions' OR 'divest*')) AND (title-abs-key ('family firm' OR 'family business' OR 'family enterprise' OR 'family control*' OR 'family influence' OR 'family involve*' OR 'family own*'))).
3. Exclusion criteria
   a. Editorials, commentaries, errata, and corrigenda.
   b. Articles not published in English.
   c. Books, book chapters, and conference papers.
4. Article selection
   a. Removing articles due to reasons listed in Step 3 regarding the exclusion criteria.

    b. The author team reviewed the title, abstract, and keywords of all articles to determine if articles were relevant to the topic of corporate diversification in family firms.

5. Article coding

    a. The author team independently reviewed the full text of each article to extract information to categorize and code each article.

    b. Coded for information related to the independent, dependent, and moderating variables; type of article (e.g., conceptual, case study, empirical, review); theoretical framework; topic area; empirical sample details (e.g., country, firm size, etc.); family definition operationalized; and the key findings.

# APPENDIX B: GENERIC SYSTEMATIC LITERATURE REVIEW PROCEDURE: THE CONDUCTING PHASE

1. Source of information
   a. Consider multiple sources of bibliographical databases to search for peer-reviewed journal articles (e.g., Scopus, EBSCO, ABInform, etc.).
2. Search method
   a. Establish a timeframe to search for published articles.
      i. **Search Criteria:** (pubyear >XXXX AND pubyear <XXXX).
   b. Generate a list of journals to search across. Using the 'OR' phrasing allows you to search across multiple journals simultaneously.
      i. **Search Criteria:** (srctitle ('XXX' OR 'XXX' OR 'XXX')).
   c. Use different combinations of search criteria pertaining to the topic of interest to identify articles relevant to the review. For example, searching the title, abstract, and keywords is a good way to capture specific topics. Using the * at the end of the keyword generates all different iterations of that word to be searched.
      i. **Search Criteria:** ((title-abs-key ('XXX*' OR 'XXX*')) AND (title-abs-key ('XXX' OR 'XXX' OR 'XXX*'))).
3. Exclusion criteria
   a. Based on the scope of your review it may be appropriate to exclude search results that are categorized as editorials, commentaries, errata, and corrigenda. Or articles not published in English. You may determine that books, book chapters, and conference papers also do not fit the objective of your systematic review.
4. Article selection
   a. Removing articles due to reasons listed in Step 3 regarding the exclusion criteria.
   b. Review the title, abstract, and keywords of all articles to determine if articles are relevant to the topic of the review.
5. Article coding
   a. The author team should independently review the full text of each article to extract information to categorize and code each article.
   b. Code for information related to the independent, dependent, and moderating variables; type of article (e.g., conceptual, case study, empirical, review); theoretical framework; topic area; empirical sample details (e.g., country, firm size, etc.); and the key findings.

# PART II

# Qualitative challenges and solutions

# 8. Making the case for single-case research on family business

## Lori Tribble Trudell, Theodore Waldron, and James Wetherbe

The founding, maturation, and persistence of family businesses is a journey, a dynamic, evolutionary process that qualitative research is particularly well suited to explain (Brigham & Payne, 2015). Calls for qualitative research continue to increase within the entrepreneurship and family business domains (e.g., Dawson & Hjorth, 2012; Payne, 2018; Short & Payne, 2020). However, qualitative methodologies are still highly underutilized within the family business literature. For example, since the inception of the *Family Business Review*, only 71 of over 700 articles (about 10%) classify as qualitative research articles (excluding mixed-methods studies). These numbers are consistent across journals. An analysis in 2012 showed only 18 of the 215 most cited family business studies (8.4%) utilized qualitative methods (De Massis, Sharma, Chua, & Chrisman, 2012). A review of family business research in 2014 showed 78 of 656 articles (about 11.9%) utilizing such methods (Reay & Zhang, 2014).

The underutilization of qualitative methods in the family business literature is surprising. Family firms typically have fewer short-term changes but can be very dynamic over time. Family firms are often 'subject to ongoing changing conditions,' such as succession, environmental, and/or more general family issues, leading to their long-term, transitional nature (Brigham & Payne, 2015, p. 1340). Characterized by family involvement and ownership, family firms tend to demonstrate unique and often more complex processes across levels of analysis. Qualitative methods offer family business researchers the opportunity to analyze these more longitudinal, historical, and interdependent processes that would not be possible using quantitative methods. However, utilizing qualitative methods becomes difficult due to the lack of guidance on when to use them, and how to collect, analyze, and report qualitative data (Fletcher, De Massis, & Nordqvist, 2016; Kammerlander & De Massis, 2020).

The templates that qualitative researchers typically use are the multiple-case approach and the single-case approach (Kammerlander & De Massis, 2020). The multi-case approach, which draws on established theories and answers specific research questions regarding specific constructs (Kammerlander & Diaz-Moriana, Chapter 9 in this book), is used much more often than the single-case approach. When we reviewed the over 700 *Family Business Review* journal articles, of the 10 percent of qualitative papers, only 1.7 percent utilized the single-case design.[1] Yet the single-case approach, which focuses on providing rich description, describing the context, and telling the full story, allows for a much more nuanced understanding of family owners and members and how they interact and evolve (Leppäaho, Plakoyiannaki, & Dimitratos, 2016). Indeed, the single-case approach often yields rich theory that uncovers new insights, encouraging the development of new research directions and conversations (Gehman et al., 2018). Importantly, for family business to take shape as an independent domain, new theoretical development must occur that addresses family business processes. Utilizing the single-case approach in family business research could better explain family business dynamics and complexities, enabling the creation of family business theories rather than simply elaborating theories of management and/or entrepreneurship (Dawson & Hjorth, 2012).

In this chapter we focus on addressing the following questions, all to emphasize the value of the single-case method to family business researchers: (1) What features make the single-case approach uniquely useful for explaining family business phenomena? (2) When should researchers utilize the single-case approach? (3) What areas of the family business literature would benefit from more single-case approach research?

To answer these questions, we first identify and discuss the distinguishing features of the single-case approach that are particularly useful for family business research. Next, we discuss important questions that family business researchers should ask themselves when choosing which methodological approach to utilize. We then discuss areas where applying single-case research would help better define family business theory. Finally, we offer pragmatic considerations for those interested in conducting, publishing, and reviewing such work.

## HOW IS THE SINGLE-CASE APPROACH USEFUL FOR FAMILY BUSINESS PHENOMENA?

The case study approach can be defined as a method that 'explores a real-life, contemporary bounded system (a case) or multiple bounded systems (cases) over time, through detailed, in-depth data collection involving multiple sources

---

[1]    We utilized *Family Business Review* to review because it is the preeminent and oldest academic journal dedicated to the study of family business.

*Table 8.1*    Comparison of the single-case approach and multi-case approach

|  | Single-Case Approach | Multi-Case Approach |
|---|---|---|
| *Approach* | Within case, ethnographic, narrative, interpretive | Case comparison, comparison approach |
| *Ontology* | Relativism (Cunliffe, 2011) | Realism (Cunliffe, 2011) |
| *Epistemology* | Subjectivism (Denzin & Lincoln, 1994) | Objectivism (Eisenhardt, 1991) |
| *Theoretical Perspective* | Interpretivism (researcher interprets elements of the study) (Nordqvist, Hall, & Melin, 2009) | Positivism (researcher observes elements of the study using scientific methods) (Langley & Royer, 2006) |
| *Analytical Perspective* | Narrative development, thick interpretations and descriptions (Dyer & Wilkins, 1991) | Case comparison to discover facts and make observations about reality (Leppäaho et al., 2016) |
| *Methodological Techniques* | Narrative analysis, ethnography, discourse analysis, life story analysis, grounded theory | Historical analysis, structured interviews, focus groups, within-case analysis, between-case analysis, surveys |
| *Output* | New theory regarding unique phenomena and processes (Siggelkow, 2007) | Specific, testable propositions that reflect various aspects of processes (Leppäaho et al., 2016) |
| *Family Business Exemplar* | Barbera, Stamm, & DeWitt (2018) | Kotlar & De Massis (2013) |

of information ... and reports a case description and case themes' (Creswell, 2013, p. 97). The benefits and drawbacks of single-case versus multi-case approaches have been long debated (see Dyer & Wilkins, 1991; Eisenhardt, 1991). Single-case studies emphasize thick descriptions of processual phenomenon and consider how those processes produce focal outcomes (Dyer & Wilkins, 1991). Alternatively, multi-case studies analyze links between behaviors and outcomes, often yielding testable propositions about emergent constructs (Eisenhardt, 1991). Single-case approaches help researchers understand the nuanced interplay of context and behavior, while multi-case designs help researchers to understand discrete construct relationships embedded in and pertaining to those processes. Essentially, the two approaches differ in their philosophical and theoretical foundations, methodological approaches, and their analytical outputs. Indeed, single-case studies culminate in explanations that are a mile deep and an inch wide, whereas multi-case studies provide the opposite. Table 8.1 summarizes these differences (see Kammerlander & Diaz-Moriana, Chapter 9 in this book for a full description of the multi-case approach).

Multi-case studies are much more common than single-case studies. However, single-case studies are often the most cited articles or even distinguished as best papers in management journals (Pratt, Kaplan, & Whittington, 2020). This is likely because the single-case approach has many strengths that offset the weaknesses of the multi-case approach. The more phenomenologically anchored nature of single-case design can help family business researchers to answer research questions that uniquely advance family business theory (Hamilton, Cruz, & Jack, 2017), notably by making closer connections to real family business problems and developing more grounded insights. Three strengths make the single-case approach useful for family business research.

First, the single-case approach and the richness it provides allows for a deeper understanding of family firm dynamics (Leppäaho et al., 2016). Because of the many moving parts that make up the family, the business, and the combination of the two, analyzing multiple subjective perspectives is important for generating family business theory. For example, as seen in Barbera et al. (2018), taking multiple generational perspectives is vital in understanding family firm succession issues. As noted by Salvato and Corbetta (Chapter 10 in this book), entrepreneurial families do not often disclose private family dynamics. While subjectivity may be viewed as a weakness, engaging with the context and participants of the case allows researchers to understand diverse perspectives and generate trust with the family (Easterby-Smith, Golden-Biddle, & Locke, 2008). This engagement facilitates understanding of more 'open-ended, iterative, and contingent process[es]' (Easterby-Smith et al., 2008, p. 423), which helps to build new family business theory.

Second, single-case research is useful for understanding the intricate contextual workings of processual phenomena. Single-case design is effective in elaborating the contexts, behaviors, and interactions that make up complex processes over time (Dyer & Wilkins, 1991). While the single-case approach lacks between-case analysis, it produces rich data needed to examine a phenomenon holistically. Context is arguably the most important aspect of family business research, as family business researchers must analyze the organization with the 'family' at 'the heart of the research' (Hamilton, 2006, p. 253). Because context is important in family business research, single-case approaches can provide a more thorough understanding of the evolving interplay of actors, actions, and outcomes that occur in such businesses (Dyer & Wilkins, 1991).

Finally, single-case research is better equipped to develop initial theoretical understanding of previously underexplored processual phenomena (Gehman et al., 2018). Family businesses behave and make decisions very differently from other businesses. Therefore, we need to generate new theory that features the family firm context to delineate family business research from other fields. When researchers aim to build theory in a unique setting like family firms, the single-case approach is well suited due to the context-dependent insights it provides (Pratt et al., 2020). Encouraging a deeper investigation of the contextual characteristics of family firms rather than surface-level analyses could provide richer understanding of family business phenomena. Single-case approaches also better facilitate the search for underlying causal mechanisms, enabling more precise understanding of family and business integration (Astrachan, 2003) and relationship dynamics (Ainsworth & Cox, 2003). Overall, single-case research supports more nuanced, accurate accounts of family firm dynamics (Leppäaho et al., 2016).

## WHEN SHOULD RESEARCHERS UTILIZE THE SINGLE-CASE APPROACH?

Given the relative infrequency of single-case research, we pose six questions that researchers interested in this approach might ask when deciding whether to adopt a single-case or a multi-case approach. Figure 8.1 visualizes when to ask these six questions and summarizes what their answers mean for selecting the appropriate case design.

**Question 1**. *Does the prospective study aim to explain the intricate dynamics and outcomes of a process?* If it does, a single-case design is appropriate. Although longitudinal studies may be completed using the multiple-case approach or more quantitative methods, process research tries to understand participant interpretations of events and how those interpretations evolve (Gehman et al., 2018). Understanding the evolution of events requires interpretive work, wherein researchers are involved more in depth with the data and the participants, such as that within single-case design (Denzin & Lincoln,

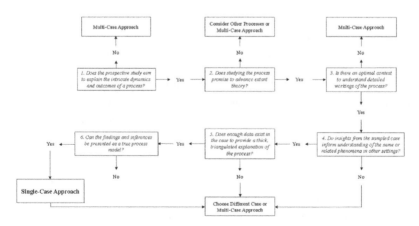

*Figure 8.1    When to use a single-case versus multi-case approach*

1994). Alternatively, multi-case approaches are more efficient if researchers are looking to explain discrete relationships embedded within a process, rather than the intricate workings of the process itself. By identifying a processual phenomenon and research question based on it, researchers can build family business theories that are based on the actual problems that families encounter in their firms (Pieper, Astrachan, & Manners, 2013). Single-case design is thus well suited to process research and theorizing.

**Question 2.** After confirming interest in a processual phenomenon, researchers might ask: *Does studying the process promise to advance extant theory? If so, how?* By studying the phenomenon via a single-case approach, would we generate novel theoretical insights? Beginning with a theoretical frame of reference in mind, researchers may use the case study to search for new theoretical ideas and interpretations (Nordqvist et al., 2009). In family business research, where several interpretations can emerge due to the multiple points of view in a family firm, single-case research can effectively create new theoretical insight. However, if analyzing a process would not generate new theoretical insights, the researcher may need to either (1) consider if conducting a multi-case design would add to existing theory or (2) identify other, more theoretically relevant processes to investigate. For example, multi-case approaches may be better suited to when researchers are proposing or testing constructs and relationships.

**Question 3.** After advancing the potential for theoretical contribution, researchers might ask: *Is there an optimal context to understand detailed workings of the process?* Finding an appropriate case to study a phenomenon can be difficult. The case should allow 'the researcher to examine the ebb and flow of social life over time and to display the patterns of everyday life as they change' (Orum, Feagin, & Sjoberg, 1991, p. 12). The case should also account for the empirical features of the focal process, capture the entirety of the process from inception to conclusion, and promise insights about the theoretical considerations of interest to the study. Finally, deep access to family firms to study longitudinal processes is necessary to obtain the in-depth data that is needed for single-case research (Nordqvist et al., 2009). Lacking an optimal context to understand the process of interest, the researcher may wish to consider the multi-case approach, where multiple contexts of the phenomenon can be studied at a more general level.

**Question 4.** If an optimal context is available, researchers should ask: *Do insights from the sampled case inform understanding of the same or related phenomena in other settings?* Single-case studies favor accuracy over generalizability (Pratt et al., 2020). If the researcher aims to build accurate understanding of the phenomenon, then a single case is better suited to this endeavor than other methods. However, if the researcher aims to generalize their findings to different phenomena, a multi-case approach would be a better fit.

**Question 5**. When researchers confirm interest in accuracy, the next question is: *Does enough data exist about the case to provide a triangulated explanation of the process?* Researchers must gather enough data on the phenomenon from multiple sources to provide thick, believable accounts of critical process components and dynamics. Consider how Barbera et al. (2018) collected data as an example. They solicited life stories from three generations of a family firm and asked participants to tell them every family and firm event they could recall. This resulted in over 13 hours of interviews. In addition, the researchers collected dozens of newspaper articles regarding the firm, three radio interviews, and various company materials. If available data are insufficient, researchers should consider a different case or the multi-case approach. Analytical techniques may be helpful to consider, too, including narrative, ethnographic, discourse, and grounded theory techniques (Cunliffe, 2011).

**Question 6**. Once researchers identify their data sources, they should ask: *Can the findings and inferences be presented as a true process model?* Single-case studies produce rich empirical descriptions and theoretical inferences about contextually influenced construct interplays over time. The findings of such studies are more intricate and complex than those of multiple-case studies, which propose discrete, variance-oriented relationships between constructs. For example, in Meier and Schier's (2016) process study, they explore the detailed interplay of 17 variables across three levels of analysis (i.e., individual, group, and organizational) over time. Scholars also vary in their presentation of theoretical inferences about empirical findings. Some create separate theoretical process models, whereas others weave theory into empirical findings. Whatever the approach, researchers should feature the rich details and conceptual meanings of the processes being studied.

## WHAT AREAS WOULD BENEFIT FROM MORE SINGLE-CASE RESEARCH?

Our chapter has underscored that the family business literature needs more single-case research, as well as offered guidance on how to make that happen. We conclude by identifying three possible areas, out of many, in the family business literature that would benefit from single-case research, as well as providing some pragmatic considerations for those interested in publishing such work.

Within the family business literature, single-case process research that allows a more complete understanding of family firm dynamics must be encouraged (Leppäaho et al., 2016). Doing so would allow novel family business theories to be developed (Payne, 2018), helping the field to hone a unique theoretical identity. Because of the strengths of single-case research, researchers can observe, analyze, and describe fluid, transformative, family business processes that may be different from other non-family entrepreneur-ship processes. Given the need for more defining theory and the usefulness of the single-case approach, we now identify three areas where researchers might conduct such work.

First, more research is needed regarding family firm goals and the potential paradoxes that exist due to the complexities of these firms (Miller, Wright, Le Breton-Miller, & Scholes, 2015). Distinct to family firms are the interactions between founders, their families, the business, and its customers. For example, goals are tough to analyze as both business goals and family goals must be addressed and reconciled (De Massis & Foss, 2018). While business-oriented goals may be vital for success, the more family-oriented goals may be more important for family members (Vazquez & Rocha, 2018). Studies show that family members are more interested in pursuing noneconomic goals, such as socioemotional wealth (Debicki, Van de Graaff Randolph, & Sobczak, 2017), while non-family members are generally more focused on economic goals, such as shareholder returns (Vazquez & Rocha, 2018). Research is scarce on how these multiple goals are formulated, determined, enacted, and reconciled.

Understanding these changing and evolving processes requires the collec-tion and analysis of more in-depth, multi-source data and the development of thick processual descriptions. Indeed, Vazquez and Rocha (2018) note the importance of asking more 'why' questions when it comes to future goal research, focusing more on the processual nature of goal development. We take this a step further and suggest that future research not only ask why different goals are important in family firms, but also how those goals are for-mulated. For instance, how are contradictory goals manifested in family firms? How are seemingly contradictory goals integrated in a synergistic way? How can family firm owners, CEOs, and TMTs become successful at managing the paradoxical goals that exist between the family and business? We suggest that, through single-case studies, new theory may be developed regarding family firm goal reconciliation.

Second, family business succession is a highly debated – yet incompletely understood – process in the family business literature, making it a fruitful area for continued research. For example, we do not yet know the 'goal of family business succession, who (i.e., which actors) determines such goals, and how such a goal is related to the purpose of the family business' (De Massis & Foss, 2018, p. 392). Many complex, interrelated factors must be considered to understand a succession event. Indeed, succession is a processual phenomenon that may occur over years or even decades of planning. Succession planning not only includes the founder, but also considers the social environment within which the family firm is situated (Steyaert, 2007).

Succession events as discrete turnover events lend themselves well to more quantitative approaches to research. However, family firm succession entails more thought and planning over an extended period than analogous processes at non-family firms. With single-case approaches, researchers can follow family firms for long periods to answer questions that have been overlooked in the family succession literature. For example, single-case process studies could answer questions such as: How do family businesses approach the lead-up to succession? How do family business goals factor into succession? How do family firm owners make sense of their own succession? Single-case approaches would enable researchers to create a theory of family firm succession, which could be elaborated with other methods.

Finally, family business strategizing would benefit from further study. Many organizational, industrial, and other contextual factors contribute to how a family business is run, including the strategies they develop and enact. These factors influence the goals, beliefs, and behaviors of family firm owners (Fletcher et al., 2016). For example, the culture within which the business operates may affect how owners approach strategic decision-making (Basco, Calabrò, & Campopiano, 2019). Further, the industry context where family firms operate can affect how goals, innovation, and strategy are handled (De Massis & Foss, 2018).

While controlling for contextual industry-level factors is common in family business research, the processes and mechanisms through which contextual factors influence family firm strategies, behaviors, and decisions lack adequate theoretical coverage (Fletcher et al., 2016). However, by studying a single family firm in depth and over time, researchers can answer key questions. For example, how does the industry shape family business strategies, routines, and behaviors over time? How does the cultural context impact family business decision-making? How do family firm decision makers change and grow with the changing environment? These questions beg for the sort of processual answers than single-case research is designed to provide.

## WHAT MIGHT SINGLE-CASE RESEARCHERS CONSIDER?

Three considerations might help researchers in their attempts to publish single-case studies. The first consideration is that single-case research must be accurately executed by researchers and evaluated by editors and reviewers. Single-case research is often executed and evaluated utilizing the same standards as that of quantitative research (Pratt et al., 2020). According to Pratt et al. (2020), 'the inappropriate transfer of quantitative logics to qualitative research potentially puts in jeopardy a great deal of important work' (p. 3). Most scholars are trained to be quantitative empiricists and the multi-case method has thus become the dominant qualitative method, perhaps due to its more quantitative leanings and features. Yet, single-case studies are philosophically and empirically different from multi-case and quantitative studies.

Generally, neither authors nor review teams adequately understand what single-case studies can and cannot do, or what they should and should not do. For example, many have called for single-case studies to be generalizable and have questioned how resulting theories can be generalized. However, single-case studies intentionally sacrifice generalizability to optimize accuracy and specificity (Dyer & Wilkins, 1991). Making this tradeoff is critical to the development of rich new theory that can be extended, tested, and adapted through other methods (Siggelkow, 2007). Accordingly, editors and reviewers encouraging single-case researchers to increase their replicability or generalizability are promoting 'unhelpful' and 'potentially even dangerous' research (Pratt et al., 2020).

The second consideration involves applying case research techniques from other fields. For example, in the medical field, it is common to employ single-case experimental designs (SCED) (Bentley et al., 2019). In SCED, researchers examine a participant, give the participant a treatment, and then examine the participant again. In this type of quasi-experiment, strong inferences can be made about the effect of the intervention (Thomson et al., 2017). Family business researchers could implement SCEDs that either examine a case where treatments naturally unfold or implement treatments artificially. By utilizing methods from other fields, single-case approaches may gain more traction and offer more contribution to the field.

The third consideration deals with the interpretive skills of the researchers. Such skills are critical in developing, reviewing, and learning from case study research. Single-case approaches offer opportunities for readers who possess high levels of interpretive skill and sophistication to extract diverse meanings from the findings of such work. Their rich, diverse meanings make single-case studies very useful to academics and practitioners, particularly when they possess the skill needed to identify the implications of relevance to their situations. However, to produce practically relevant case studies, researchers must remain intimately connected with practitioners to know what problems in the field need to be solved (Nobel, 2016).

To conclude, the family business literature is ripe with complex processual phenomena that merit further study. Single-case research promises to build new theory that explains these phenomena, thereby helping to bolster the unique theoretical identity of family business. We hope this chapter helps researchers interested in answering this call.

# REFERENCES

Ainsworth, S. & Cox, J. W. (2003). Families divided: Culture and control in small family business. *Organization Studies*, 24(9), 1463–1485.

Astrachan, J. H. (2003). Commentary on the special issue: The emergence of a field. *Journal of Business Venturing*, 18(5), 567–572.

Barbera, F., Stamm, I. & DeWitt, R. L. (2018). The development of an entrepreneurial legacy: Exploring the role of anticipated futures in transgenerational entrepreneurship. *Family Business Review*, 31(3), 352–378.

Basco, R., Calabrò, A. & Campopiano, G. (2019). Transgenerational entrepreneurship around the world: Implications for family business research and practice. *Journal of Family Business Strategy*, 10(4), 100249.

Bentley, K. H., Kleiman, E. M., Elliott, G., Huffman, J. C. & Nock, M. K. (2019). Real-time monitoring technology in single-case experimental design research: Opportunities and challenges. *Behaviour Research and Therapy*, 117, 87–96.

Brigham, K. H. & Payne, G. T. (2015). Article commentary: The transitional nature of the multifamily business. *Entrepreneurship Theory and Practice*, 39(6), 1339–1347.

Creswell, J. W. (2013). *Qualitative Inquiry and Research Design: Choosing Among Five Approaches* (3rd edition). Sage.

Cunliffe, A. L. (2011). Crafting qualitative research: Morgan and Smircich 30 years on. *Organizational Research Methods*, 14(4), 647–673.

Dawson, A. & Hjorth, D. (2012). Advancing family business research through narrative analysis. *Family Business Review*, 25(3), 339–355.

Debicki, B. J., Van de Graaff Randolph, R. & Sobczak, M. (2017). Socioemotional wealth and family firm performance: A stakeholder approach. *Journal of Managerial Issues*, 29(1), 82–111.

De Massis, A. & Foss, N. J. (2018). Advancing family business research: The promise of microfoundations. *Family Business Review*, 31(4), 386–396.

De Massis, A., Sharma, P., Chua, J. H. & Chrisman, J. J. (2012). *Family Business Studies: An Annotated Bibliography*. Edward Elgar Publishing.

Denzin, N. L. & Lincoln, Y. (1994). *Handbook of Qualitative Research*. Sage.

Dyer Jr, W. G. & Wilkins, A. L. (1991). Better stories, not better constructs, to generate better theory: A rejoinder to Eisenhardt. *Academy of Management Review*, 16(3), 613–619.

Easterby-Smith, M., Golden-Biddle, K. & Locke, K. (2008). Working with pluralism: Determining quality in qualitative research. *Organizational Research Methods*, 11(3), 419–429.

Eisenhardt, K. M. (1991). Better stories and better constructs: The case for rigor and comparative logic. *Academy of Management Review*, 16(3), 620–627.

Fletcher, D., De Massis, A. & Nordqvist, M. (2016). Qualitative research practices and family business scholarship: A review and future research agenda. *Journal of Family Business Strategy*, 7(1), 8–25.

Gehman, J., Glaser, V. L., Eisenhardt, K. M., Gioia, D., Langley, A. & Corley, K. G. (2018). Finding theory–method fit: A comparison of three qualitative approaches to theory building. *Journal of Management Inquiry*, 27(3), 284–300.

Hamilton, E. (2006). Whose story is it anyway? Narrative accounts of the role of women in founding and establishing family businesses. *International Small Business Journal*, 24(3), 253–271.

Hamilton, E., Cruz, A. D. & Jack, S. (2017). Re-framing the status of narrative in family business research: Towards an understanding of families in business. *Journal of Family Business Strategy*, 8(1), 3–12.

Kammerlander, N. & De Massis, A. (2020). Frequently asked questions in qualitative family business research and some guidelines to avoid risky paths. In A. De Massis & N. Kammerlander (Eds.), *Handbook of Qualitative Research Methods for Family Business* (pp. 1–22). Edward Elgar Publishing.

Kotlar, J. & De Massis, A. (2013). Goal setting in family firms: Goal diversity, social interactions, and collective commitment to family-centered goals. *Entrepreneurship Theory and Practice*, 37(6), 1263–1288.

Langley, A. & Royer, I. (2006). Perspectives on doing case study research in organizations. *M@n@gement*, 9, 81–94.

Leppäaho, T., Plakoyiannaki, E. & Dimitratos, P. (2016). The case study in family business: An analysis of current research practices and recommendations. *Family Business Review*, 29(2), 159–173.

Meier, O. & Schier, G. (2016). The early succession stage of a family firm: Exploring the role of agency rationales and stewardship attitudes. *Family Business Review*, 29(3), 256–277.

Miller, D., Wright, M., Le Breton-Miller, I. & Scholes, L. (2015). Resources and innovation in family businesses: The Janus-face of socioemotional preferences. *California Management Review*, 58(1), 20–40.

Nobel, C. (2016, September 19). *Why Isn't Business Research More Relevant to Business Practitioners?* HBS Working Knowledge. Retrieved November 3, 2021, from https://hbswk.hbs.edu/item/why-isn-t-business-research-more-relevant-to-business-practitioners.

Nordqvist, M., Hall, A. & Melin, L. (2009). Qualitative research on family businesses: The relevance and usefulness of the interpretive approach. *Journal of Management and Organization*, 15(3), 294–308.

Orum, A. M., Feagin, J. R. & Sjoberg, G. (1991). Introduction: The nature of the case study. In J. R. Feagin, A. M. Orum, & G. Sjoberg (Eds.), *A Case for the Case Study* (pp. 1–26). The University of North Carolina Press.

Payne, G. T. (2018). Reflections on family business research: Considering domains and theory. *Family Business Review*, 31(2), 167–175.

Pieper, T. M., Astrachan, J. H. & Manners, G. E. (2013). Conflict in family business: Common metaphors and suggestions for intervention. *Family Relations*, 62(3), 490–500.

Pratt, M. G., Kaplan, S. & Whittington, R. (2020). Editorial essay: The tumult over transparency: Decoupling transparency from replication in establishing trustworthy qualitative research. *Administrative Science Quarterly*, 65(1), 1–19.

Reay, T. & Zhang, Z. (2014). Qualitative methods in family business research. In L. Melin, M. Nordqvist & P. Sharma (Eds.), *The SAGE Handbook of Family Business* (pp. 573–593). Sage.

Short, J. C. & Payne, G. T. (2020). In their own words: A call for increased use of organizational narratives in family business research. *Family Business Review*, 33(4), 342–350.

Siggelkow, N. (2007). Persuasion with case studies. *Academy of Management Journal*, 50(1), 20–24.

Steyaert, C. (2007). 'Entrepreneuring' as a conceptual attractor? A review of process theories in 20 years of entrepreneurship studies. *Entrepreneurship & Regional Development*, 19(6), 453–477.

Thomson, C., Wilson, R., Collerton, D., Freeston, M. & Dudley, R. (2017). Cognitive behavioural therapy for visual hallucinations: An investigation using a single-case experimental design. *The Cognitive Behaviour Therapist*, 10(10), 1–20.

Vazquez, P. & Rocha, H. (2018). On the goals of family firms: A review and integration. *Journal of Family Business Strategy*, 9(2), 94–106.

# 9. The multicase study approach in family businesses: opportunities and challenges

**Nadine Kammerlander and Vanessa Diaz-Moriana**

## INTRODUCTION

Since its inception, family business studies have drawn on multicase studies to advance knowledge in our field. The reasons for this methodological interest have been multifaceted. First, given the often-observed privacy concerns, dearth of transparency, and lack of regulatory pressure to publish data, it is difficult for researchers to study family businesses based merely on publicly available databases. Second, many of the important issues of family businesses relate to 'soft topics': the importance of nonfinancial goals, emotions in decision-making, the role of individuals (such as spouses outside the business sphere), the succession process, and multifaceted conflicts among family members, to name just a few. Third, and maybe most importantly, we recognized that conducting multicase studies can provide researchers with much joy due to direct contact with—often inspiring—individuals, mostly owner-managers of impressive family businesses. As such, it is no surprise that we have dedicated much of our career to the study of family businesses through multicase studies. Like us, many of our colleagues have followed the same path, as observed by the large number of multicase-study-based articles, as well as articles on qualitative work in family businesses (e.g., Calabrò et al., 2016; Clinton et al., 2018; Hashim et al., 2020; Howorth et al., 2016; Jaskiewicz et al., 2015; Erdogan et al., 2020; De Massis et al., 2016; Glover & Reay, 2015; Parada et al., 2010; Kotlar & De Massis, 2013; Salvato & Corbetta, Chapter 10 in this book).

Despite the many benefits of a multicase approach, we must acknowledge that conducting this type of research is not an easy task. Looking back at our own 'early work' throughout our PhD studies, we recognize many methodological or processual mistakes that could have been avoided if we had known more about the pitfalls and the 'do's and don'ts' that we know now. Moreover, as editors (e.g., of FBR) and editorial review board members (e.g., of AMJ, ETP, JOM, JPIM, and SEJ) we often feel confronted with multicase study manuscripts that begin with a good idea but fail to deliver methodological rigor. More often than not, we have to reject multicase study-based articles tackling an interesting phenomenon due to methodological flaws. The following book chapter is based on our own experiences as authors, editors, reviewers, as well as on beginning researchers' perspectives. To gather the perspective of young researchers, we sent out a questionnaire to the (former) PhD students of the first author, asking them about their experience with qualitative multicase study work (see Table 9.1 for the PhD students' perspective).

## UNIQUE CHALLENGES AND GUIDELINES TO OVERCOME THEM

### Appropriate Research Questions

The rather large number of qualitative studies (as well as the difficult access to data on family businesses) may suggest to novices in the field that multicase studies are the 'default' methodological option and always an appropriate research design; this is not the case, however. Multicase studies should be used if there is a relevant research gap that cannot sufficiently be answered by existing (conceptual or empirical) research. Research questions that are adequately answered by multicase studies mostly refer to 'how' and 'why' questions. The first author vividly remembers writing a chapter of her dissertation based on a qualitative research design and a research question that could be easily answered based on a systematic literature review and deductive theorizing. Once aware of that fact, the author realized the lack of novelty in her analysis and had to rephrase the research question, collect new data, and effectively had to go through the entire research process again. While this endeavor eventually resulted in a well-cited publication, much time, effort, and stress could have been avoided by appropriate questioning from the beginning: 'Can this question be answered based on extant research?'. Moreover, these how and why questions should be related to family aspects, e.g., how the family character of a business affects specific behavior (i.e., family as an explanatory variable) or how family-related variables are affected (i.e., family conflicts, family harmony, SEW as variables to be explained).

In the papers we receive as editors and reviewers, we often see an extended theoretical background section with knowledge that already exists. For instance, authors elaborate in detail on extant frameworks and explain that they will use those frameworks in their multicase studies. We then ask ourselves: Why is a qualitative study required? Wouldn't another research approach, such

*Table 9.1*   Best practices in multicase study research

| | What would you have done differently? | Tips for new researchers |
|---|---|---|
| **Research Question** | • Allow research question to be adapted throughout the process—there might be more and different interesting insights in the data than originally thought | • Invest sufficient time in the early phases of qualitative research<br>• Talk to researchers (senior and junior; at conferences, seminars, or just approach them via email) who investigate similar topics (but diverse methods) but also similar methods (but diverse topics) |
| **Case Selection** | • Send official and professional letter to potential interviewees (ideally paper-based with signatures, increases professionality and seriousness, also as differentiating factor from dozens of other less professional studies) including short description of institute/team, yourself, goals of study<br>• Plan sufficient time for interviewee sourcing<br>• Follow up with nonresponding interviews after one week (later it might feel awkward to them) | • Be as specific as possible with your case selection criteria<br>• Leverage your own network and region (contact and networks as key success factors) and make use of social platforms such as LinkedIn<br>• For multicase studies, derive a longer list of potential cases (e.g., based on published books, websites) and based on defined criteria, select a few cases for deeper investigation (not directly select cases)<br>• Ask interviewees for preferred interview mode (daytime, personal vs. online), then provide three suggestions; be flexible regarding scheduling<br>• Make sure to follow up with thank-you mails and provide interviewees with an executive summary of your results |

| | What would you have done differently? | Tips for new researchers |
|---|---|---|
| **Case Depth** | • Sign up for interviewer training<br>• Run pilots of questionnaire with practitioners AND researchers<br>• Focus more on depth than breadth—try to also interview family members<br>• Get as much information on history as possible<br>• Interview the firm's competitors as experts<br>• Try to understand the relationships among the interviewees<br>• Take extensive notes (even if you record the interview)<br>• Ask follow-up questions and for more and precise examples<br>• Remain balanced and examine potential negative aspects | • Have an NDA prepared to offer<br>• Include sufficient open questions that allow interviewees to also comment on related topics they consider important (MP)<br>• Ask interviewees to refer you to other potential interviewees in the organization—especially the names mentioned in the interviews (MP)<br>• Use interview guide as a 'rough guide' and try to make it a nice discussion atmosphere (MP)<br>• If someone declines an interview, ask if s/he can recommend an alternative interviewee<br>• Spend as much time as possible with the interviewees—not just in the interviews<br>• Try to interview organizational members of many different hierarchies |
| **Analysis** | • Start first analysis after conducting 15 interviews (not later) and come up with first propositions; then adapt your interview guide accordingly<br>• Accept that your findings might contradict extant literature<br>• Be more open—do not jump on the first pattern/finding that emerges | • From the beginning, store documents in an ordered way and keep them up-to-date—keep a 'research log book'<br>• Start writing case studies early on<br>• Use the case summaries to think about potential models<br>• Transcribe the interviews as soon as possible<br>• Think about additional data (mixed methods) and computer-based analysis that may further support your qualitative analysis |

| | What would you have done differently? | Tips for new researchers |
|---|---|---|
| **Presentation of Findings** | • Make sure to also incorporate secondary data in your findings part | • Draw as many different models as possible—and make sure to store them |
| **Further Aspects** | • Be in contact with other PhD students doing qualitative research (for exchanging experience, etc.) | • Stay in contact with interviewees (e.g., through updates on study, final outcome, campus, or just Christmas wishes)<br>• Read as many multicase studies published in top journals as possible, contact the authors, read the AMJ 'From the Editors'<br>• Find out at what time of the day/week you perform best—try to allocate your interviews to those slots<br>• Even if you feel lost throughout data collection and analysis: Trust the process!<br>• 'Enjoy the ride'—you cannot plan everything from the beginning; multi-case study work requires patience and adaptability |

*Note:* This table is based on a survey of 12 current and prior PhD students of the first author who have all completed at least one multicase study project.

as a large-scale survey, better answer the research question? The second author conducted her entire PhD through a qualitative multiple case study research design. While the main phenomenon studied in her work had not been studied through qualitative research, her work needed to clearly highlight (1) why doing qualitative work on the phenomenon was going to advance knowledge in the field and (2) why doing it through multiple case studies was the most appropriate research design. This issue seems particularly salient in family business research, where we often must rely on theories from other disciplines, such as sensemaking (Strike & Rerup, 2016), institutional theory (Reay et al., 2015), socialization (Bika et al., 2019), stewardship theory (Calabrò et al., 2016; Neubaum et al., 2017), or attention-based view (Kammerlander & Ganter, 2015). There is always a fine balance of incorporating extant theory into multicase studies. If too much theory is presented upfront, the manuscript appears 'overengineered.' In such cases, interesting insights from the data do not have the opportunity to emerge; instead, any novel insight might be over-shadowed by the existing theory. Naturally, such 'theoretical handcuffs' will limit the potential theoretical contributions (Micelotta, Chapter 2 in this book). However, if no (or hardly any) theory is included, the likelihood of the paper reinventing the wheel is high, and these types of theory-free articles do not join any 'scholarly conversation' (Huff, 1999). When we start our own qualitative research projects, we try to read as much as possible on the phenomenon—and potentially relevant theories—before drafting the interview guidelines. We also have theories in mind that could become relevant during the course of our analysis, although these theories often change. The process usually involves iteratively analyzing qualitative data by alternating between qualitative evidence and theoretical arguments that respond to established theory (Miles & Huberman, 1994; Reay, 2014).

When analyzing the interviews with family members from our cases, we often realize that specific aspects that we have not thought of before are much more relevant than the ones we originally considered. One should pay special attention to family specifics that might affect the phenomenon to study (i.e., family factors that are unique in a family business setting and might not be relevant/present in a nonfamily business). This often results in a prolonged rereading of extant literature and adaption of the theories in mind. We then search the literature for existing frameworks that could help explain the observations emerging from our data and could help to answer our research questions. While this process is time-consuming, this step makes the study more robust and, as a desired byproduct, increases the researchers' knowledge.

Another specific challenge for family business researchers is to think about the following aspect: Has this research question already been addressed in the nonfamily business context? If so, researchers need to carefully think about what justifies an additional investigation in the family business context.

A potential reason for studying a general research question in the family business context might be that the researchers expect that family-specific aspects affect the relationships under investigation. As an example, one might expect that transgenerational conflicts between senior and junior generations affect the adoption of digital technologies. This makes the investigation of top management team (TMT) relationships in the digitalization context worthwhile to be studied in the family firm context.

## Selection of and Access to Cases

As a first challenge, researchers need to carefully select family businesses to be included in their research design. Which organizations are appropriate largely depends on the research question. If the study is intended to investigate family influence on, for instance, working atmosphere or culture, researchers need to focus on firms in which such influence is likely to be salient—e.g., smaller organizations and/or those with a family member as CEO. For instance, with more than 120,000 employees and a firm-external CEO, car producer BMW might not be an adequate case to study how employees identify with the owning family. However, given the strong influence of owning family members Susanne Klatten and Stefan Quandt on the supervisory board, BMW would be an adequate case to study the influence of family-related aspects on important strategic decisions such as offshoring. Hence, for many research questions, smaller and medium-sized family businesses might be very appropriate—also because our experience shows that those firms' decision-makers are typically more open to share their true thoughts rather than offering 'PR talk.' However, in some cases, firms need to be a certain size to be considered appropriate for the study. For instance, if the research question requires the existence of certain structures and routines (such as in Kammerlander et al., 2018), then researchers might select family businesses of a certain size (e.g., at least 50 employees). Other research questions might require researchers to focus on family businesses with a certain number of completed successions (e.g., when studying legacy), in a certain industry (e.g., when studying innovation behavior, see DeMassis et al., Chapter 6 in this book), or with a certain minimum number of generations involved (e.g., when studying transgenerational entrepreneurship).

In family businesses, many of our research questions relate to the top management or the owners of the company and their preferences and behavior. As many—although not all—qualitative research projects rely largely on interviews,[1] this poses both a unique challenge and opportunity to family business researchers. On the one hand, we must clearly outline who are the ideal interviewees, i.e., who is most likely to provide insights that are necessary to study our research question, prior to the data collection. If the research question—as it often does—refers to the owning family, then it is important to also interview family members—not only organizational nonfamily members. This is a challenge, as those family members are often part of an 'elite' group who are busy and not easily accessible. On the other hand, discussions with those individuals often prove to be particularly interesting.

There are several ways to overcome this challenge. One very promising way is to work with established consortia such as the STEP project. The Successful Transgenerational Entrepreneurship Practices (STEP) project was founded in 2005 by Babson College and seeks to investigate the impact of resources and entrepreneurial attitudes on financial, entrepreneurial, and social performance outcomes across generations of family businesses. To be included in the STEP project, a business needs to meet the following criteria: (1) the owning family must see their business as a family business; (2) the family must hold majority ownership in the main operating business; (3) there must be at least one active operating business; (4) generational involvement in ownership and/or management must span at least two generations; (5) at least 50 employees must be employed by the main operating business; and (6) the owning family must have an ambition to pass on the business to the next generation (Nordqvist & Zellweger, 2010). These criteria directly narrow the family business cases that one could use for their research. Furthermore, STEP provides its members with interview guidelines. Being a partner of this project helped the second author of this book chapter collect data for her research and use data already collected to enhance the robustness of the findings she found in her previously collected data.

Another promising way is to utilize university contacts. For instance, the Institute of Family Business and Mittelstand at WHU—Otto Beisheim School of Management, codirected by the first author, dedicates substantial time and effort to building meaningful connections with family businesses across the nation by organizing a practitioner conference every year and by being present in the local and national media and events. We often receive feedback that the presence on social, online, and offline media—enhanced by positive word

---

[1]    Other valuable data sources for qualitative research projects include, for instance, archival books or (video) interview material. Moreover, in the future, data sources such as social media posts might also be used increasingly by researchers applying qualitative designs. However, taking into account that most currently published qualitative studies are based on interviews, we focus on interview-based studies in this section.

of mouth by other families—encouraged family business owner-managers to participate in our studies.

Throughout our projects, we also realize that there might be 'optimal ways' of how to contact owner-managers of family businesses. In the German-speaking context, this is a physical letter, labeled 'personal' with handwritten salutation (preferably with fountain pen instead of ballpoint pen) and handwritten greetings—often completed with an (also handwritten) note, such as congratulations for a recent award. Roughly two weeks after the physical mailing, a telephone follow-up further explaining the purpose for the study is helpful. Before sending out the letters, we typically show them to family business owner-managers within our network (representing the target group) asking for feedback. In some cases (e.g., Schickinger et al., 2021), this leads to several rounds of (partly minor yet still important) adaptations to language and format before we finally send out the letter. Similarly, the second author is part of the DCU National Centre for Family Business (Ireland), where they have been gathering interviews, observations, and archival data on Irish family businesses since 2013. The center is committed to Ireland's family business community, providing annual seminars, workshops, conferences, and executive education. Through these events, the research team gathers data and contacts the family businesses, which increases the likelihood of approaching them at a later stage to be interviewed for a specific research project.

**Case Depth**

With regard to the number of cases, the classical work by Eisenhardt (1989) originally referred to an ideal number of four to eight cases—that is, mostly four to eight family businesses in our context. Unfortunately, many researchers equate the number of cases with the number of interviews required. Often, we see papers submitted with only 10–15 interviews. Although there is no clear 'threshold' of required interviews and although there might be cases where such numbers are sufficient, our experience tells us that with more than 30 interviews (per submitted paper), reviewers feel comfortable about the amount of knowledge collected during the study; with more than 50–70 interviews (depending on the journal) they start to become impressed. With more than approximately five interviews per case, readers gain confidence that the authors have built substantial knowledge about the case, including the perspective of various stakeholders such as active and nonactive family members, nonfamily managers, etc. There might always be cases of one interviewee having totally different perspectives on the firm than other members (e.g., on the digitalization level of the business or on its culture due to personal biases) and some interviewees (unfortunately) turn out to be excellent marketing people—that hide any critical aspects of their business and thereby inhibit the deep reflection of the researchers. We also recognize that this happens, not always and not exclusively, but often, with family-external managers of larger family businesses that fear making any critical comments, even if confidentiality and anonymity are guaranteed. Moreover, nonfamily managers might substantially diverge in their strategic assessments compared to family members that are emotionally attached to the firm.

Another common pitfall is to be too 'dazzled' about the interesting stories that family business owner-managers tell—leading to an increasing number of cases to be added. This particularly happens when family business owner-managers refer to other family business owner-managers as potentially interesting cases. The first author, in one of her early projects, ended up having a total of 14 cases in one project, which clearly exceeded the number of eight provided by Eisenhardt. This did not only pose challenges regarding appropriate case explanation in the paper (you just cannot elaborate on 14 cases in detail!) but also led an Editor to reject the paper in a top journal in the second round, suggesting that other methods instead of multicase study analysis (e.g., fsQCA) would be more applicable. Hence, setting up a multicase study design also requires the discipline to limit the number of cases.

As noted above, to gain sufficient depth, at least 5–8 interviews per case should be collected. Very often, this is a high number for family businesses, especially if they are smaller in size (as is often the case for family businesses) and cannot afford for their employees to be spending too much time on interviews. However, based on our experience, these requirements should be communicated openly at the beginning of the data collection process to the respective organizations. It is also important to explain why this number of interviews is needed and how the data will be used. Many family business owner-managers are concerned about data confidentiality in the first place (especially because of their desire to fully control everything and because of their reputation concerns) but are willing to participate once they understand that academic articles are based on pseudonyms only. At the same time, it is also very promising to ask for further interviewees in a 'snowballing-like' manner. When the first author collected data in family-owned publishing houses (Kammerlander et al., 2018), she asked, during the interviews, questions such as 'Who was the employee driving this digital initiative? Can I talk to him?' This often increased the number of interviews conducted for a case by 50 percent (compared to the ones initially scheduled). Here, we can rely on 'centralized decision-making,' often available in family businesses. This means that once the owning family supports your project, the rest of the organization will follow suit! Our recommendations about the number of interviews to be conducted are done on a general basis; however, there might be exceptions where the study is carried out in microfamily businesses and the number of people to be interviewed is less than three per firm. In those cases, a researcher would need to think creatively about other valuable data sources to gather sufficient knowledge on the phenomenon, such as real-life observations from meetings or interactions with customers. Moreover, we use pictures such as that of 'treasure hunters' or 'detectives' when collecting data on cases. You need to gather *all* the information that you can get. In addition to interviews, this means, for instance, browsing through the archival webpages of the focal family businesses (e.g., via web.archive.org), visiting the family businesses at their headquarters, or visiting them at industry fairs. The more information you can get, the better!

## Analysis of Cases

Several important pitfalls occur when analyzing the data. One of the primary challenges when analyzing family business multicase studies is: Do we pay attention to the process or do we pay attention to heterogeneity or differences among cases? While the classical, Eisenhardt-style multicases pay attention to patterns among businesses, a new trend—fostered by Denny Gioia's data structure approach (Gioia et al., 2013)—looks at analyzing the processes.

The problem is that many family business studies combine both elements. Since qualitative research in the family business domain is increasingly moving from purely explorative studies identifying patterns (e.g., the 'what') to explaining mechanisms (e.g., Strike & Rerup, 2016; the 'how' and 'why'), a process perspective becomes more important. To analyze processes within family businesses, appropriate—often longitudinal—data are required. Longitudinal research studies, with interviews over multiple years, are the exception (though preferred!), but often the additional study of archival (printed and online) material can help gather material covering longer time periods. Here, another family business research advantage comes into play: the existence of long-tenured employees may help you recap events that happened a longer time ago. Moreover, some centennial businesses decide to write about the family business history in a book to have as a tribute from previous generations and a memory for the next generations. This type of data—which is often not available for nonfamily businesses—is very rich in details about the history of the family and the business and often about the community.

Despite the importance of process-based investigations, recent research has increasingly emphasized that family businesses are not the same but that there is substantial heterogeneity among them (Rau et al., 2019; Neubaum et al., 2019; Memili & Dibrell, 2018). Hence, most researchers building on multicase studies do not only reveal a universal process but also identify substantial variance among family businesses. While this likely outcome—process with variation—is quite common in family business research (e.g., Strike & Rerup, 2016), it still poses challenges in the review process. From our own experience (e.g., Diaz-Moriana et al., 2020; Gamble et al., 2021; Kammerlander et al., 2018), it is helpful to clearly outline the research purpose early in the paper, e.g., 'We aim to unveil the process of xyz and, simultaneously, scrutinize the family-related contingency factors influencing this process'. Often, we found it helpful to put the identified process—e.g., an attention-based process of radical innovation in family businesses (e.g., Kammerlander & Ganter, 2015)—center stage, and label the variation as a secondary contribution. In such a case, a generalized process model could be the central figure of the manuscript, while a table showing case-specific antecedents and behavior could highlight heterogeneity across cases.

Another somewhat related issue is the use of theory in data analysis. Frequently, family business researchers present their work as 'inductive analysis' that 'builds grounded theory', while at the same time presenting predefined theoretical frameworks (often from nonfamily business fields) that are reflected in the semistructured interview guidelines. This is, in itself, a contradiction! From our experience, the review process becomes much smoother if authors explicitly (and frankly) explain their approach to theory. This could go from 'we took a theory-informed approach and combined deductive and inductive data analysis' to 'we started out with the broad research question X, yet while analyzing the data we found that Y is particularly important and hence decided to adopt an ABC-theory informed lens'. There is also a new trend to combine both deductive and inductive methods by accommodating the continuous interplay between induction and deduction (Mantere & Ketokivi, 2013; Shepherd & Sutcliffe, 2011; Staat, 1993; Thomas, 2010). The approach begins with existing conceptualizations, which aim to advance research about a (family business or business family) phenomenon already known through theory development (Mantere & Ketokivi, 2013; Thomas, 2010; Staat, 1993; Wirth, 1999). For instance, Erdogan and colleagues (2020) linked their multicase empirical evidence on family firms to theory by abductively grounding their arguments in imprinting theory. Likewise, Parada et al.'s (2010) multicase study research goes back and forth between the data and their initial institutional theory framework. Through this approach, family business researchers can provide new insights based on existing theories. Thus, the development of theory emerges through the constant interplay between empirical data and the researcher's developing conceptualizations.

As an additional challenge, many researchers feel overwhelmed when confronted with the huge amount of data to be analyzed—especially in the field of family businesses, where owner-managers tend to enjoy sharing information about various aspects of their business. In the data collection phase, the researcher's day seemed to be rather structured due to the scheduled interviews. However, in the data analysis phase, the researchers find themselves in a rather 'unstructured' situation with huge staples of endless transcripts that are left to be analyzed. Here, it is important that researchers set up a plan for themselves to systematically analyze their data. Furthermore, as one of the surveyed beginning researchers explains, 'Craft case summaries right from the beginning as an orientation throughout the data collection and analysis phase!' Hence, summarizing the histories and stories of each of the family businesses will help researchers to easily recognize the differences and similarities across family businesses.

## Presentations of Findings

'Focus, focus, and focus—keep it simple' (PhD student survey, 2021). Often, the conducted interviews are very extensive and cover a broad array of topics. From our own experience, we know that family business owner-managers especially like to talk extensively about their business, its history, their approaches, culture, achievements, strategies, processes, etc. While all those stories tend to be extremely interesting (and provide important insights to the researchers), they might not be relevant for the final goal (i.e., the publication of a paper, see Brigham & Payne, Chapter 1 in this book).

As editors and reviewers, we often see submitted family business articles that aim to provide overarching solutions to the world. For instance, those studies aim to tackle 'the succession process of family businesses' or 'innovation in family businesses' in general and fail to recognize that there is an entire—and quite extensive—research stream on this topic already. As mentioned before, multicase studies in family businesses require discipline on the part of researchers. One aspect of discipline is focusing on one specific research question—one specific, theoretically interesting, aspect addressed in the interviews and other data. This specific aspect should be investigated as much as possible. All other potentially interesting aspects need to be removed from the submitted manuscript. (As this can be frustrating, especially for the interviewers, the first author made it a habit to additionally publish practitioner reports—in the local language and in plain language—capturing all the interesting details and side stories that ultimately did not make it into the academic paper.)

A well-known recommendation for multicase study researchers is: Show your data! The question remains: How much data? In our own publishing experience, we have received diverse feedback, often criticizing our paper for providing too few (e.g., only 1–2 quotes per proposition) or too many (e.g., in sum 40 quotes) verbal quotes. Additionally, we have received comments about our quotes either being too short (two lines or less) or too long (10+ lines). As always, authors need to find a balance here (and remove interesting quotes and observations to an appendix if necessary (e.g., De Massis et al., 2015; Kammerlander & Ganter, 2015; de Groote & Bertschi-Michel, 2021)).

What is even more important is to sufficiently draw on the 'further (archival or secondary) material' when showing your evidence—especially for family businesses, in which long-term employees or family members might assess the history in a very positive light. Often, authors refer to such data (e.g., brochures, websites, observations, etc.) in their methods section, but fail to 'show' any such evidence in the findings section. In the family business context, we found it useful to refer to historical events or statements (documented, e.g., in letters or press interviews) in the findings section to support our interpretation (see Diaz-Moriana et al., 2020).

## FUTURE DIRECTIONS

Multicase studies have made an important contribution to family business research in the past, and they will hopefully do so even more in the future. While we hope that our observations and guidelines may help researchers conduct and publish their studies, we also expect (and hope) that there will be sufficient innovation and progress in the coming years.

One already observable change is the increased use of video-taped interviews. When the COVID-19 pandemic hit in early 2020, we were quite worried about our multicase studies. While technology (e.g., Zoom, Teams, Skype) was available, we were unsure about how our interviewees would react to this mode. To our surprise, it turned out quite favorably. While personal, direct contact is missing, we noticed that the home office setting—often with children and pets in the background—immediately created an open and intimate atmosphere filled with trust. One family business owner-manager even told us, 'I couldn't have agreed to this interview in a physical setting at the headquarters, because I don't want my sister to know that I am talking to you.' Nevertheless, researchers need to be aware that one important source of information—observations in the headquarters and informal chats in the hallway with further employees—is disappearing in the digital world. However, these changes may offer up additional opportunities as well.

As such, it is important to become creative about other potential data sources. These could include, for instance, social media posts, podcasts, participation in online meetings, etc. Indeed, depending on the specific topic, researchers are encouraged to creatively think about which further sources may add to the overall picture.

We also want to encourage researchers to think more broadly about the research questions asked. Qualitative multicase studies are often at the forefront of research, tackling interesting questions that are difficult to explain through quantitative methods. As such, we would expect to see much more research on novel and important topics such as sustainability, ethics, new work, climate change, and big data, among others, in family businesses.

## CONCLUSION

Multicase studies are a fascinating part of family business research. They match many of the requirements of contemporary family business research; they have the potential to substantially advance family business theory—and last, but not least, they are fun to conduct. Nevertheless, the path from research idea to publication has many pitfalls for multicase study researchers. In this book chapter, we aimed to build on our own experience, as well as that of others, to highlight critical junctures and decisions in multicase study work, share our learning, and some best practices.

## ACKNOWLEDGMENTS

We thank Alexandra Bertschi, Moritz Feninger, Jana Hermle, Raphael Langenscheidt, Charlotte Layher, Larissa Leitner, Anna Schade, Jonas Soluk, Hubertus Theissen, Marina Palm, Stephanie Querbach, and Conrad Wiedeler for their valuable input.

## REFERENCES

Bika, Z., Rosa, P., & Karakas, F. (2019). Multilayered socialization processes in transgenerational family firms. *Family Business Review*, *32*(3), 233–258.

Calabrò, A., Brogi, M., & Torchia, M. (2016). What does really matter in the internationalization of small and medium-sized family businesses? *Journal of Small Business Management*, *54*(2), 679–696.

Clinton, E., McAdam, M., & Gamble, J. R. (2018). Transgenerational entrepreneurial family firms: An examination of the business model construct. *Journal of Business Research*, *90*, 269–285.

de Groote, J. K., & Bertschi-Michel, A. (2021). From intention to trust to behavioral trust: Trust building in family business advising. *Family Business Review*, *34*(2), 132–153.

De Massis, A., Frattini, F., Kotlar, J., Messeni Petruzzelli, A., & Wright, M. (2016). Innovation through tradition. *Academy of Management Perspectives*, *30*(1), 93–116.

De Massis, A., Frattini, F., Pizzurno, E., & Cassia, L. (2015). Product innovation in family versus nonfamily firms: An exploratory analysis. *Journal of Small Business Management*, *53*(1), 1–36.

Diaz-Moriana, V., Clinton, E., Kammerlander, N., Lumpkin, G. T., & Craig, J. B. (2020). Innovation motives in family firms: A transgenerational view. *Entrepreneurship Theory and Practice*, *44*(2), 256–287.

Eisenhardt, K. M. (1989). Building theories from case study research. *Academy of Management Review*, *14*(4), 532–550.

Erdogan, I., Rondi, E., & De Massis, A. (2020). Managing the tradition and innovation paradox in family firms: A family imprinting perspective. *Entrepreneurship Theory and Practice*, *44*(1), 20–54.

Gamble, J. R., Clinton, E., & Díaz-Moriana, V. (2021). Broadening the business model construct: Exploring how family-owned SMEs co-create value with external stakeholders. *Journal of Business Research, 130*, 646–657.

Gioia, D. A., Corley, K. G., & Hamilton, A. L. (2013). Seeking qualitative rigor in inductive research: Notes on the Gioia methodology. *Organizational Research Methods, 16*(1), 15–31.

Glover, J. L., & Reay, T. (2015). Sustaining the family business with minimal financial rewards: How do family farms continue? *Family Business Review, 28*(2), 163–177.

Hashim, S., Naldi, L., & Markowska, M. (2020). 'The royal award goes to…': Legitimacy processes for female-led family ventures. *Journal of Family Business Strategy*. https://doi.org/10.1016/j.jfbs.2020.100358.

Howorth, C., Wright, M., Westhead, P., & Allcock, D. (2016). Company metamorphosis: Professionalization waves, family firms and management buyouts. *Small Business Economics, 47*(3), 803–817.

Huff, A. S. (1999). *Writing for Scholarly Publication*. Sage.

Jaskiewicz, P., Combs, J. G., & Rau, S. B. (2015). Entrepreneurial legacy: Toward a theory of how some family firms nurture transgenerational entrepreneurship. *Journal of Business Venturing, 30*(1), 29–49.

Kammerlander, N., & Ganter, M. (2015). An attention-based view of family firm adaptation to discontinuous technological change: Exploring the role of family CEOs' noneconomic goals. *Journal of Product Innovation Management, 32*(3), 361–383.

Kammerlander, N., König, A., & Richards, M. (2018). Why do incumbents respond heterogeneously to disruptive innovations? The interplay of domain identity and role identity. *Journal of Management Studies, 55*(7), 1122–1165.

Kotlar, J., & De Massis, A. (2013). Goal setting in family firms: Goal diversity, social interactions, and collective commitment to family-centered goals. *Entrepreneurship Theory and Practice, 37*(6), 1263–1288.

Mantere, S., & Ketokivi, M. (2013). Reasoning in organization science. *Academy of Management Review, 38*(1), 70–89.

Memili, E., & Dibrell, C. (2018). *The Palgrave Handbook of Heterogeneity among Family Firms*. Palgrave Macmillan.

Miles, M. B., & Huberman, A. M. (1994). *Qualitative Data Analysis: An Expanded Sourcebook*. Sage Publications.

Neubaum, D. O., Kammerlander, N., & Brigham, K. H. (2019). Capturing family firm heterogeneity: How taxonomies and typologies can help the field move forward. *Family Business Review, 32*(2), 106–130.

Neubaum, D. O., Thomas, C. H., Dibrell, C., & Craig, J. B. (2017). Stewardship climate scale: An assessment of reliability and validity. *Family Business Review, 30*(1), 37–60.

Nordqvist, M. & Zellweger, T. (2010). *Transgenerational Entrepreneurship*. Edward Elgar Publishing.

Parada, M. J., Nordqvist, M., & Gimeno, A. (2010). Institutionalizing the family business: The role of professional associations in fostering a change of values. *Family Business Review, 23*(4), 355–372.

Rau, S. B., Werner, A., & Schell, S. (2019). Psychological ownership as a driving factor of innovation in older family firms. *Journal of Family Business Strategy, 10*(4), 100246.

Reay, T. (2014). Publishing qualitative research. *Family Business Review, 27*, 95–102.

Reay, T., Jaskiewicz, P., & Hinings, C. R. (2015). How family, business, and community logics shape family firm behavior and 'rules of the game' in an organizational field. *Family Business Review*, *28*(4), 292–311.

Schickinger, A., Bertschi-Michel, A., Leitterstorf, M. P., & Kammerlander, N. (2021). Same same, but different: Capital structures in single family offices compared with private equity firms. *Small Business Economics*, 1–19.

Shepherd, D. A., & Sutcliffe, K. M. (2011). Inductive top-down theorizing: A source of new theories of organization. *Academy of Management Review*, *36*(2), 361–380.

Staat, W. (1993). On abduction, deduction, induction and the categories. *Transactions of the Charles S. Peirce Society*, *29*(2), 225–237.

Strike, V. M., & Rerup, C. (2016). Mediated sensemaking. *Academy of Management Journal*, *59*(3), 880–905.

Thomas, G. (2010). Doing case study: Abduction not induction, phronesis not theory. *Qualitative Inquiry*, *16*(7), 575–582.

Wirth, U. (1999). Abductive reasoning in Peirce's and Davidson's account of interpretation. *Transactions of the Charles S. Peirce Society*, *35*(1), 115–127.

# 10. Qualitative research interviewing in family firms

## Carlo Salvato and Guido Corbetta

## 1. THE UNIQUE CHALLENGES AND OPPORTUNITIES OF QUALITATIVE INTERVIEWING IN FAMILY FIRMS

Qualitative research has been widely used as the main approach to building theory in the family business field (Chenail, 2009; Reay, 2014). Although qualitative researchers use a wide spectrum of data sources including secondary and archival data, interviews are by far the most widely adopted source of information in qualitative studies (Seidman, 2013; Weiss, 1994). An interview can be defined as 'an inter-change of views between [at least] two persons conversing about a theme of mutual interest' (Kvale & Brinkmann, 2009, p. 2). In research interviewing, one of the two persons is the researcher (or interviewer), while the other is the participant (informant or interviewee). In this chapter, we will offer guidelines to perform qualitative interviewing in family business settings. Many of the suggestions illustrated in this chapter apply to qualitative research interviewing in any nonfamily empirical setting and they are aligned with established literature in qualitative methods (e.g., Creswell, 2013; Golden-Biddle & Locke, 2007; Patton, 2002; Spradley, 1979; Wengraf, 2001). However, interviewing informants (both family *and* nonfamily members) within a family business setting involves unique challenges and opportunities. These are due to the overlap of family and business logics and dynamics, which affects all dimensions of the business organization.

The main *challenges* result from the risk that informants will not disclose the subtle family-related facts and dynamics that may explain a significant part of the investigated phenomena. For instance, a family CEO may explain the choice to diversify into the unrelated business of luxury hotels as resulting from the need to diversify corporate risk. She may conceal, however, that the main reason is offering a top managerial position to her youngest male child who has a passion for the luxury and hospitality industries, whereas top management positions in the main business are already covered by his older siblings.

Correspondingly, the main *opportunities* result from the possible emergence of interesting, counter-intuitive, and often surprising phenomena that have the potential to illuminate and expand existing knowledge on the object of the study. The same CEO may, for example, reveal that the controlling family performed past acquisitions only in highly related businesses, to avoid the loss of family control resulting from the need to entrust nonfamily managers to run businesses the family had little knowledge about.

Unfortunately, family dynamics do not easily emerge in data collection for at least three reasons. First, members of an entrepreneurial family – members of *any* family, for that matter – do not easily and willingly disclose private family issues to strangers. Second, both family and nonfamily managers find it inappropriate to reveal that some company decisions and actions are driven by family dynamics, due to the prevalent negative bias that is usually attached to family control. Third, nonfamily employees are often worried about the personal consequences of revealing the family dynamics that they observe in everyday operations, in particular those revealing family conflicts or a departure from managerial logics.

Interviewing in family firms is thus difficult yet exciting and rewarding at the same time. Issues such as quality of access, building trust, and designing interview questions that acknowledge and anticipate the possible reluctance of informants becomes paramount. This chapter offers some guidance on how to design and implement effective qualitative interviews in family-controlled firms.

## 2.    A STEP-BY-STEP GUIDE TO PERFORMING QUALITATIVE INTERVIEWING IN FAMILY FIRMS

### 2.1    Gaining Access and Building Trust

Gaining access means finding and securing participants for research (Buchanan, Boddy, & McCalman, 1988; Feldman, Bell, & Berger, 2003). The unique features of family firm interviewing suggest that lacking excellent access and the openness of informants to provide candid information, interviews will only scratch the surface of the dynamics that actually drive observed phenomena. There are two main approaches to gaining access: (1) through direct contact or (2) through a gatekeeper (Peticca-Harris, deGama, & Elias, 2016).

## 2.1.1 Gaining access through direct contact

Particular care needs to be taken when you directly approach interviewees – both family *and* nonfamily members of family firms. Direct approaches would include those occurring at a conference, workshop, or through an email or telephone call following such events. These approaches must be carefully prepared. The potential informant is going to interpret whatever the researcher says and fit it into a mental frame that will shape the informant's willingness to give the interview and the information disclosed during the possible interview (Foddy, 1993). This framing is usually unconscious. Therefore, the researcher must anticipate it, and try to avoid the 'wrong framing' by the informant (Wengraf, 2001). An example is when the researcher does not clearly explain that the interview is a data-collection effort aimed at gathering evidence for scientific purposes. Some families are reluctant to give interviews to the media and may therefore deny access. To avoid wrong framings that may prevent access or alter collected data, the researcher must be clear, precise, authentic, and to the point.

The researcher should practice the phrases used to describe the research project, its goals, and, importantly, why and how access to that specific family firm will be important. The researcher should clearly state (1) who he or she is and in what capacity he or she is performing the research ('I am a PhD student, a university professor …' vs. 'a journalist, a consultant, an entrepreneur in the same industry…'), (2) the purpose of the research in plain language and avoiding academic jargon, and (3) the outcome of the whole process ('I am working on an academic paper, a PhD thesis, a book …'). The researcher should also make sure to mention the verb 'to tell' or an equivalent, to avoid giving the impression that what is required is some kind of difficult abstraction, synthesis, or conceptualization (e.g., 'from your speech at yesterday's conference, I realized that you have interesting stories you could tell me about the topic of CEO succession').

## 2.1.2 Gaining access through gatekeepers

Everything is much easier if the researcher is first introduced by a gatekeeper. Gatekeepers help in granting permission to make the first contact with potential informants, and to keep them committed across the entire research process. Gatekeepers in family business research are usually family business employees or next-generation members of the controlling family. The closer the gatekeeper is to members of the controlling family (e.g., the son of the Chairman and majority owner of the firm), the better will be the chance for good access. However, even contact with a young, nonfamily junior manager of a large family group may be enough to break the initial barrier due to lack of mutual knowledge and trust.

Despite their valuable role, gatekeepers do not necessarily guarantee that informants will accept participating in the research or that they will remain fully committed over time (Clark, 2010; Wanat, 2008). Therefore, in their direct contacts with participants, interviewers should also exercise the particular care described in the previous section.

### 2.1.3    Ethical issues of confidentiality and anonymity

Due to the highly personal, sensitive, and sometimes intimate nature of the information that is disclosed within a family setting, participants often raise issues of confidentiality before agreeing to participate in an interview-based research project (research grounded on surveys or secondary data allows families to exercise a significantly greater degree of control on the information that they disclose). Some prominent families may even require a preliminary contact with their lawyers, before accepting the offer to participate. These concerns may prompt families, or researchers themselves, to request or propose the signing of a *non-disclosure agreement (NDA)*.

There are no straightforward guidelines on how to behave in these circumstances. The requested level of confidentiality usually depends on the nature and theme of the study (e.g., past strategic decisions vs. current family conflicts) and on the degree of previous familiarity and trust. Generally, the researcher should constantly and consistently assure participants that the information they indicate as confidential will be kept that way, and that, in general, anonymization will be maintained, as they require.

Most importantly, however, researchers should always fully respect the privacy of participating families and the deep value and importance that persons, relationships, and feelings have for them (Lee, 1993). Our own research objectives and career goals should never prompt us to overlook these needs. We should always ask ourselves: 'How would I, or my relatives, feel if someone were disclosing this information about *my own* family?' Once this level of care is exercised, however, we should also remember that committing to high levels of anonymity and confidentiality – which families may require – may give access to the case, but it may later prevent us from fully exploiting collected data. A possible solution is, for instance, to ensure (in writing, if needed) that collected information will only be available to members of the research team during the data analysis phase, that drafts of research outcomes will be sent to the informants before publication, and that nothing will be published without their explicit consent. An abridged example of an NDA is reported in Box 10.1.

## BOX 10.1 EXAMPLE OF NON-DISCLOSURE AGREEMENT (*EXCERPT, SIMPLIFIED*)

- The Research Team will protect Confidential Information (i.e., information which is not already of public domain) disclosed by the Company in any form.
- The Research Team may use Confidential Information solely to complete the research project and for no other purpose, and may not share Confidential Information with anyone outside the Research Team.
- All Confidential Information shall at all times remain the property of the Company.
- The Company authorizes the Recipient to process the Confidential Information to elaborate research findings and to disclose the name of the Company in the final research reports of the Project.
- The Research Team is entitled to request prior written permission to the Company to publish non-anonymized quotes from interviews in the final research report or non-anonymized information resulting from documents received from the Company.
- The Research Team will share a draft of the final research reports with the Company before publication to identify any information that the Company does not wish to disclose. The Research Team commits to anonymize or to eliminate this information from the research reports, as the Company will indicate.

### 2.2    Developing a Research Design

Before writing the questions for a research interview, the researcher should draw an analytical design of the investigated phenomenon, its conceptual understanding, the research questions, and the methods intended to answer them. A *research design* is a detailed plan allowing a researcher to rigorously and efficiently move through the following stages (Creswell, 2013, 2014): (a) a *conceptual framework* describing the phenomenon of interest; (b) the *central research questions* that the researcher aims at answering through the development or test of a theory; (c) a description of the *methods* that the researcher intends to use to answer those questions (operationalization of concepts, choice of units and sampling, techniques of data collection and fieldwork); and (d) *results* expected from data-processing and analysis through strategies and procedures that lead to testing or developing *theory and theoretical propositions*.

Research designs span through a range that goes from highly *deductive* '*model-*' or '*theory-testing*' approaches (where the researcher aims at testing propositions derived from existing theory) to highly *inductive* '*model-*' or '*theory-building*' approaches (where the researcher aims at building new theory derived from the collected data). Interviews can be used in both approaches (Figure 10.1). Deductive research usually requires *fully structured* (i.e., multiple-choice, such as in surveys) or *heavily structured* questions (i.e., questions addressing a narrow and very specific issue, often entailing short answers grounded on data and facts). Inductive research usually requires *lightly or semi-structured* (i.e., relatively broad questions, each followed by a number of alternative sub-questions to further direct the informant's attention) or *unstructured* questions (i.e., very broad questions allowing the informant to freely touch upon the issue of interest, followed by additional questions improvised by the researcher as the conversation unfolds).

## 2.3    Developing the Interview Guide

### 2.3.1    Developing interview questions from the research design

*Breaking up the central research question.* There is no structured technique to develop research questions. However, researchers who carefully developed their research design can proceed by gradually breaking up their central research question/s along dimensions that are meaningful to their research project. Examples of dimensions (see also Figure 10.2) can be time (e.g., calendar time, or before/during/after an event), levels of analysis (e.g., macro: industry/social community; meso: firm/family; micro: individual managers/ family members), or components of a phenomenon (e.g., affective, cognitive, behavioral, organizational, financial, relational).

*Capturing stories, data, hard facts.* Qualitative research is aimed at explaining complex family and business phenomena. The complexity is often so huge that the researcher has a hard time developing questions that could elicit specific-enough information to address the study's questions. An effective way to address this common problem in qualitative research is to ask questions related to specific facts, events, or phenomena that punctuate the history of a family or a firm, rather than asking for a description of the full story. For example, a researcher could develop a comparative case study design to understand how long-lived family firms accomplish continuity across generations (Kammerlander & Diaz-Moriana, Chapter 9 in this book). The option of asking informants to recollect the entire story of the family and the business is obviously difficult to pursue. As an alternative, the researcher could assume that families and businesses that survive across generations are those that survive disruptions and shocks. The researcher may thus identify a small number of these disruptions, and focus interviews on how the family and the firm managed (or failed) to address such disruptions.

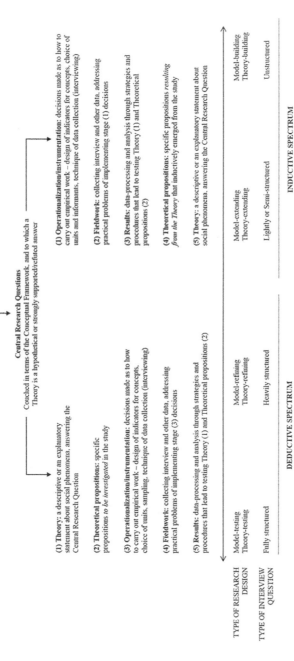

**Conceptual Framework**
a set of concepts in terms of which questions about the investigated phenomena can be asked and answers can be given, theories and theoretical propositions hypothesized (deductive) or built (inductive).

**Central Research Questions**
Coupled in terms of the Conceptual Framework, and to which a Theory is a hypothetical or strongly supported/refuted answer

**(1) Theory:** a descriptive or an explanatory statement about social phenomena, answering the Central Research Question

**(2) Theoretical propositions:** specific propositions *to be investigated* in the study

**(3) Operationalization/instrumentation:** decisions made as to how to carry out empirical work – design of indicators for concepts, choice of units, sampling, technique of data collection (interviewing)

**(4) Fieldwork:** collecting interview and other data, addressing practical problems of implementing stage (3) decisions

**(5) Results:** data-processing and analysis through strategies and procedures that lead to testing Theory (1) and Theoretical propositions (2)

**(1) Operationalization/instrumentation:** decisions made as to how to carry out empirical work – design of indicators for concepts, choice of units and informants, technique of data collection (interviewing)

**(2) Fieldwork:** collecting interview and other data, addressing practical problems of implementing stage (1) decisions

**(3) Results:** data-processing and analysis through strategies and procedures that lead to testing Theory (1) and Theoretical propositions (2)

**(4) Theoretical propositions:** specific propositions *resulting from the Theory* that inductively emerged from the study

**(5) Theory:** a descriptive or an explanatory statement about social phenomena, answering the Central Research Question

|  | DEDUCTIVE SPECTRUM |  |  | INDUCTIVE SPECTRUM |  |
|---|---|---|---|---|---|
| TYPE OF RESEARCH DESIGN | Model-testing Theory-testing | Model-refining Theory-refining | | Model-extending Theory-extending | Model-building Theory-building |
| TYPE OF INTERVIEW QUESTION | Fully structured | Heavily structured | | Lightly or Semi-structured | Unstructured |

*Figure 10.1  How the research design drives the research process and the type of interview questions in deductive and inductive research*

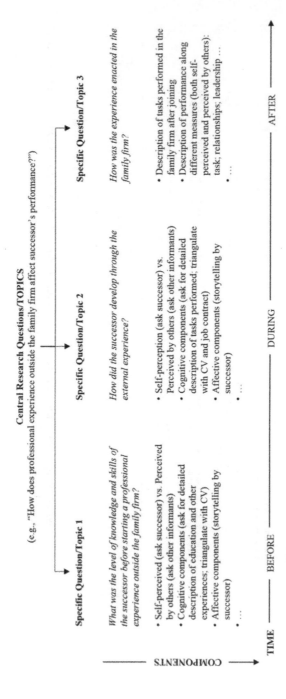

*Figure 10.2    How to structure interview questions from the central research questions*

*Asking for counter-examples.* The richness of a research and the conclusiveness of its results are substantially enhanced if the researcher offers counter-examples or surprising and puzzling exceptions to the explanations offered by the study. Qualitative research runs the risk of offering smooth or linear accounts of extremely rich and complex phenomena, or intuitive, 'so what?' answers to the research questions, which could often be derived from the existing literature. These weaknesses are often due to the type of questions asked by the researcher. If the research question is: 'How does the involvement of the Board reduce family conflict in succession processes?', the risk is that all interview questions aim at eliciting instances of conflict-reduction through Board involvement. The research will likely result in a straightforward account of how and why the Board reduces conflict. The researcher should design questions prompting informants to illustrate instances in which the Board could *not* reduce conflict, or at least not entirely. These questions may unveil the presence of moderating factors (e.g., the seniority or level of independence and charisma of Board members, or the length or location of Board meetings), or valuable extensions of the research (e.g., evidence that the Board helps in reducing some types of conflict, but not others).

*Triangulating data sources.* A central tenet of qualitative research is data triangulation, although it applies to all types of research (Patton, 1999, 2002). Triangulating information means collecting data on a specific phenomenon or issue from more than one, but ideally three or more sources. With triangulation, researchers avoid recollection bias of single informants, socially acceptable answers, and attempts at misleading the researcher for a number of possible reasons. To perform triangulation, researchers should plan to ask the same questions to multiple informants, or to the same informants across multiple interviews. Moreover, researchers should plan to collect secondary and archival data, when available, to corroborate the evidence collected through interviews.

### 2.3.2 Writing interview questions

Interview questions should not only rigorously flow from the research design. They should also be written in a way that makes them easy and, possibly, pleasant to answer. The following are some key suggestions that may help the researcher in framing the interview as a smooth and pleasant conversation that will yield valuable research insights.

*Avoiding 'abstract' or 'conceptual' questions.* Qualitative interviewing aims at collecting data to illustrate or develop theory, such as the relationship between two variables (e.g., the involvement of a Board of directors and the emergence of conflict in succession processes), or a detailed description of a process (e.g., how Board involvement in succession unfolds over time). The task of the researcher is to collect enough 'raw' empirical evidence to suggest the relationship or to describe the process. It is not the informant's task to theorize. Usually, the researcher should not ask informants the study's research questions: 'How does the involvement of the Board of directors reduce/ increase conflict in succession processes?' or 'What are the stages of involvement of the Board in the succession process?' Rather, the researcher should ask informants to tell stories about succession, from which the researcher will be able to infer the conceptualization allowing to answer the research questions. 'Conceptual' questions are extremely difficult for an informant to answer and, importantly, they risk driving the respondent in specific directions.

*Avoiding yes/no and nominal/ordinal questions.* Qualitative interviewing aims at capturing 'rich' and 'thick' information on complex phenomena. When writing a question, the researcher should try to anticipate: (a) the richness and nuance that the question will elicit in the respondent's answer; (b) the possibility to obtain a 'power quote' that could be used in the paper or report. For this reason, the researcher should avoid asking questions that can be answered with a simple 'yes/no' ('Did you ...'), or with a nominal ('Which ...') or ordinal ('Higher or lower?') response. Rather than asking: 'Did you involve an advisor in the selection of the successor?', the researcher may ask: 'Can you describe the selection process in terms of what happened and who was involved?'. Similarly, rather than asking: 'Who makes the final decision about a candidate: the Board or the Shareholders' Assembly?' the researcher may ask: 'Can you describe how the decision-making process unfolds, and why you set up these rules?' Exceptions are questions aimed at capturing a specific piece of information or an opinion, to be followed by questions exploring the 'why' and 'how' of the investigated phenomenon.

*Framing 'tricky' questions.* If the researcher anticipates a question as particularly 'tricky' for the informant (e.g., 'Can you please describe the conflict that erupted between you and your children when you informed them that only one of them could join the business?'), he or she may introduce it with a statement framing the possibly discomforting answer as 'acceptable' (e.g., 'Decades of research showed that setting up rules for joining the business often determines some form of conflict between the Senior and Junior generation'). However, the researcher should avoid 'framing' the respondent's answer with these introductory statements. Trickier questions should be placed at the end of the interview, when trust has been developed and informants have become less vigilant.

*Using plain vs. formal wording.* Questions should be written in plain language, avoiding formal phrases. After writing a question, the researcher should always read it aloud, ideally to a test person such as a colleague, to hear how it 'sounds.' An interview is a conversation, not an interrogation or an exam. Questions should thus flow smoothly if they intend to elicit smooth answers.

## 2.4     Planning and Performing Interviews: Who, Where, When, and How

### 2.4.1     Who: selecting informants

Selecting interviewees is a difficult and important task. Generally speaking, qualitative interviewing is about collecting rich insights from multiple viewpoints. Interviewees should be selected to develop a three-dimensional view of the investigated phenomenon. For example, research on leadership development in family CEO successors should not only address successors to capture how they developed their leadership skills over time. The researcher should also interview the incumbent CEO, advisors, and coaches who supported the candidate. The researcher should also interview 'followers' (e.g., junior and middle managers), who will provide evidence of developed leadership (or lack thereof). Finally, the researcher should also interview family members who are not active in the business, to understand if, how, and why they supported or hindered the successor's leadership development (for a detailed example see Salvato and Corbetta, 2013).

Besides aiming at richness in viewpoints, the choice of informants should be guided by the more or less deductive or inductive nature of the study (Figure 10.1). Deductive studies aim toward precision and they usually require a large number of informants, pre-selected by how representative they are of the category of interest (e.g., family CEOs, independent Board members). Inductive studies aim at richness and at novel and surprising insights. Informants for inductive theory-building studies are often selected through a 'snowballing' technique, which implies starting from a key informant and identifying subsequent participants from the first interviews, as novel facts and insights emerge.

Most research designs involve a plan for one or, at most, two sessions with each interviewee. However, when interviewing subsequent interviewees, reading the transcripts, or writing up the study, researchers may realize that they need additional information on specific issues from some of the interviewees. Therefore, at the end of each session the researcher should ask permission to contact the interviewee again, should the need emerge for a follow-up session, perhaps only on the phone, 'to clear up questions that may arise during the period of analysis.' Having already created some rapport with the researcher, and with the prospect of concluding the interview at last, participants will seldom say no.

### 2.4.2     Where: location matters in family business interviewing

The researcher should keep in mind that the success of an interview depends in part on the context. The ideal context is a time and place where the researcher will be alone in a one-to-one situation, without interference. Informants will most of the time suggest to be interviewed in their office. This is usually acceptable, provided continuous interruptions can be avoided. However, in a family business setting the researcher may try to hold at least some of the interviews in a different setting, such as the company showroom or the informant's house.

One clear advantage of getting outside of the office and into a company or family setting is that rich story-based descriptions may be generated that can 'connect what people say with where they say it' (Jones et al., 2008, p. 2). Moreover, in family business research, interesting information may emerge on the informant's and the family's values, interests, relationships, and conflicts.

### 2.4.3 When: interview length

Qualitative interviews in family business settings tend to be longer, on average, than in nonfamily settings. The overlap of business and family logics and dynamics, and the need to collect stories about the entire life span of an individual, a family, and a firm, often requires addressing the phenomenon of interest (e.g., M&A decisions or family conflicts) from multiple viewpoints (Atkinson, 1998; McCracken, 1988). Moreover, participants – family members, in particular, and long-tenured nonfamily managers – tend to be passionate about anything that refers to the business and its relations with the family. Researchers in family business will thus often be engaged in long interviews. We define long interviews as interviews lasting approximately three or more hours, either in a single session or over multiple sessions with the same participant.

Long interviews allow researchers and participants to co-experience material objects and spaces and, thus, to co-generate ideas, insights, and knowledge. Long interviews are a form of highly adaptable and creative explorations (Douglas, 1985). By slowing down, researchers can 'wait and be open to what may unfold.' Douglas (1985, pp. 67–68), for example, characterized long interviews as an intimate process of discovery. Thus, long interviews represent one tool that gives the researcher permission to become ever more human and 'deviate from the ideal of a cool, distant, and rational interviewer' in order to explore more deeply (Fontana & Frey, 1994, p. 366; Hansen & Trank, 2016). The importance of long interviews is especially evident in Dundon and Ryan's (2010) model for building rapport with reluctant respondents, which relies on a four-hour interview to move through its five developmental stages, for which shorter interviews provide insufficient scope.

### 2.4.4 How: recording interview data

Researchers should record each interview and transcribe it *verbatim* (i.e., word-by-word). Recording and transcribing interviews is the standard for rigorous qualitative research. The only rare exceptions are informal encounters with informants (e.g., in the office corridor, at the coffee machine, or in a noisy production facility) or in extreme situations (e.g., the informant starts crying and, to show respect for his or feelings, the researcher turns the recorder off).

Researchers are often concerned about asking if they may record the interview, with the fear that the informant may refuse (both the recording and the interview), or that he or she may reluctantly accept and then alter or conceal valuable information. However, informants very rarely deny permission to record, if the request is properly advanced. First, the researcher should build some minimal relationship with the informant. The small talk that occurs before the interview, when the researcher may mention something personal about him or herself, is usually enough to build the minimum amount of trust required. For the same reason, the request to record should not be mentioned before the meeting, for example by email or over the phone. Without a previously established relationship, most respondents will deny permission to record. Second, the request should be dropped casually in the interview, right before asking the first question. It should be motivated with the need to attentively focus on what the informant will be saying ('rather than wasting time taking notes ... by the way, with the use of computers we're no longer accustomed to write, and I can barely read my own handwriting!'). Third, the researcher should warrant full confidentiality and care for how the recording will be used, mentioning that the recording will be transcribed by the research team and the transcripts will only be used for the purposes of the research.

## 2.5    Interview Data Analysis and Use

Some of the readers are familiar with the question that inexperienced students writing their dissertation sometimes ask their advisor: 'Shall I include the interview transcripts in the data chapter?' It is obviously the researcher's job to analyze the transcripts, and to only report those quotes that support the conceptual insights resulting from the analysis.

It is beyond the scope of this chapter to explain how interview data are analyzed and incorporated in the final paper or report. However, there are three broad approaches to analyzing qualitative data and to build theory from them: single-case studies, comparative case studies, and process studies (Gehman et al., 2018; Langley, 1999). Moreover, qualitative data analysis can be more or less inductive or 'grounded' (Eisenhardt, 1989; Gioia, Corley, & Hamilton, 2013; Trudell, Waldron and Wetherbe, Chapter 8 in this book; Kammerlander and Diaz-Moriana, Chapter 9 in this book).

An important aspect related to using qualitative interview data is the use of quotes from the interviews, which is closely related to the scope of this chapter. In collecting and transcribing interview data, researchers should first make sure to collect multiple forms of evidence from multiple sources and the core concepts of the research (multiple informants, multiple interviews to the

same informant, interviews and secondary/archival data), to allow data triangulation. These data (or a selection) are usually reported in summary tables
that can be included in the report or paper. Second, researchers should identify
'power quotes' in the interview that will be used to provide vivid examples
of the core concepts and insights emerging from the analysis. The researcher
should never report the same quote twice (e.g., as a 'power quote' in the text
and in the summary tables). This choice signals that the empirical evidence is
very thin and, thus, unconvincing (Silverman, 2017).

## 3.    EXPERIENCING THE QUALITATIVE RESEARCH INTERVIEW

### 3.1    Emotional Involvement with Participants

Qualitative interviewing in family firms almost always involves touching
upon emotion-laden family-related issues. However, even the most empathic
researcher runs the risk of considering such issues simply as 'cold' and abstract
constructs. For instance, 'I've not been talking with my father since then' is
simply recorded by the researcher as 'a cutoff in the relationship', and the
emotional account of the informant mother's death simply results in drawing
a cross over the related circle in the family genogram.

This is not how informants experience the interview. Whoever had the
experience of being interviewed about their family knows that even apparently
simple questions such as: 'How can you describe the relationship with your
father?' can immediately trigger a highly emotional response. Blood pressure
rises, heart rate accelerates, and the interview abruptly turns from 'a cold
collection of data to help these academics perform their research' into 'an
intrusion into my most intimate thoughts and feelings.' Researchers should
be aware that informants often may not have discussed certain issues even
with their closest relatives. As experienced family business researchers know,
sometimes family informants introduce their most intimate answers with:
'I have never told this to anyone, not even to my husband/father/son.'

There are two main consequences of the high intensity of emotions that
researchers' questions may raise. First, and most important, researchers should
respect their informants' feelings and thoughts. Besides the central ethical
considerations, this has a profound impact on the researcher–informant trust
relationship and, thus, may influence the likelihood of continuing forward
with the study. An informant whose recollection of intimate information is
coldly listened to and recorded by the researcher, will feel disrespected, thus
losing the motivation to support the research. Second, as we said, family firms
are unique because of the unavoidable combination of rational and emotional
factors. Researchers who disregard or trivialize emotionality may thus result

in overlooking the uniqueness of the phenomena they are investigating, thus missing the most insightful potential contributions.

To avoid this risk, the researcher should show compassion in their data-collection activities. Besides being respectful to their informants, they will capture opportunities for emergent theoretical insights that can lead to both new theoretical insights and the alleviation of suffering in the immediate research context (Hansen and Trank, 2016).

## 3.2    Exchanging Roles, Breaking the Rules

Unlike survey research and highly structured theory-testing studies, qualitative interviewing requires creativity and improvisation. This is particularly relevant in a family business setting, in which the researcher often needs to elicit information on highly sensitive if not private events. Researchers may use different approaches to access the required information, often requiring a break with traditional rules and roles.

One approach to breaking the rules of standard interviewing is to use show-and-tell to allow informants to connect with the material world in order to more easily and effectively illustrate otherwise abstract or tricky concepts (Crawford, Chiles, & Elias, 2020). For example, to answer a question about personal or family values, the informant may prefer to walk the researcher through the family business museum or home, rather than attempting difficult generalizations and abstractions. Similarly, to describe conflict with a relative, the informant may want to show an email or a short video in which individuals in conflict are engaged or represented.

Breaking with the rules can extend as far as a wholesale role reversal, where – at least intermittently throughout the interview – the participant asks questions and the researcher responds to them, leading to more balanced and fluid conversations (Kvale & Brinkmann, 2009). This may refer, for example, to the researcher's personal experience with his or her family, which would also balance the emotional effort inherent in asking about personal issues. A researcher may let a participant lead the way as they explore material objects and spaces together. After all, researchers aim to understand the informants' social worlds. Therefore, researchers may empower participants to show what they perceive as important, rather than overlay the researcher's explanations onto the interview. Participants are thus treated as collaborators and asked to co-generate ideas together.

## 4.    CONCLUSION

Qualitative interviewing is a complex mix of art and science. As suggested in this chapter, researchers should move from carefully planning and developing a research design, to identifying their informants, and to writing, or partially writing, the questions to be asked. Simultaneously, however, researchers should keep their mind and approach open to understanding when they risk stumbling into a tricky personal issue, and when they are facing a unique opportunity for developing a novel insight and contribution by digging deeper into a situation described by the informant. This chapter offered guidance to address both the more structured and the creative side of qualitative interviewing. Some key suggestions are summarized in Box 10.2. However, becoming a skilled qualitative research interviewer also requires a significant amount of experience and respect for the personal and family context in which participants live and act.

BOX 10.2   A CHECKLIST OF GOOD PRACTICES
                IN QUALITATIVE RESEARCH
                INTERVIEWING IN FAMILY FIRMS

Before the interview

- Develop a Research Design
- Develop interview questions from the Central Research Question/s described in the Research Design
- Place 'tricky' questions at the end of the interview
- Rehearse interview questions (ideally with a test person, or read them aloud)
- Ask participants whether they can identify a location for the interview that is particularly meaningful to them and in relation to the topic of the interview (e.g., company workshop, showroom, museum, family house, etc.)
- Bring new batteries for your recorder (or charging device for your smartphone/laptop)
- Be on time, if not a few minutes ahead of time; small talk before the actual interview is essential to build a relationship of trust with informants, but it reduces the time available for the actual interview

During the interview

- Ask participants whether they can show objects or artifacts allowing them to more effectively illustrate complex and difficult concepts and situations
- If allowed to record the interview, focus on the informant, not on your notes or, worse still, your laptop; try to build a relationship with inform-

ants, in particular when they are talking about personal or private issues; show empathy and interest

- If needed, and in specific circumstances, 'exchange roles' by mentioning something about yourself, your job, your family, and even by allowing the informant to ask you questions
- Avoid interrupting informants, in particular when they are illustrating exactly what you were looking for; refrain from the urge to ask for further clarification and confirmation of what you anticipated; failing to do so may result in interrupting valuable 'power quotes' you could use in the final report
- Keep recording until the very end of the meeting (not just the formal interview); highly insightful summary statements are often made by informants after the 'formal' questions, to summarize, exemplify, or restate the essence of their answers
- At the end of the interview, ask permission to contact the interviewee again, should the need emerge for a follow-up session

After the interview

- Send a thank you note to your informants, briefly mentioning how insightful and valuable it was for your research; remind them about the possibility to go back to them for clarifications or missing details
- Go through your written notes (and, ideally, the recording) and add additional information, impressions, and emerging insights by the end of the interview day (or within 24 hours); field notes are an important component of your field data
- Transcribe (or have it transcribed) the interview verbatim as quickly as possible
- Read the transcriptions as soon as they are ready (even if you performed them) to check for possible mistakes and to recall additional impressions to be added to your notes

If you did not perform the transcription, check if the whole transcription (or at least samples of it) carefully matches the recording.

# REFERENCES

Atkinson, R. (1998). *The Life Story Interview*. Thousand Oaks, CA: Sage.

Buchanan, D., Boddy, D., & McCalman, J. (1988). Getting in, getting on, getting out, and getting back. In A. Bryman (Ed.), *Doing research in organizations* (pp. 53–67). London: Routledge.

Chenail, R.J. (2009). Communicating your qualitative research better. *Family Business Review, 22*: 105–108.

Clark, T. (2010). Gaining and maintaining access: Exploring the mechanisms that support and challenge the relationship between gatekeepers and researchers. *Qualitative Social Work, 10*(4), 485–502.

Crawford, B., Chiles, T.H., & Elias, S.R.S.T.A. (2021). Long interviews in organizational research: Unleashing the power of "Show and Tell". *Journal of Management Inquiry, 30*(3), 331–346. https://doi.org/10.1177/1056492620930096

Creswell, J.W. (2013). *Qualitative Inquiry & Research Design*. Thousand Oaks, CA: Sage.

Creswell, J.W. (2014). *Research Design: Qualitative, Quantitative, and Mixed Methods Approaches*. Thousand Oaks, CA: Sage.

Douglas, J.D. (1985). *Creative Interviewing*. Thousand Oaks, CA: Sage.

Dundon, T., & Ryan, P. (2010). Interviewing reluctant respondents: Strikes, henchmen, and Gaelic games. *Organizational Research Methods, 13*(3), 562–581.

Eisenhardt, K.M. (1989). Building theories from case study research. *Academy of Management Review, 14*, 532–550.

Feldman, M.S., Bell, J., & Berger, M.T. (2003). *Gaining Access: A Practical and Theoretical Guide for Qualitative Researchers*. Walnut Creek, CA: Altamira Press.

Foddy, W. (1993). *Constructing Questions for Interviews and Questionnaires: Theory and Practice in Social Research*. Cambridge, UK: Cambridge University Press.

Fontana, A., & Frey, J.H. (1994). Interviewing. In N.K. Denzin & Y.S. Lincoln (Eds.), *Handbook of Qualitative Research* (pp. 361–376). Thousand Oaks, CA: Sage.

Gehman, J., Glaser, V.L., Eisenhardt, K.M., Gioia, D., Langley, A., and Corley, K.G. (2018). Finding theory–method fit: A comparison of three qualitative approaches to theory building. *Journal of Management Inquiry, 27*(3), 284–300.

Gioia, D.A., Corley, K.G., & Hamilton, A.L. (2013). Seeking qualitative rigor in inductive research: Notes on the Gioia methodology. *Organizational Research Methods, 16*, 15–31.

Golden-Biddle, K., & Locke, K. (2007). *Composing Qualitative Research*. Thousand Oaks, CA: Sage.

Hansen, H., & Trank, C.Q. (2016). This is going to hurt: Compassionate research methods. *Organizational Research Methods, 19*(3), 352–375.

Jones, P., Bunce, G., Evans, J., Gibbs, H., & Hein, J.R. (2008). Exploring space and place with walking interviews. *Journal of Research Practice, 4*(2), 1–9.

Kvale, S., & Brinkmann, S. (2009). *InterViews*. Thousand Oaks, CA: Sage.

Langley, A. (1999). Strategies for theorizing from process data. *Academy of Management Review, 24*, 691–710.

Lee, R. (1993). *Doing Research on Sensitive Topics*. London: Sage.

McCracken, G. (1988). *The Long Interview*. Thousand Oaks, CA: Sage.

Patton, M.Q. (1999). Enhancing the quality and credibility of qualitative analysis. *Health Services Research, 34*(5), 1189–1208.

Patton, M.Q. (2002). *Qualitative Research and Evaluation Methods*. Thousand Oaks, CA: Sage.

Peticca-Harris, A., deGama, N., & Elias, S.R.S.T.A. (2016). A dynamic process model for finding informants and gaining access in qualitative research. *Organizational Research Methods, 19*(3), 376–401.

Reay, T. (2014). Publishing qualitative research. *Family Business Review, 27*(2), 95–102.

Salvato, C., & Corbetta, G. (2013). Transitional leadership of advisors as a facilitator of successors' leadership construction. *Family Business Review, 26*(3), 235–255.

Seidman, I. (2013). *Interviewing as Qualitative Research*. New York: Teachers College Press.

Silverman, D. (2017). How was it for you? The Interview Society and the irresistible rise of the (poorly analyzed) interview. *Qualitative Research, 17*(2), 144–158.

Spradley, J.P. (1979). *The Ethnographic Interview*. Long Grove, IL: Waveland.

Wanat, C.L. (2008). Getting past the gatekeepers: Differences between access and cooperation in public school research. *Field Methods, 20*(2), 191–208.

Weiss, R.S. (1994). *Learning from Strangers: The Art and Method of Qualitative Interview Studies*. London: Simon and Schuster.

Wengraf, T. (2001). *Qualitative Research Interviewing: Biographic Narrative and Semi-structured Methods*. Thousand Oaks, CA: Sage.

# 11. Computer-aided text analysis in family business research: guidelines and considerations

**Danuse Bement and Jeremy C. Short**

Analyzing naturally occurring organizational narratives using content analysis represents a fruitful but under-utilized research stream in the family business literature (Short & Payne, 2020). The term content analysis refers to a broad umbrella of approaches where the 'content' of narratives is coded, categorized, or otherwise assigned value through manual or computer-assisted means to assess potential underlying meaning. Examples of content analysis in family business include developing a taxonomy of family firms by manually coding organizational values from narratives collected from company websites (Rau et al., 2019), coding minutes of meetings to uncover how outside business advisors mediate the negative emotions of incumbents and successors during family business succession events (Bertschi-Michel et al., 2020), and analyzing interview transcripts from a four-generation family firm to design a multi-layered model of family socialization (Bika et al., 2019).

Content analysis is an appealing technique as it allows scholars to examine a host of constructs in scenarios where traditional survey techniques are unlikely to yield sufficient sample sizes required for multivariate tests (Rutherford & Phillips, Chapter 14 in this book; Short et al., 2018). Family businesses are often reluctant to participate in surveys or otherwise reveal sensitive data, and family members may also hesitate to directly share information with researchers that could compromise the reputation of the business or the family. Content analysis leverages naturally occurring language that family members project through conversations, social media, or in more formal documents such as press releases. Consequently, scholars can use content analysis to capture and make sense of words, phrases, and language used by individuals and organizations in a broad variety of narrative texts (McKenny et al., 2012). Information gleaned from content analysis can be used as a standalone source, or it can be used to increase the accuracy of research findings by triangulating it with other data sources. For example, scholars could use content analysis to build on previous research comparing private and public statements in corporate communications (cf., Fiol, 1995).

We focus on one particular content analytic technique: Computer-aided text analysis (CATA). This approach uses any number of available software packages to assess rhetorical content systematically and objectively (Short et al., 2018). The key advantages of CATA are driven by its ability to process large quantities of data, consistently implement a predetermined coding scheme, and evaluate texts in a manner that constitutes unobtrusive measurement (Short et al., 2018; Short & Palmer, 2008). More than a decade ago, scholars reviewing content analysis in organizational studies noted relatively sparse use of this approach (Duriau et al., 2007). Since that time, advancement in empirical techniques and the availability of commercial software have led CATA to be more affordable, practical, and accepted in organizational studies. Indeed, several studies have applied this approach to family business (e.g., McKenny et al., 2012; Moss et al., 2014; Payne et al., 2011; Zachary et al., 2011b).

Data analysis using CATA is possible with either primary data, such as interview reports or open-ended surveys, and/or secondary data, such as annual reports, proxy statements, shareholder letters, 'About Us' pages and other online content, or press releases (Duriau et al., 2007; Short & Payne, 2020). Given the challenges and limitations related to primary data collection and measurement, such as the potential for recall or nonresponse bias (Rutherford & Phillips, Chapter 14 in this book) and difficulty to capture cognition-related constructs, family business researchers commonly utilize secondary data (Short & Payne, 2020). In particular, archival databases and publicly accessible sources such as social media (e.g., Twitter, Facebook, or Twitch) or crowdfunding platforms (e.g., Kickstarter or Kiva) allow researchers to leverage large sample sizes at a relatively low cost, with the added potential to engage in replication (Gomez-Mejia et al., 2011).

Our work presents a brief tutorial of key steps and considerations when using CATA in family business studies. We provide an overview of CATA, along with step-by-step suggestions for choosing appropriate narratives, measuring constructs to ensure validity and reliability, and creating research designs that maximize knowledge for family business scholars. We apply our approach using the construct of humility (Tangney, 2002; Weidman et al., 2018) and leverage text from annual shareholder letters of family firms in the S&P 500 (e.g., Anglin et al., 2017; Zachary et al., 2011b). We conclude by identifying future opportunities for the use of CATA in family business research and considerations for authors and review team members when encountering CATA.

## OVERVIEW OF CATA

Family business researchers can leverage the power of CATA using both inductive and deductive research methodologies. Application of a deductive approach typically involves using existing or newly developed *dictionaries,* or word lists associated with theoretical constructs, to quantitatively analyze the salience of each construct in a sample of narratives (Short et al., 2018). This 'bag-of-words' approach to CATA is based on the notion that the frequency of certain words or phrases used in a narrative is indicative of their relative importance. For example, Short and colleagues (2009) discovered that differences exist between family and non-family firms with respect to entrepreneurial orientation, because family firms use fewer words in CEO letters that refer to the entrepreneurial orientation dimensions of autonomy, proactiveness, and risk taking.

A growing number of statistical packages can be used to analyze text. For example, LIWC includes several dictionaries validated from the perspective of psychology (Pennebaker et al., 2015), while DICTION focuses on dictionaries drawn from political science (cf., Short & Palmer, 2008). Each of these software packages includes built-in dictionaries that can be used to process texts. For example, family business researchers can leverage the existing *family* dictionary included in LIWC to identify the extent to which family firms identify as such in their 'About Us' pages. The dictionary captures words that are directly related to aspects of family, such as 'family', 'relatives', or 'paternal', and it has been used by researchers in family business to provide evidence of the representativeness of their sample (Anglin et al., 2017). LIWC contains over 90 psychological and grammar-related dictionaries in several languages, such as positive and negative affect, filler words, or analytical thinking, which researchers have used to study psychological phenomena (Pennebaker et al., 2015). Developed to study political rhetoric, DICTION offers similar features as LIWC, with 31 predefined dictionaries used to create five master variables—certainty, optimism, activity, realism, and commonality. DICTION also includes a series of *metrics*, or calculated variables, that reflect patterns found in a text rather than counts of words from a dictionary (Short et al., 2018). CAT Scanner, a free CATA tool designed by Aaron F. McKenny and Jeremy C. Short, can also be used for dictionary-based analysis. CAT Scanner additionally helps facilitate several potentially challenging processes surrounding CATA, such as the removal of special characters that obscure analysis by causing words to be recognized as distinct text, or generating a list of words frequently used within a text sample to ensure the content validity of new dictionaries.

Researchers using an inductive approach to content analysis can also use CATA to analyze and interpret organizational narratives to develop and refine theoretical frameworks. Analyzing interviews collected during case studies (Salvato & Corbetta, Chapter 10 in this book), for example, presents a practical way to use a qualitative approach to inductively generate theory about family business (Kammerlander & Diaz-Moriana, Chapter 9 in this book; Trudell et al., Chapter 8 in this book). Researchers following the inductive method commonly use packages such as ATLAS.ti or NVivo. Although both packages can replicate the dictionary-based CATA approach, they are particularly well suited for manual coding and allow users to organize, locate, code, and annotate findings. Other options for analyzing data using CATA include programming languages such as R, Python, or Java, including the application of topic modeling and machine learning (e.g., Choudhury et al., 2021).

## SELECTING NARRATIVES FOR CATA IN FAMILY BUSINESS

Scholars using content analysis often begin by identifying a particular organizational narrative to analyze and then selecting a useful sampling frame. These decisions are important as they affect the external validity of research findings across different populations and potentially allow for comparisons to previous research efforts. In deciding which documents to analyze, researchers should initially assess if the construct of interest can reasonably be expected to be detected in a narrative by informally examining potential study texts. Their decision, therefore, should be informed by a qualitative perspective regarding examining texts carefully before a study is begun to explore if the phenomena or construct of interests seems to be apparent in existing texts; at the same time, researchers should also begin projects with a theoretical explanation of why a particular narrative presents an adequate fit for the research question of interest (Short et al., 2010).

Researchers using content analysis should also consider the level of analysis at which they are conducting their study (cf., McKenny et al., 2013). Statements made by CEOs of public companies, for example, have been used to assess CEO personality (see, for example, Harrison et al., 2019). The outcome of such measurements can be used to understand either the private behavior of the CEO, such as personal donations to political parties, or to extrapolate firm-level decisions in the spirit of Upper Echelons theory (e.g., Carr et al., 2021). In family business research, the unit of analysis may also be the family itself. Because families are nested within their businesses yet do not constitute the whole business, the narratives used to examine a family's psychometric tendencies should potentially be seen as originating from the families themselves, rather than from the organization or an individual.

The choice of sampling frame represents a second crucial decision to ensure that the conclusions of the current research efforts can be generalized to other contexts (Short et al., 2002). The S&P 500 is a commonly chosen sampling frame for family business research (e.g., Anglin et al., 2017; Brigham et al., 2014). The S&P 500 is attractive to researchers because it features publicly traded companies that are required to release organizational narratives such as annual reports and shareholder letters that offer insights into firm values, beliefs, identity, and decision-making processes (Short et al., 2009).

Although the S&P 500 is a popular sampling frame due to its accessibility and the large impact factor of the firms it includes, other sampling frames used in family research include firms from the S&P 600 Growth index (Brigham et al., 2014), firms undergoing initial public offerings on the NASDAQ and NYSE during a specific timeframe (Chandler et al., 2019), or Australian private family firms (McKenny et al., 2012). Content analysis may be a particularly useful method to study private family firms because archival data originating from such firms is usually scarce. Because owners of private firms have greater latitude in setting company objectives, their firms constitute a distinct population of interest to which conclusions gleaned from other samples may not be applicable (Carney et al., 2015). Researchers should provide a convincing, theory-driven explanation justifying their sampling decision (Short et al., 2002), keeping in mind that allowing comparisons to other similar sampling frames provides an opportunity to replicate data and improve the generalizability of research findings (Tsang & Kwan, 1999).

For illustrative purposes, we collected three years of shareholder letters published between the years 2010 and 2012 from our sampling frame of S&P 500 firms. We use data from our previous research to identify 70 family firms that were listed in the S&P 500 index and had data available for all three years (Anglin et al., 2017). Researchers may increase the stability of their measure, and thereby decrease the likelihood of measurement error variance (McKenny et al., 2018), by collecting a longitudinal dataset and averaging the measures and study variables over a designated period of time (e.g., Short et al., 2009). Datasets spanning longer time periods may also allow for an examination of changes in family business measures over time (e.g., Allison et al., 2014; Anglin et al., 2017).

To provide an exemplar of a construct that could be brought to the family business literature we examine the usage of humility-related narratives of family firms (Table 11.1 summarizes the steps and recommendations described in this chapter). Personality characteristics exert a sizeable influence on business decisions of top managers (e.g., Colbert et al., 2014). Psychologists have labeled humility as one of the most influential personality traits (Tangney, 2002), and recent studies have focused on understanding the role humility plays in organizational success (e.g., Petrenko et al., 2019).

*Table 11.1        Recommended CATA steps*

| Step | Recommendation | Examples |
| --- | --- | --- |
| Select a Construct of Interest | Find an existing, validated measure (e.g., entrepreneurial orientation) or create and validate a new measure (for detailed guidance on construct validation, see Short et al., 2010) | Psychological capital, market orientation, narcissism, humility |
| Select a Sampling Frame | Select a sampling frame that presents an adequate fit with the research question and population of interest | S&P 500, all privately held family firms in a country or area |
| Select a Narrative | Choose a narrative with a reasonable chance of including construct of interest to ensure validity | Interview transcripts, 'About Us' sections of company websites, shareholder correspondence |
| Select a Sample | Identify family firms (e.g., firms with 10% or more family-ownership stake), and use the *family* dictionary in LIWC to measure the usage of family-related terms in the 'About Us' pages on websites | Compare family firms to non-family firms belonging to the S&P 500 within a specific timeframe |
| Analyze Data | Choose software package based on the dictionaries it includes, intended usage, and availability Process narratives to obtain measurements of each construct, standardize to a 'per word' or 'per 100 words' metric | DICTION, LIWC, CAT Scanner, NVivo |
| Check Measurement Reliability | Improve measurement reliability by addressing transient error, specific factor error, and algorithm error | Assess stability of measure over time by collecting a longitudinal dataset and averaging measure across time Compare measures to results collected from a different sampling frame Compare to a manually coded subsample (of about 10% of sample or 100 narratives, whichever is lower) Analyze narratives in a second software package |
| Assess Content Validity | Check discriminant validity by comparing measure to other related constructs | Compare measure to existing measures of related constructs (e.g., narcissism or modesty when measuring humility) |

# ANALYZING DATA USING CATA

Two common research designs have been used to leverage CATA in family business research. One approach provides a comparison between family firms and non-family firms (Zachary et al., 2011b). More recently, family business scholars have called for more research examining variance within different family firms (Sharma et al., 2014). In line with this call, Allison and colleagues (2014) use an established CATA measure of organizational ambidexterity (Uotila et al., 2009) to examine variance in ambidexterity over time.

Deductive approaches to CATA utilize validated dictionaries to measure constructs of interest. Examples of constructs used by family researchers include market orientation (Zachary et al., 2011b), family involvement (Chandler et al., 2019), or long-term orientation (Brigham et al., 2014). Scholars traditionally use previously developed surveys or definitions to generate dictionaries associated with constructs of interests (Nunnally & Bernstein, 1994). Short and colleagues (2010) demonstrate the development of entrepreneurial orientation using a deductive process. Relying on the five dimensions stemming from an established definition of entrepreneurial orientation by Lumpkin and Dess (1996), the authors first develop exhaustive lists of words that capture each dimension. Their word lists for each dimension are generally mutually exclusive, but include the original words as well as synonyms found in *The Synonym Finder* (Rodale, 1978). In the next step, the lists are validated by multiple raters through a multistep process of matching the words with the theoretical definition of entrepreneurial orientation, until an acceptable interrater reliability is calculated using Holsti's method (Holsti, 1969).

One issue that family scholars may encounter is construct dimensionality, or the association of measurement to a single construct (Nunnally & Bernstein, 1994). For example, although humility has historically been conceptualized as a unidimensional construct (e.g., Petrenko et al., 2019), Weidman and colleagues (2018) created two separate word lists—each belonging to a potentially discrete dimension of humility—as part of an effort to examine the psychological underpinnings of humility. The word lists include words that were classified by experts as being characteristic of appreciative humility, such as 'collaborative', 'modest', and 'open-minded', as well as words relating to self-abasing humility, such as 'apologetic', 'self-critical', and 'remorseful'. Scholars using newly generated or unvalidated word lists must, therefore, make a theory-based assessment regarding whether measures of each dimension should be used separately or added together, as well as assess construct dimensionality by visually comparing the correlation matrix of the multiple word lists (Short et al., 2010).

For our illustrative analysis we relied on a single word list without phrases (cf. Petrenko et al., 2019). Further research should validate the humility measure using previously established word list validation techniques (Short et al., 2010). For example, Weidman and colleagues' (2018) conceptualization of humility also included short phrases, such as 'not having an ego' or 'valuing others' virtues'. Although DICTION, CAT Scanner, and LIWC can handle short phrases, NVivo's capacity to examine larger phrases may be better suited for word lists where phrases are predominant.

We used CAT Scanner to measure humility-related rhetoric found in shareholder letters. CAT Scanner analyzes the frequency with which S&P 500 firms use words from the humility dictionary developed by Weidman and colleagues (2018). A common concern in research utilizing CATA is that the length of texts used may vary significantly, potentially resulting in longer texts having higher CATA scores than lower texts (Short et al., 2018). Researchers often control for the length of the document by dividing each variable by the total number of words (some software packages automatically standardize their measures, so be sure to check the associated user manual). In our sample, for instance, family firms used between 0.17 and 1.15 words related to humility per each 100 words (see Table 11.2 for examples of how such words are used in text), with an average of 0.53 words. A one-sample $t$ test compared to a test statistic of zero (which would suggest that firms did not use humility-related language) indicated that humility language existed within shareholder letters originating within our subset of family firms ($t = 23.31$, $p < .001$). Future research could use this approach to examine substantive research questions related to uncovering if differences exist between family firms and non-family firms in their usage of humble rhetoric.

CATA provides significant advantages over other measurement techniques with respect to internal, construct, and external validity. Researchers must be mindful, however, of how to identify and minimize potential measurement error (McKenny et al., 2018). For instance, we averaged three years of available data to minimize transient error (error resulting from fluctuations in psychological processes over time) to obtain a more reliable measure of firm humility (McKenny et al., 2018). Algorithm error (error that exists due to differences in software estimation approaches) can be assessed by using multiple software packages to measure the same variable and calculating Krippendorff's alpha interrater agreement estimate (Krippendorff, 2018). Finally, manual content analysis of a portion of the computer-analyzed text provides researchers with a parallel forms reliability check. Because dictionary-based CATA is sensitive to context, manual coding of a subset of at least 10 percent of the sampled texts to obtain stable estimates provides researchers with a point of comparison for their CATA findings (McKenny et al., 2018).

## OPPORTUNITIES FOR FUTURE RESEARCH

Ample opportunities exist for family business researchers to apply content-analytic techniques to build knowledge about how family firms operate and differ from non-family businesses. Sources originating directly

*Table 11.2      Examples of humility language in family firms*

| Humility-related Words from Weidman et al. (2018) | Examples from Shareholder Letters |
|---|---|
| Grateful | 'I am proud and **grateful** for the commitment of our employees worldwide...' |
| Open | 'We cultivate a work environment that is **open** and allows good ideas to flourish.' |
| Mutual; collaborative | '...collegially and with **mutual** respect, in a spirit of **collaboration**...' |
| Compassionate; respectful | '...we value integrity, **compassion**, **respect** for individuals and relationships...' |
| Understanding | '[Our company] **understands** that the health of small business is key...' |
| Dialogue | '...we hosted screenings at colleges and universities across the country to engage students in the **dialogue**.' |
| Aware | '... to raise **awareness** of and identify solutions to common challenges.' |

from individuals, such as CEOs, can also be analyzed using CATA, and may provide a fruitful avenue for future research. Although shareholder letters from the CEO have been used by scholars for decades, family business scholars may examine statements by key representatives of family businesses on social media such as Twitter (e.g., Grafström & Falkman, 2017), or online streaming or other video-mediated communication such as recorded speeches or other social media such as Facebook or Twitch (e.g., Woodcock & Johnson, 2019) (see Table 11.3 for suggestions of future research applications of CATA to family business).

Recently, researchers have also called for the need to investigate the microfoundations of family business where study of actions and relationships at a lower level of analysis helps explain macro-level phenomena (e.g., De Massis & Foss, 2018). Such calls may inspire family business researchers to embrace CATA to examine the cognition of individuals where the family itself is considered as the key level of analysis. Further, family business scholars can use combinations of narratives, such as emails from all family members as a collective, as compared to emails from individual family members, to investigate the dynamics between firms, the families who own them, and individual actors such as outside CEOs or other members of the top management team. Scholars have noted that movies often mimic organizational phenomena (Zachary et al., 2011a), and content analysis could examine how family dynamics are portrayed in popular films that feature family business such as *The Godfather*, *Knives Out*, and *Yellowstone*.

*Table 11.3*     *Future research opportunities using CATA in family business*

| Topic | Potential Text | Research Question | Description |
|---|---|---|---|
| Gendered language (Pietraszkiewicz et al., 2019) | Podcast transcripts of interviews with family firm executives | Do family firm executives use more communal language than their non-family counterparts? | Agentic characteristics tend to be preferred in leaders (Koenig et al., 2011), but family firms may be more open to communal leadership. This preference may manifest in executives using more communal language, which includes softer words such as 'helpful', 'team-player', or 'collaboration', rather than agentic language, which includes words like 'assertive' or 'dominant'. |
| Corporate heritage (Balmer & Burghausen, 2015) | Advertising materials | Does family legacy communicated through advertising materials improve firm performance? | Family firms may benefit from communicating their heritage, such as their founding story, to increase their legitimacy with customers and other stakeholders. |
| Political ideology (Jones et al., 2018) | Twitter | Are family firm executives more likely to express their political ideology on social media than non-family firm executives? | Executives whose family owns the firm they manage may be less concerned with jeopardizing their employment and, as a result, share their political beliefs more freely with the public. |
| Organizational time horizon (DesJardine & Bansal, 2019) | Shareholder letters | Do family firms exhibit greater long-term orientation than non-family firms? | Organizations often default to focusing on short-term time horizons, such as profit maximization. Family firms, however, may be more likely to emphasize long-term gains due to their interest in value creation over extended time periods. |
| Humility (Weidman et al., 2018) | Transcripts of earnings calls | Do CEOs use more humble rhetoric following unmet analyst expectations? | CEO humility tempers stock market analyst expectation (Petrenko et al., 2019), but CEOs may also exhibit more humility after failing to meet their performance targets to influence the reaction of the stock market. |

| Topic | Potential Text | Research Question | Description |
|---|---|---|---|
| CEO dominance (Brown & Sarma, 2007) | Transcripts of recorded board meetings | Do family CEOs who use dominating language during board meetings get better approval rates for their proposals? | CEOs who own large amounts of company shares have structural power over their boards (e.g., Shen, 2003) which may reflect in boardroom dynamics, such as the frequency with which the CEO speaks or the language they employ. Dominating the board may increase the likelihood of favorable outcomes for CEOs. |
| Management of historical rhetoric (Suddaby et al., 2020) | 'About Us' sections of websites | Do family firms manage their historical narratives (i.e., as objective past, as interpretive rhetoric, or as imaginative future-perfect thinking) differently from non-family firms? | Firms differ in how they describe their history to stakeholders, and family firms may be more likely to exhibit a particular narrative style as compared to non-family firms. |
| Machine learning for pattern recognition (Choudhury et al., 2021) | Shareholder letters | Do the narrative patterns of CEOs of family firms follow more closely the patterns of other family firms or their industry and sector competitors? | Isomorphic pressures contribute to the proliferation of certain managerial practices through peer groups and board interlocks (e.g., Krause et al., 2019), but it is unknown whether CEOs of family firms are more likely to imitate other family firms or their direct competitors. |
| CEO cognitive complexity (Graf-Vlachy et al., 2020) | Transcribed CEO speeches | Do insider CEOs of family firms possess an advantage at the beginning of their tenure by having greater cognitive complexity than outsiders? | Longer-tenured CEOs engage in more complex thinking as a result of their role-specific knowledge or expertise. However, family firm insiders may already possess firm-specific information that would increase their cognitive complexity and improve their understanding of company strategy at the beginning of their tenure as CEOs. |

Family business researchers may continue to draw from other research domains such as entrepreneurship, strategic management, or organizational behavior to identify constructs relevant to family business. For instance, rhetoric related to individual characteristics of writers, such as narcissism or the Big Five characteristics (Anglin et al., 2018; Harrison et al., 2019), cognitive complexity (Graf-Vlachy et al., 2020), or the political ideology of top executives (Gupta et al., 2020) could answer research questions about the relationship of these constructs with firm performance, as well as identify their prevalence among family business firms. Scholars have recently found that standing out from the crowd in terms of narrative content is advantageous for microfinance campaigns led by men but often associated with worse performance for women-led campaigns (Williamson et al., 2021); such findings might provide a basis for scholars seeking to explore a deeper knowledge of family-based insights based on the roles of language and gender as they relate to critical family firm outcomes.

## CONCLUSION

CATA is an increasingly popular method for capturing individual and organizational constructs with noted advantages over methods such as surveys or interviews allowing scholars to more confidently measure difficult-to-capture cognition-based constructs from large samples. Editors and reviewers should be aware of the potential benefits of applying CATA methodologies to research questions in the field of family business, despite—or perhaps because of—its limited usage in the field to date. They should also encourage scholars to help build trust in the method by approaching their research designs carefully and systematically, utilizing recent advancements in the field to improve the reliability of their results.

## REFERENCES

Allison, T. H., McKenny, A. F., & Short, J. C. (2014). Integrating time into family business research: Using random coefficient modeling to examine temporal influences on family firm ambidexterity. *Family Business Review, 27*(1), 20–34.

Anglin, A. H., Reid, S. W., Short, J. C., Zachary, M. A., & Rutherford, M. W. (2017). An archival approach to measuring family influence: An organizational identity perspective. *Family Business Review, 30*(1), 19–36.

Anglin, A. H., Wolfe, M. T., Short, J. C., McKenny, A. F., & Pidduck, R. J. (2018). Narcissistic rhetoric and crowdfunding performance: A social role theory perspective. *Journal of Business Venturing, 33*(6), 780–812.

Balmer, J. M., & Burghausen, M. (2015). Explicating corporate heritage, corporate heritage brands and organisational heritage. *Journal of Brand Management, 22*(5), 364–384.

Bertschi-Michel, A., Kammerlander, N., & Strike, V. M. (2020). Unearthing and alleviating emotions in family business successions. *Entrepreneurship Theory and Practice, 44*(1), 81–108.

Bika, Z., Rosa, P., & Karakas, F. (2019). Multilayered socialization processes in transgenerational family firms. *Family Business Review, 32*(3), 233–258.

Brigham, K. H., Lumpkin, G. T., Payne, G. T., & Zachary, M. A. (2014). Researching long-term orientation: A validation study and recommendations for future research. *Family Business Review, 27*(1), 72–88.

Brown, R., & Sarma, N. (2007). CEO overconfidence, CEO dominance and corporate acquisitions. *Journal of Economics and Business, 59*(5), 358–379.

Carney, M., Van Essen, M., Gedajlovic, E. R., & Heugens, P. P. (2015). What do we know about private family firms? A meta-analytical review. *Entrepreneurship Theory and Practice, 39*(3), 513–544.

Carr, J. C., Vardaman, J. M., Marler, L. E., McLarty, B. D., & Blettner, D. (2021). Psychological antecedents of decision comprehensiveness and their relationship to decision quality and performance in family firms: An upper echelons perspective. *Family Business Review, 34*(1), 33–47.

Chandler, J. A., Payne, G. T., Moore, C., & Brigham, K. H. (2019). Family involvement signals in initial public offerings. *Journal of Family Business Strategy, 10*(1), 8–16.

Choudhury, P., Allen, R. T., & Endres, M. G. (2021). Machine learning for pattern discovery in management research. *Strategic Management Journal, 42*(1), 30–57.

Colbert, A. E., Barrick, M. R., & Bradley, B. H. (2014). Personality and leadership composition in top management teams: Implications for organizational effectiveness. *Personnel Psychology, 67*(2), 351–387.

De Massis, A., & Foss, N. J. (2018). Advancing family business research: The promise of microfoundations. *Family Business Review, 31*(4), 386–396.

DesJardine, M., & Bansal, P. (2019). One step forward, two steps back: How negative external evaluations can shorten organizational time horizons. *Organization Science, 30*(4), 761–780.

Duriau, V. J., Reger, R. K., & Pfarrer, M. D. (2007). A content analysis of the content analysis literature in organization studies: Research themes, data sources, and methodological refinements. *Organizational Research Methods, 10*(1), 5–34. https://doi.org/10.1177/1094428106289252

Fiol, C. M. (1995). Corporate communications: Comparing executives' private and public statements. *Academy of Management Journal, 38*, 522–536.

Gomez-Mejia, L. R., Cruz, C., Berrone, P., & De Castro, J. (2011). The bind that ties: Socioemotional wealth preservation in family firms. *Academy of Management Annals, 5*(1), 653–707.

Graf-Vlachy, L., Bundy, J., & Hambrick, D. C. (2020). Effects of an advancing tenure on CEO cognitive complexity. *Organization Science, 31*(4), 936–959.

Grafström, M., & Falkman, L. L. (2017). Everyday narratives: CEO rhetoric on Twitter. *Journal of Organizational Change Management, 30*(3), 312–322.

Gupta, A., Fung, A., & Murphy, C. (2020). Out of character: CEO political ideology, peer influence, and adoption of CSR executive position by Fortune 500 firms. *Strategic Management Journal, 42*(3), 529–557.

Harrison, J. S., Thurgood, G. R., Boivie, S., & Pfarrer, M. D. (2019). Measuring CEO personality: Developing, validating, and testing a linguistic tool. *Strategic Management Journal, 40*(8), 1316–1330.

Holsti, O. R. (1969). *Content analysis for the social sciences and humanities.* Addison-Wesley.

Jones, K. L., Noorbaloochi, S., Jost, J. T., Bonneau, R., Nagler, J., & Tucker, J. A. (2018). Liberal and conservative values: What we can learn from congressional tweets. *Political Psychology, 39*(2), 423–443.

Koenig, A. M., Eagly, A. H., Mitchell, A. A., & Ristikari, T. (2011). Are leader stereotypes masculine? A meta-analysis of three research paradigms. *Psychological Bulletin, 137*(4), 616–642.

Krause, R., Wu, Z., Bruton, G. D., & Carter, S. M. (2019). The coercive isomorphism ripple effect: An investigation of nonprofit interlocks on corporate boards. *Academy of Management Journal, 62*(1), 283–308.

Krippendorff, K. (2018). *Content analysis: An introduction to its methodology.* Sage.

Lumpkin, G. T., & Dess, G. G. (1996). Clarifying the entrepreneurial orientation construct and linking it to performance. *Academy of Management Review, 21*(1), 135–172.

McKenny, A. F., Aguinis, H., Short, J. C., & Anglin, A. H. (2018). What doesn't get measured does exist: Improving the accuracy of computer-aided text analysis. *Journal of Management, 44*(7), 2909–2933.

McKenny, A. F., Short, J. C., & Payne, G. T. (2013). Using computer-aided text analysis to elevate constructs: An illustration using psychological capital. *Organizational Research Methods, 16*(1), 152–184.

McKenny, A. F., Short, J. C., Zachary, M. A., & Payne, G. T. (2012). Assessing espoused goals in private family firms using content analysis. *Family Business Review, 25*(3), 298–317.

Moss, T. W., Payne, G. T., & Moore, C. B. (2014). Strategic consistency of exploration and exploitation in family businesses. *Family Business Review, 27*(1), 51–71.

Nunnally, J. C., & Bernstein, I. H. (1994). *Psychometric theory* (3rd edn). McGraw-Hill.

Payne, G. T., Brigham, K. H., Broberg, J. C., Moss, T. W., & Short, J. C. (2011). Organizational virtue orientation and family firms. *Business Ethics Quarterly, 21*(2), 257–285.

Pennebaker, J. W., Boyd, R. L., Jordan, K., & Blackburn, K. (2015). *The development and psychometric properties of LIWC2015.* University of Texas at Austin.

Petrenko, O. V., Aime, F., Recendes, T., & Chandler, J. A. (2019). The case for humble expectations: CEO humility and market performance. *Strategic Management Journal, 40*(12), 1938–1964.

Pietraszkiewicz, A., Formanowicz, M., Gustafsson Sendén, M., Boyd, R. L., Sikström, S., & Sczesny, S. (2019). The big two dictionaries: Capturing agency and communion in natural language. *European Journal of Social Psychology, 49*(5), 871–887.

Rau, S. B., Schneider-Siebke, V., & Günther, C. (2019). Family firm values explaining family firm heterogeneity. *Family Business Review, 32*(2), 195–215.

Rodale, J. I. (1978). *The synonym finder.* Rodale.

Sharma, P., Salvato, C., & Reay, T. (2014). Temporal dimensions of family enterprise research. *Family Business Review, 27*(1), 10–19.

Shen, W. (2003). The dynamics of the CEO–board relationship: An evolutionary perspective. *Academy of Management Review, 28*(3), 466–476.

Short, J. C., & Palmer, T. B. (2008). The application of DICTION to content analysis research in strategic management. *Organizational Research Methods, 11*(4), 727–752.

Short, J. C., & Payne, G. T. (2020). In their own words: A call for increased use of organizational narratives in family business research. *Family Business Review, 33*(4), 342–350.

Short, J. C., Broberg, J. C., Cogliser, C. C., & Brigham, K. H. (2010). Construct validation using computer-aided text analysis (CATA): An illustration using entrepreneurial orientation. *Organizational Research Methods, 13*(2), 320–347.

Short, J. C., Ketchen Jr, D. J., & Palmer, T. B. (2002). The role of sampling in strategic management research on performance: A two-study analysis. *Journal of Management, 28*(3), 363–385.

Short, J. C., McKenny, A. F., & Reid, S. W. (2018). More than words? Computer-aided text analysis in organizational behavior and psychology research. *Annual Review of Organizational Psychology and Organizational Behavior, 5*, 415–435.

Short, J. C., Payne, G. T., Brigham, K. H., Lumpkin, G., & Broberg, J. C. (2009). Family firms and entrepreneurial orientation in publicly traded firms: A comparative analysis of the S&P 500. *Family Business Review, 22*(1), 9–24.

Suddaby, R., Coraiola, D., Harvey, C., & Foster, W. (2020). History and the micro-foundations of dynamic capabilities. *Strategic Management Journal, 41*(3), 530–556.

Tangney, J. P. (2002). Humility. In C. R. Snyder & S. J. Lopez (Eds.), *Handbook of positive psychology* (pp. 411–419). Oxford University Press.

Tsang, E. W., & Kwan, K.-M. (1999). Replication and theory development in organizational science: A critical realist perspective. *Academy of Management Review, 24*(4), 759–780.

Uotila, J., Maula, M., Keil, T., & Zahra, S. A. (2009). Exploration, exploitation, and financial performance: Analysis of S&P 500 corporations. *Strategic Management Journal, 30*(2), 221–231.

Weidman, A. C., Cheng, J. T., & Tracy, J. L. (2018). The psychological structure of humility. *Journal of Personality and Social Psychology, 114*(1), 153–178.

Williamson, A. J., Short, J. C., & Wolfe, M. T. (2021). Standing out in crowdfunded microfinance: A topic modeling approach examining campaign distinctiveness and prosocial performance. *Journal of Business Venturing Insights, 16.* https://doi.org/10.1016/j.jbvi.2021.e00261

Woodcock, J., & Johnson, M. R. (2019). Live streamers on Twitch.tv as social media influencers: Chances and challenges for strategic communication. *International Journal of Strategic Communication, 13*(4), 321–335.

Zachary, M. A., McKenny, A. F., Short, J. C., & Ketchen, D. J. (2011a). Strategy in motion: Using motion pictures to illustrate strategic management concepts. *Business Horizons, 55*, 5–10.

Zachary, M. A., McKenny, A. F., Short, J. C., & Payne, G. T. (2011b). Family business and market orientation: Construct validation and comparative analysis. *Family Business Review, 24*(3), 233–251.

# PART III

# Quantitative challenges and solutions

# 12. Advancing the study of family firms through the use of experimental designs

## Isabel C. Botero and Tomasz A. Fediuk

## INTRODUCTION

Experiments are a powerful research tool for determining causality (Highhouse, 2009), and drawing causal inferences (i.e., determine cause and effect, identifying active ingredients of a relationship, and ruling out alternative explanations; Cook & Campbell, 1979; Grant & Wall, 2009). The experimental method is an invaluable resource for building, refining, accumulating, and applying knowledge about organizational life into theories (Grant & Wall, 2009). However, many organizational scholars view experiments as contrived, irrelevant, and even misleading (Highhouse, 2009). These perceptions are tied to the belief that experiments result in low levels of external validity, which prevents generalization across populations, settings, and variables (Grant & Wall, 2009). On the other side of the argument, researchers like Highhouse (2009, p. 555) suggest that: 'experiments do not need to mirror the external environment for us to generalize inferences across populations, settings, and variables. There is a real danger in confusing ecological validity (generalizing to) with external validity (generalizing across).' These scholars argue that the general purpose of experiments is to test theory and theoretical propositions. Thus, experiments should focus on generalizability at the theoretical level. Independent of the approach taken, experiments provide important information in the theory development process.

Although the use of experimental design in family business research has grown in the last decade (Lude & Prügl, 2021), the use of experimental approaches in family business research is limited. There are multiple reasons for this. One reason may be how the family business field has evolved. Starting with a very practical focus, the family business field initially explored field settings, which make the use of experiments much more complex. Additionally, as the field has evolved, scholars that conduct research in this area commonly come from backgrounds in strategy or entrepreneurship where experimentation is not a common methodological approach. It may also be that the limited use of experimentation is tied to the type of research questions and dependent variables that have been explored in the field so far. Research questions in family business studies tend to focus on internal processes of the business and are more likely to focus on comparisons between family and non-family firms, making the use of experimentation less relevant. Similarly, the primary dependent variables of study (i.e., performance, strategy, social and economic impact, succession, family business roles, family dynamics, and governance) are at the firm or family level (Yu et al., 2012), which makes experimentation much more complex. Thus, up to now, the experimental method has not been frequently utilized.

An important part of gaining legitimacy in the broader academic space is dependent, in part, on the variety and rigor of methodological approaches used when studying topics (Evert et al., 2016). Although previous work highlights the important methodological changes that have occurred within the family business field (Litz et al., 2012; Lude & Prügl, 2021; Reilly & Jones, 2017; Payne et al., 2017; Wilson et al., 2014), these researchers also point out the important gaps in the field's development. The use of experimental design is one of those methodological gaps that needs to be addressed to help this field move forward.

Good experimental work requires researchers to clearly understand the purpose of experiments as well as the different components to consider when designing, collecting data, and writing up experiments. To help family business researchers better understand experiments and incorporate them within their research, this chapter is organized with two goals in mind. First, we examine what constitutes an experiment and the types of questions that lend themselves to be explored using this approach. Second, we outline guidelines and a three-step process to design and publish sound experiments within the family business field.

## WHAT IS AN EXPERIMENT AND WHEN SHOULD WE USE THEM?

Determining causality is at the center of experimental design (Shadish et al., 2002). Relationships are causal when they fulfill three conditions: (1) the cause (X) precedes the effect (Y) in time (i.e., temporal precedence); (2) the cause and effect are related to one another (i.e., covariation); and (3) there are no rival explanations of the observed relation between the cause and effect (i.e., absence of confounds) (Cook & Campbell, 1979). At their core, experiments test causality by determining what happens when you vary the conditions of the cause. In other words, the goal is to find whether one operationalization of

a construct (an independent variable) causes a change in another operationalization of a construct (a dependent variable), while holding all else constant
(Highhouse, 2009).

To illustrate this idea, let's consider the following causal statement: explicitly communicating the family business brand (FBB) (i.e., formal and informal
communication of the family element of firm essence; Binz Astrachan et
al., 2018) is likely to result in positive customer perceptions. To understand
whether this statement is true we would have to show that: (1) The FBB is
communicated before customers develop cognitive associations; (2) when the
FBB is communicated customers will have positive perceptions due to the
exposure to the FBB message; and (3) it is the communicating of the FBB
message that leads to the perceptions – and not other factors, messages, or
pre-existing conditions. The best way to test causal relationships is through an
experiment. In an experiment, the researcher alters some feature of the independent variable (in this case, the communication of the FBB message) and
observes whether the dependent variable (i.e., customer perceptions) is altered
due to the manipulation of the independent variable.

Experiments can be described as exploring effect-based research questions
(i.e., what happens when I do 'x'?). In its broadest sense, experimental designs
involve the manipulation or control of an independent variable, a comparison
between or within groups, and the measurement of a dependent variable
(Shadish et al., 2002). However, there are three different experimental designs.
*Randomized experiments*, also referred to as pure experiments, offer the most
stringent design. In these types of experiments, participants are randomly
assigned to experimental conditions to create groups that are probabilistically
comparable to one another (Shadish et al., 2002). The goal is to remove any
systematic differences or spurious relationships that can alter the observed
outcomes. For instance, the likelihood that one experimental condition is composed of members of a family business while participants in another condition
are all non-family business members is eliminated by chance selection into
experimental conditions. Thus, observed differences that are found can be
attributed to the experimental condition and not some participant characteristic
within the experiment.

*Quasi-experiments* are different from a pure experiment in that they do not
necessitate the random assignment of participants into conditions. Further,
quasi-experiments differ from experiments in that the control/comparison
groups are not equivalent to the treatment group. In these experiments, assignment to conditions is done by the experimenter or through self-selection by
participants. Lacking equivalence across groups, researchers need to be able
to anticipate alternative explanations to what they are studying so that they
can collect either pre-test measures or additional measures to rule out these
alternatives (Shadish et al., 2002).

Finally, in a *natural experiment*, researchers compare naturally existing groups in an environment. In these experiments, the goal is to expose the naturally existing groups to condition(s) and assess the differences between the groups after their exposure within the naturally occurring environment (Shadish et al., 2002). Such experiments are often conducted in applied research. An example of this can be studying the impact that implementing a dividend policy in a business family can have on the commitment of family members toward the family and the business. In this case the experimenter can find a group of business families that are implementing a dividend policy, and others that are not and assess the level of commitment of family members.

Although experiments are very useful, generalizability using this methodology is dependent on the attention that is given to the operationalization of constructs (i.e., in the sense of psychometric validity and domain representativeness) and the planning for data collection (Highhouse, 2009). In the next section we discuss important considerations when designing and conducting experiments.

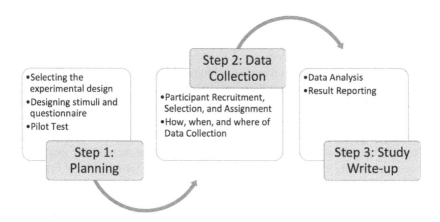

*Figure 12.1     Steps for conducting sound experiments*

## CONSIDERATIONS IN DESIGNING EXPERIMENTS

The success of experimental studies requires researchers to pay close attention to the preparation and planning of the experiment, to the data collection process, and the writing of the manuscript (see Figure 12.1; Aguinis & Bradley, 2014; Grant & Wall, 2009; King et al., 2013). In the following sections, we explain what is included in each of the three steps and outline important considerations for researchers. However, before going down this path, researchers need to be sure there is a good fit between the research question and experimental approach. As we mentioned before, experiments are primarily designed to test causation (i.e., does X cause Y and to what degree). Thus, the research question should be concerned with causal relationships between theoretical constructs.

## Step 1 – Planning

The best way to make sure that an experiment can help answer a research question and generate knowledge that is of publishable quality is to spend time planning what to do and pre-test this approach before the official data collection process. Confidence in experimental results requires that researchers maximize the realism of context, precision of measurement, and generalizability of their results (McGrath, 1981). Thus, the planning stage is crucial. There are several areas that the researcher needs to work on within this step. *First is selecting the experimental design that will be used* (Aguinis & Bradley, 2014; King et al., 2013). Researchers need to select how they want to collect their data. Will they collect data using a randomized experiment, a quasi-experiment, or a natural experiment? The answer to this will depend on the desire and capability of the research team to randomly assign participants to conditions. Random assignment is the approach used to position participants in the different treatment groups within an experiment. The goal is to have treatment and control groups that are like each other in key characteristics to allow comparisons. When random assignment is not possible, the researcher will need to make sure that they identify key factors that will affect the way that individuals behave or react to the treatment condition so that they can use statistical approaches to control for those factors. For example, when conducting experiments about consumer perceptions of family firms, it is important to assess participants' previous experiences with family firms. Random assignment would conceptually randomize these experiences across all experimental conditions. When random assignment to conditions is not possible, the researcher should measure the participant's perceptions of family business before they are exposed to any information about family firms. In this sense, the choice of the experimental design will determine the type of additional information that needs to be collected to explore the researcher's ideas, and the considerations that need to be implemented to ensure realism of the experiment.

Selecting the design also involves determining whether the researcher will collect data using a *within-subjects or between-subjects design.* A within-subject experiment is one in which the participant is exposed to more than one of the experimental conditions (Charness et al., 2012). With these designs the causal estimates are made based on changes observed in participants over time. In a between-subject experiment, each participant is exposed to only one treatment (Charness et al., 2012). Testing causal estimates with between-subject experiments is dependent on having comparable groups. This step is important because it will help the research team determine which validity threats to consider and how they can prepare to address them (see Shadish et al., 2002 for a detailed discussion of validity threats).

A second aspect of the planning process involves *designing the stimuli and measurement tool*. The stimuli represent the information, object, or event that is expected to create differences in participants. A key consideration when designing experimental stimuli is that the researcher needs to make sure that the information provided to participants in each condition differs only in what is manipulated and nothing else. This means that when there are written messages, each stimulus condition needs to be similar in length, content, language, and tone. For example, in their 2017 paper, Kahlert and colleagues are interested in understanding whether information about family ownership and organization size influences attractiveness to a firm. To test their ideas, they exposed participants to the following messages (emphasis provided for our example):

> In the process of looking for a job you came across an employment ad of a company that is seeking applicants in your area of interest and for your preferred region or city. This company is a leading provider for premium consumer products and has been in business over 70 years. In their ad, this company mentions that they are *A FAMILY-OWNED AND OPERATED COMPANY WITH 500 EMPLOYEES* seeking highly motivated individuals with clever ideas who can help the company improve their international position. In their effort to recruit for different entry-level positions, the company has asked the university to inquire who would be interested in attending a presentation at the university to recruit and set up an interview with applicants. (*Family Business – Large Condition*)

> In the process of looking for a job you came across an employment ad of a company that is seeking applicants in your area of interest and for your preferred region or city. This company is a leading provider for premium consumer products and has been in business over 70 years. In their ad, this company mentions that they are *A COMPANY WITH 70 EMPLOYEES* seeking highly motivated individuals with clever ideas who can help the company improve their international position. In their effort to recruit for different entry-level positions, the company has asked the university to inquire who would be interested in attending a presentation at the university to recruit and set up an interview with applicants. (*No family ownership information – small*)

In this example, the only difference between conditions is the information related to family ownership and size. By doing this, the researchers avoid potentially creating differences in responses that are a product of the variance in the stimuli instead of the variance in the independent variables that are tested.

Parallel to designing the stimuli is determining what is going to be assessed and how it will be measured. Measures can be behavioral (i.e., obtained through direct observation) or perceptual (i.e., obtained through question-naire). In either case, the researcher should make sure that they have a clear way to assess their variables of interest and other variables that may influence the behaviors and responses of participants. Determining what additional measures to include is dependent on the type of design and the assessment of potential validity problems. An important consideration when developing the measurement tool is to assess manipulation checks when possible. A manipu-lation check tests whether participants reacted to your stimuli in the way you intended. Too often, the experimental manipulations result in a minimal effect when evaluating the manipulation check, which introduces error into observed statistical effects as well as issues in the interpretation of results.

As researchers design the questionnaire, they should keep in mind any potential ordering effects (i.e., where a preceding question may influence the interpretation of or response to the following questions) and the length of the questionnaire (to avoid fatigue). Additionally, it is important not to forget to collect important demographic information from the sample. Researchers need to make sure that the most important questions are placed earlier in the ques-tionnaire and the less important later. For experiments, capturing the variables studied is more important than demographic information (unless they are part of the hypotheses/research questions). If questionnaire fatigue sets in, it is better to lose demographic information than items that are critical to the testing of hypotheses.

The third step of the planning and design step is to *pilot test your materials with similar audiences.* It is important to make sure that the stimuli and meas-ures are understood by study participants. The best way to assess this is by testing the materials prior to launching the large-scale study. A pilot test can be done by asking a smaller sample of participants to read the stimuli material and assess their understanding of the materials as well as assess the realism of the stimuli scenarios. These first responders will help polish the information because they can answer questions as they go through the process to make sure that they are understanding the variable manipulations in the way that is intended. Following this approach can help researchers modify their stimuli and questionnaire before they put resources into collecting their data. It also helps identify and account for unexpected issues that may arise during the experiment.

Throughout the planning stage the researcher should work on maximizing both internal and external validity to enhance the use of the results for theory development. Once the planning steps are completed, the researcher is ready for data collection.

## Step 2 – Data Collection

The data collection step involves two broad aspects: *specification of the sample* and *collecting data*. Researchers have acknowledged that the quality of the data in any research project is dependent on the respondent (Cavanaugh & Fritzsche, 1985). Respondents need to reflect the population of interest and need to be able to interact with the information that is presented to them (Aiman-Smith et al., 2002; Highhouse, 2009). Sample sizes can be determined by assessing the number of conditions and the power needed to detect differences (see Cohen, 1988 for different approaches to calculate the minimum sample size). The larger the number of included conditions and levels, the larger sample required.

A second consideration in the specification of the sample is ensuring comparability between experimental groups. This is in part determined by the design that the researcher selects. In randomized experiments, this similarity is created through the way that participants are assigned to groups. However, when using other experimental designs, the authors need to make sure that they are measuring the characteristics of the sample. During data analysis, the researcher can determine if there are any substantial differences across conditions based on these characteristics. For example, previous experience with a family business can influence how participants react to a branding message from a family business. Thus, when conducting an experiment, it is advised that researchers assess the previous experience that participants have with family businesses to ensure that the effects observed are due to the stimuli (i.e., message) and not due to previous experiences. In this case if no differences are observed between groups on the participants' experience with family firms, the data analysis can continue as if these were comparable groups. When differences are observed, this variable can be entered as a control variable in the analysis. These additional measures will help the researchers control differences that can influence the dependent variable and understand processes when they do not work in the expected ways.

Data collection is the stage in which planning meets execution. In experimental designs, the researcher needs to consider the setting and timing of the experiment. Variations in the timing and setting of the experiment can influence participants' responses and perceptions, affecting the validity of experiments. For example, if a researcher is interested in understanding the effect of communicating that a firm is family owned on applicant intentions to work for a business, and the data is collected in a time where there is high unemployment, the desirability for work may be driving the intentions of respondents instead of the message communicating whether the business is family owned or not. If data collection takes a longer time-period, changes in the environment (such as economic downturns and perceptions of employment opportunities) may impact subject responses. A useful tip during the data collection stage is to have a diary to take notes of the conditions under which the data are collected and the presence of unique occurrences during this time. These notes can help when there are inconsistencies in the data that may affect the results.

**Step 3 – Study Write-up**

The final stage of an experimental project involves *data analysis* and results *write-up*. Although this chapter is not specifically about data analysis, there are critical points to be made in analyzing and reporting experimental data. It is a common belief that the best way to analyze experimental data is using analysis of variance. However, reporting of this data analysis technique tends to provide insufficient information for follow-up studies and meta-analyses. These studies report unstandardized statistical differences and fail to adequately report effect sizes. Thus, even if conducting analysis of variance, researchers should include basic descriptive statistics (i.e., mean and standard deviation) and zero order correlation tables.

Although analysis of variance can be a useful data analytic approach, there are other ways to analyze experimental data. For example, building on work on message effects from the communication field (i.e., O'Keefe, 2003), some family business researchers (Arijs et al., 2018; Kahlert et al., 2017) use manipulation checks as a continuous independent variable within a regression model to analyze their data. Given that most research hypotheses are interested in the participants post-manipulation psychological state instead of the experimental condition, using the manipulation check is appropriate to explore differences in the data analysis.

The write-up of the methodology and results of an experiment is one of the most important parts of the process of sharing the findings with the research community. Researchers should discuss as much information as possible to help the reader understand what was done and to facilitate the replication of the work. Table 12.1 provides a list of the sub-sections that need to be considered in the write-up phase. From our experiences as editors and authors, clarity in the methodology and data analysis is essential when publishing experimental work.

*Table 12.1     Components of the methodology section in experimental designs*

| Area | Content |
| --- | --- |
| **Methodology** | |
| Sample | This section should provide information about the demographics of the sample. It should include general demographics (age, sex, education), and specific areas that are of relevance in the experimental context. |
| Design | This section summarizes all the design choices made by the researchers including type of experimental design and clarity regarding between or within structure. |
| Procedure | This section describes all the steps that were followed to collect the data. |
| Stimuli | This section explains the factors that were manipulated and how they were manipulated. It often provides an example for the reader. |
| Measurement | This section outlines the variables that were measured and how they were measured. |
| Measurement Model | This section presents the results of the factors' structure of the measures of the study. |
| Common Method Bias | In cases where all the data is collected from the respondents, this section presents the results of common bias tests. |
| **Results** | |
| Descriptives & Correlations | The first part of the results should always include reference to the descriptives and bi-variate correlation table. |
| Manipulation Checks | This section presents the results to test whether the inductions from the experiments worked in anticipated ways. |
| Hypotheses Testing | The final part of the results section is explaining how data was analyzed and how hypotheses were tested, including its results. |

# BUILDING THE FUTURE OF EXPERIMENTAL RESEARCH IN FAMILY FIRMS

As we mentioned at the opening of the chapter, there is not a lot of research that uses an experimental methodology in the family business field. Part of the reason for this is that most of the interest in the family business field has been dedicated to the exploration of topics that do not lend themselves easily to be explored using an experimental design. As we move toward an exploration of perception and individual-level behaviors, we believe that experimentation will gain popularity as a methodology to use in the field. An example of this is the work of family business branding. This is one of the few areas now that relies on experimental methodology for most of its work. Thus, as researchers in the field become more interested in external stakeholders, their perceptions/behaviors (i.e., purchase intention, supportive behaviors, punitive

*Table 12.2*     *Illustrative family business research questions that could be addressed using experimental designs*

| Research Area | Sample Questions to Address with Experiments |
| --- | --- |
| Branding | What are the negative effects of communicating your family brand? |
| Crisis | Does emphasizing the family business nature impact the way that crisis responses are received by an audience? |
| | Are we more likely to believe crisis responses that come from a family business? |
| | Are we more likely to forgive a family business after a crisis? |
| Human Resources | *Internal HR* – What effects does the implementation of family favoring policies have on perceptions of justice of non-family employees? |
| | *External HR* – Does communicating that a firm is family owned affect intentions to work of applicants? |
| Marketing | What is the effect of communicating the family brand on intention to buy? |
| | What are the added effects (i.e., above communicating that you are family owned) of other factors such as locally owned on intentions to buy? |
| Next Generation | Does having previous experience working inside the family firm affect the perceptions of legitimacy of next generation members? |
| | Does having outside work experience make a next generation more credible in the eyes of non-family employees? |
| Governance | What is the effect of having a family constitution on the conflict levels within a business family? |
| | What is the effect of having a board of advisors on the strategic decisions of a family firm? |
| Investing | Does being family owned affect the willingness to invest or buy stock of consumers? |

behaviors, willingness to work, willingness to invest), and the effects of these perceptions/behaviors we believe the use of experimental research will grow. Similarly, as researchers become interested in the implication of human resource management choices in the perceptions and behaviors of potential applicants, and family and non-family employees, the use of experiments will also grow. For example, experimental studies can be used to understand the reactions and justice perceptions that employees within a family firm can have based on the implementation of certain policies or practices, or how family brand messages affect intentions to work in a family firm. In Table 12.2 we provide examples of multiple areas of research that could be explored using experimental methodologies.

As we conclude this chapter, it is important to finish our work by providing some guidelines for how researchers can enhance their experimental work when they send it for publication. One practice that can make it difficult to publish experimental work is poor data reporting. Too often, researchers choose to analyze and report overly complex statistics and structural equation models when such advanced analysis are not necessary. After conducting an experiment your data should be analyzed and reported in the simplest way that sufficiently answers your hypotheses and research questions. Most experimental studies can be examined through analysis of variance techniques and correlations/regressions. More advanced path modeling is warranted with model hypotheses. But remember that one critical goal of research is understandability and encouragement for future studies. Overly complex report writing usually leads to data that is difficult to replicate and not applicable in summary types of analyses such as meta-analysis. Researchers should let their hypotheses and data guide the analysis and write-up, not the complex computations. This will help when responding to reviewers and in providing clarity in a project. Additionally, it is important to provide all the information necessary for other authors to replicate and build on your work. This will also help in the development of experimental work.

Experimental design is growing in popularity in the study of family businesses. We hope that this chapter offers some useful and practical tips and practices to advance the field, and that researchers can build on the ideas presented here to strengthen their work and to explore the experimental methodology.

## REFERENCES

Aguinis, H., & Bradley, K. J. (2014). Best practice recommendations for designing and implementing experimental vignette methodology studies. *Organizational Research Methods*, *17*(4), 351–371.

Aiman-Smith, L., Scullen, S. E., & Barr, S. H. (2002). Conducting studies of decision making in organizational contexts: A tutorial for policy-capturing and other regression-based techniques. *Organizational Research Methods*, *5*, 388–414.

Arijs, D., Botero, I. C., Michiels, A., & Molly, V. (2018). Family business employer brand: Understanding applicants' perceptions and their job pursuit intentions with samples from the US and Belgium. *Journal of Family Business Strategy*, *9*(3), 180–191.

Binz Astrachan, C., Botero, I. C., Astrachan, J. H., & Prügl, R. (2018). Branding the family firm: A review, integrative framework proposal, and research agenda. *Journal of Family Business Strategy*, *9*(1), 3–15.

Cavanaugh, G. F., & Fritzsche, D. J. (1985). Using vignettes in business ethics research. In L. E. Preston (Ed.), *Research in Corporate Social Performance and Policy* (pp. 279–293, Vol. 7). London: Jai Press.

Charness, G., Gneezy, U., & Kuhn, M. A. (2012). Experimental methods: Between-subject and within-subject design. *Journal of Economic Behavior & Organization*, *81*(1), 1–8.

Cohen, J. (1988). *Statistical Power Analysis for the Behavioral Sciences* (2nd edn). Hillsdale, NJ: Lawrence Erlbaum Associates.

Cook, T. D., & Campbell, D. T. (1979). Quasi-experimentation: Design and Analysis Issues for Field Settings. Boston, MA: Houghton Mifflin.

Evert, R. E., Martin, J. A., McLeod, M. S., & Payne, G. T. (2016). Empirics in family business research: Progress, challenges, and the path ahead. *Family Business Review, 29*(1), 17–43.

Grant, A. M., & Wall, T. D. (2009). The neglected science and art of quasi-experimentation: Why-to, when-to, and how-to advice for organizational researchers. *Organizational Research Methods, 12*(4), 653–686.

Highhouse, S. (2009). Designing experiments that generalize. *Organizational Research Methods, 12*(3), 554–566.

Kahlert, C., Botero, I. C., & Prügl, R. (2017). Revealing the family: Effects of being perceived as a family firm in the German recruiting market. *Journal of Family Business Management, 7*(1), 21–43.

King, E. B., Hebl, M. R., Botsford Morgan, W., & Ahmad, A. S. (2013). Field experiments on sensitive organizational topics. *Organizational Research Methods, 16*(4), 501–521.

Litz, R. A., Pearson, A. W., & Litchfield, S. (2012). Charting the future of family business research: Perspectives from the field. *Family Business Review, 25*(1), 16–32.

Lude, M., & Prügl, R. (2021). Experimental studies in family business research. *Journal of Family Business Strategy, 12*(1), 100361.

McGrath, J. E. (1981). Dilemmatics: The study of research choices and dilemmas. *American Behavioral Scientist, 25*, 179–210.

O'Keefe, D. J. (2003). Message properties, mediating states, and manipulating checks: Claims, evidence, and data analysis in experimental persuasive message effects research. *Communication Theory, 13*(3), 251–274.

Payne, G. T., Pearson, A. W., & Carr, J. C. (2017). Process and variance modeling: Linking research questions to methods in family business research. *Family Business Review, 30*(1), 11–18.

Reilly, T. M., & Jones III, R. (2017). Mixed methodology in family business research: Past accomplishments and perspectives for the future. *Journal of Family Business Strategy, 8*(3), 185–195.

Shadish, W., Cook, T. D., & Campbell, D. T. (2002). *Experimental and Quasi-experimental Designs for Generalized Causal Inference.* Boston, MA: Houghton Mifflin.

Wilson, S. R., Whitmoyer, J. G., Pieper, T. M., Astrachan, J. H., Hair Jr, J. F., & Sarstedt, M. (2014). Method trends and method needs: Examining methods needed for accelerating the field. *Journal of Family Business Strategy, 5*(1), 4–14.

Yu, A., Lumpkin, G. T., Sorenson, R. L., & Brigham, K. H. (2012). The landscape of family business outcomes: A summary and numerical taxonomy of dependent variables. *Family Business Review, 25*(1), 33–57.

# 13. Enhancing the validity of socio-emotional wealth: a context-focused approach

## Cristina Cruz, Mohamed Mazen M. Batterjee, and Valeriano Sanchez-Famoso

## INTRODUCTION

The socio-emotional wealth (SEW) approach is increasingly popular in family business research since the seminal work by Gómez-Mejía et al. (2007), where the authors attempted to provide a 'homegrown' theory and a 'potential dominant paradigm' to the family business field (Berrone et al., 2012, p. 258). Today, many consider the rising popularity of the SEW framework as one of the main reasons for the growth of the family business research field in the last decade (Brigham & Payne, 2019; Swab et al., 2020).

The SEW literature suggests that decision-making in family firms is driven by the family owners' desire to preserve their SEW, which refers to the non-financial utilities or 'affective endowments' that are derived from owning a business (Gómez-Mejía et al., 2011). However, as researchers highlight the confusion caused by the ambiguity in the nature, dimensions, and outcomes of SEW, it faces serious criticism that threatens its generalizability as the central theory of family business research (Brigham & Payne, 2019; Swab et al., 2020). Researchers have raised concerns regarding where or in whom SEW resides (Schulze & Kellermanns, 2015), the co-existence of negative and positive valence toward SEW (Kellermanns et al., 2012), the dimensionality of the SEW construct (Swab et al., 2020), and how the different dimensions relate to each other and to the overall construct (Brigham & Payne, 2019). Several alternatives have been proposed to overcome these challenges, such as the development of a direct measure to capture the different dimensions of SEW (Berrone et al., 2012), conceptualizing SEW as a function of stocks and flows (Chua et al., 2015), and further investigating the variance and interrelatedness of each SEW dimension (Swab et al., 2020).

However, regarding SEW challenges and developments, no study discusses the need to incorporate situational and temporal boundaries that may shape the SEW approach. This is problematic because families represent the focal decision-making group regarding SEW (Swab et al., 2020). Hence, they may operate differently based on cultural norms and institutional differences (Basco et al., 2018). As Zahra (2016) states, 'context-free research can over-look those variables that really make family firms unique' (p. 3). If SEW is considered a unique factor that differentiates family firms (Holt et al., 2018), SEW research should be contextualized.

This study sets out to identify the challenges researchers may face in con-ducting context-sensitive SEW research and provides directions for future research. The manifold facets of context that includes business, social, spatial, and even temporal dimensions (Welter, 2011), render this a difficult task. Following recent literature that calls for more research to unveil the contex-tual specificities that make family owners unique in specific regions, such as Europe (Botero et al., 2015), Latin America (Gómez-Mejía et al., 2020), and the Arab world (Krueger et al., 2021), we focus on the challenges involved in incorporating the national context into SEW research. Following previous studies (Wright et al., 2014), we use the national context as a proxy that includes the institutional, cultural, and historical contextual aspects that may shape family owners' and family firms' behavior, and thus, family SEW.

Our claim regarding the risk of conducting (national) context-free SEW research is supported by reviewing international family business research and existing attempts to measure the SEW construct directly in different countries. Next, following the suggestions of Bamberger (2008), recently applied to family firm studies by Gómez-Mejía et al. (2020) and Krueger et al. (2021), we encourage researchers to enhance SEW research by progressively introducing (national) context research in family business studies at different stages. First, we propose to conduct more SEW studies in diverse national settings (context by sampling) as well as to develop more comparative SEW studies across countries (context by comparison). Further, we encourage researchers to intro-duce context into theoretical SEW-approach arguments.

### Why Does the National Context Matter for SEW Research?

Wortman's (1995) review of international studies on family businesses concludes 'presently, there are essentially no comparative studies of family business across cultural boundaries, ethnic boundaries, and country borders. Are there really differences in the ways in which family businesses operate sub-nationally, nationally, or globally?' (p. 56). Since then, some attempts have been made to expand knowledge on cross-national comparisons of family firms. Table 13.1 summarizes some of the most representative cross-cultural comparative studies of family firms over the last three decades. The table shows two sets of cross-national studies: (1) those focused on examining the importance of culture in explaining family firms' heterogeneity, and (2) those focused on showing differences in family owners' behaviors. The first set of studies use dimensions adopted from Hofstede or the GLOBE project (Global Leadership and Organizational Behavior Effectiveness[1]) to examine how national-level attributes affect family business outcomes. These studies show differing patterns in family firm outcomes across countries. For instance, when examining performance differences between family and non-family firms, Carr and Bateman (2010) show that while family firms are as profitable as non-family firms in 'high trust countries,' such as North America and Europe, they outperform in 'low trust countries,' such as Thailand and China. Similarly, Dow and McGuire (2016) find a positive relationship between family ownership and firm performance in countries with higher uncertainty avoidance.

Gupta and Levenburg's (2010a) seminal cross-cultural study on family firms develops the Culturally Sensitive Assessment Systems and Education (CASE[2]) project to examine cross-cultural variations between family businesses in ten cultural regions and nine cultural dimensions. The project reveals interesting differences between family firms in different countries, for instance, the inter-generational succession process is more competitive in Anglo-Saxon regions than in Nordic regions, and this may be due to (1) the rejection of the institutional collectivism by Anglo family firms and (2) the cooperative behavior of Nordic family firms.

The second set of studies compares family owners' attitudes and goals across countries. For instance, Howorth et al. (2010) find that family firm owners in European countries (Spain, Greece, and Italy) and the US demonstrate a different predisposition to sell their businesses. While European family firms may be reluctant to sell a business that they view as an extension to the family, the US family firms are more comfortable selling their firms at the appropriate price. Corbetta and Montemerlo (1999) confirm differences in transgenerational intentions among family owners. The authors show that a higher percentage of US family owners may sell their company or pass their shares on to someone outside the family than that of Italian family owners.

---

[1]    The GLOBE project is a unique large-scale study of cultural practices, leadership ideals, and generalized and interpersonal trust in more than 160 countries in collaboration with more than 500 researchers.

[2]    The CASE project reviewed the literature on family business in each region and systematically analyzed 110 articles on family businesses authored by over 200 scholars worldwide.

*Table 13.1*     *Cross-national studies on family firms*

| Author | Context | Topic investigated |
|---|---|---|
| Poza (1995) | Latin America and the United States | Family firms' strategies |
| Gundry and Ben-Yoseph (1998) | Romania, Poland, and United States | Women in family firms |
| Corbetta and Montemerlo (1999) | Italy and the United States | Family involvement through ownership, management, strategic decisions, and succession |
| Welsh and Raven (2006) | Kuwait and Lebanon | Behavior of managers and employees of family firms |
| Howorth et al. (2010) | Editorial of different articles including multiple countries | Family firms' diversity, assets, liabilities, definition, context, culture, types, role of women, and ownership transfer |
| Carr and Bateman (2010) | North America, Europe, high trust countries, Anglo-Saxon regions, low trust countries, long-termist Asian countries | Performance |
| Gupta and Levenburg (2010a) | 10 regional clusters | Cross-cultural comparisons of: Regulated boundary, Business reputation, Bridging relationships, Organizational professionalism, Regulated family power, Competitive succession, Gender-centered leadership, Operational resiliency, Contextual embeddedness |
| Gupta and Levenburg (2010b) | Latin America, Eastern Europe, and Southern Europe | |
| Gupta et al. (2011) | Anglo, Germanic and Nordic nations | |
| Mueller and Philippon (2011) | 12 countries | Family ownership |
| Lussier and Sonfield (2012) | Croatia, Egypt, France, India, Kosovo, Kuwait, and the United States | Family business succession planning |
| Van Essen et al. (2015) | 27 European countries | Downsizing |
| Galve-Górriz and Hernandez-Trasobares (2015) | Spain, Mexico, Argentina, Brazil, Chile, Honduras, Costa Rica, Peru, and Colombia | Family firms' ownership and performance |
| Pittino et al. (2016) | Austria and Hungary | Employee retention |
| Dow and McGuire (2016) | 33 countries | Family ownership and firm performance |
| Ellul et al. (2018) | The United States, Canada, Germany, the United Kingdom, Japan, and South Korea | Employment stability |

| Author | Context | Topic investigated |
| --- | --- | --- |
| Basco et al. (2018) | Europe, Latin America, Asia, and North America | Transgenerational entrepreneurship |
| Arijs et al. (2018) | The United States and Belgium | Family firms' brand |
| Porfírio et al. (2019) | Portugal and Greece | Succession |
| Bennedsen et al. (2019) | 8 countries | Performance and labor volatility of family firms |
| Block et al. (2019) | 40 countries | Family firms' employment |
| Verbeke et al. (2020) | Confucian influenced, West European, English-speaking, Latin American, East European, South Asian, and African and Middle Eastern | Bifurcation bias |
| Briano-Turrent et al. (2020) | Argentina, Brazil, Chile, and Mexico | Family firms' dividend policy |

Overall, these studies suggest that cultural norms and institutional settings vary widely across countries and may have profound implications for explaining the behavior of family owners, heterogeneity of family firms across societies, and impact of family ownership on firm outcomes (Dow & McGuire, 2016). Hence, a lack of awareness of the effects of the national context presents a barrier to the nuanced understanding of family owners and family firms. Recent works (Gómez-Mejía et al., 2020; Krueger et al., 2021) warn researchers about the oversight of context in family business studies. These studies claim that a lack of focus on the context dimension may lead to incorrect interpretations of the link between family and business and a 'one-size-fits-all' approach to family firms across the world.

Conducting context-free research is especially challenging in SEW research. While where 'does SEW reside' is debatable (Schulze & Kellermanns, 2015), families represent the focal decision-making group in SEW (Swab et al., 2020). These families may operate differently based on cultural norms and institutional differences across national boundaries (Wright et al., 2014); therefore, the national context is expected to influence the relative importance that family owners assign to different SEW dimensions. Building on the behavioral agency model, the SEW model proposes that family businesses make decisions depending on the manner in which problems are framed and their main point of reference at the decision-making moment (Kotlar & De Massis, 2013). This point of reference is strongly shaped by situational aspects that occur at the family and business level (Llanos-Contreras & Jabri, 2019); therefore, context-free research may threaten the generalizability of the SEW approach. For instance, using a sample of Italian family firms, Calabrò et al. (2018) suggest that SEW is positively related to primogeniture. Nevertheless, they emphasized that context matters, as succession strategies are deeply embedded in the context in which it takes place (Bertocchi, 2006; Coli et al., 2003; Coli & Rose, 1999). Hence, their results may not hold in other national contexts with a different attitude toward firstborns.

This discussion raises two fundamental questions for SEW researchers, whether (1) a universal method to capture the affective endowment of family owners across the world is possible and (2) SEW impacts firm outcomes similarly across national boundaries.

A review of empirical studies using the FIBER scale[3] as a proxy for family SEW shows that these questions remain unsolved. The reviewed studies show important differences regarding the relationship between SEW and performance and how SEW should be measured, depending on the country in which the study was conducted. For instance, Angulo et al. (2016) find that in Mexico, firm performance is positively related to all FIBER dimensions, while Razzak and Janssen (2019) in a sample of Bangladeshi firms confirmed these findings for all FIBER dimensions except 'binding social ties'. However, Bratnicka-Myśliwiec et al. (2019) find that family control (F) and family identification (I) are negatively related to firm performance using a sample of Polish family firms. Moreover, while most empirical studies confirm the validity of a five-dimensional FIBER scale (e.g., Angulo et al., 2016; Razzak & Janssen, 2019), using a sample of 216 family firms in Austria and Germany, Hauck et al. (2016) propose that the FIBER dimension should be reduced to a three-dimensional REI scale, and Dayan et al. (2019), with 150 family firms from the United Arab Emirates, propose a four-dimensional IBER scale.

The lack of consensus regarding the validity of the construct, its measurement across national contexts, and its impact on firm outcomes, limits the general applicability of SEW as a central homegrown theory of family business. We believe that contextualizing SEW research may help to ascertain why, when, and where the dark or bright sides of SEW may emerge. Hence, to enhance the validity of the SEW approach, researchers should incorporate the interdependence of cultural aspects and formal and informal institutions within national boundaries as important issues to capture family owners' affective endowments. Therefore, we suggest various approaches in the following section.

---

[3]    The FIBER scale is one of the most influential conceptualizations of the SEW construct (Swab et al., 2020) developed by Berrone et al. in 2012. The authors proposed a 27-item scale to capture the multidimensionality of SEW through five dimensions: (F) family control and influence, (I) identification of family members with the firm, (B) binding social ties, (E) emotional attachment of family members, and (R) renewal of family bonds to the firm through dynastic succession (Berrone et al., 2012).

# INTRODUCING THE NATIONAL CONTEXT IN SEW STUDIES

Following Bamberger (2008), Gómez-Mejía et al. (2020) and Krueger et al. (2021), we contextualize SEW research through three different approaches: context by sampling, context by comparing, and context by theorizing. Although these approaches are not exclusive to SEW, they are highly relevant because the SEW construct aims to explain the essence of or dominant coalition in the firm, which is deeply influenced by the cultural and institutional norms of the country in which the firm operates.

## Context by Sampling

The context-by-sampling approach refers to the strategy used to investigate the SEW phenomenon in a specific geographical or contextual setting, which is followed by most existing empirical studies on SEW (e.g., Berrone et al., 2010). Studies that adopt a context-by-sampling approach range from those that consider context to be tangential (e.g., Berrone et al., 2010), to those that emphasize the importance of context (e.g., Calabrò et al., 2018). Nevertheless, in later cases, these studies fail to provide information on how the research setting might create boundary conditions to the SEW approach. Another challenge is related to borrowing theories and concepts that were developed in a specific context and applying them to another context, under the impression that 'one size fits all.'

Following studies that attempted to contextualize research in other fields (e.g., Welter, 2011; Maloney et al., 2016), we offer academics practical suggestions to enhance SEW research by providing more contextual knowledge from the field research, even when the study may not be specifically focused on context.

- Include a more thorough description of the national context in the research setting. For instance, scholars may share detailed information about the unique cultural aspects of the sample country (e.g., the level of power distance, individualism, masculinity, uncertainty avoidance, long-term orientation, and indulgence of Angola).
- Identify and investigate underrepresented contextual settings in contemporary SEW research (e.g., understand how SEW works in emerging economies).
- Provide deeper discussions about the dependence of the study's results on the national setting and the level of confidence regarding the generalizability of findings in other contexts (Aguinis & Edwards, 2014). For example, results showing the relationship between SEW dimensions and

performance in the US might not be applicable to countries with a low level of performance orientation, such as Argentina.

We acknowledge that encouraging researchers to describe external context details when it is not the main research focus may be a challenge, given the space constraints in most journals. Nevertheless, many journals offer online appendices that can be used to include this information.

While context by sampling is highly encouraged as an aid to build consistency in SEW research, it does not enable researchers to understand the causal or moderating relationship between the national context and SEW. Therefore, we encourage researchers to further incorporate context in the research strategy of their SEW studies. First, by developing comparative SEW studies across countries (context by comparison). Second, by theorizing how the SEW approach may be altered, modified, or constrained due to national culture (context by theorizing). We propose a research agenda for each of the two research strategies as follows.

## Context by Comparing

This research strategy conducts comparative SEW studies in different geographical contexts with the aim to highlight the heterogeneity of SEW across nations. Comparing SEW research to analyze context poses a major challenge to researchers, as they need to examine whether the available scales to measure SEW are valid across nations. The lack of valid measures across nations threatens the overall reliability and conclusions of any study. Furthermore, it limits researchers' confidence in the assumption that SEW is understood similarly across nations.

To overcome this challenge, we encourage researchers to test the cross-national measurement invariance of the instruments used to capture the SEW construct, as measurement invariance is believed to be a prerequisite to establish the validity of a survey instrument (e.g., Steenkamp & Baumgartner, 1998). Confirming measurement invariance implies that the set of indicators measures the same latent variables across contexts (Kline, 2005). Hence, assessing the cross-national measurement invariance of the SEW scale enables a meaningful comparison across countries, as it ensures that the instruments used to measure the SEW construct can be conceptualized in the same manner across countries (Steenkamp & Baumgartner, 1998). The SEW construct invariance should be confirmed following the steps recommended by Steenkamp and Baumgartner (1998), which entail confirming the configural, metric, and scalar invariance of the scale. Configural and metric invariance allow researchers to use the scale to study the relationships among values, attitudes, behavior, and socio-demographic characteristics across countries.

Scalar invariance enables researchers to compare mean values across countries (Davidov et al., 2008).

Once the measurement invariance of the SEW scale is confirmed, scholars can focus on comparative knowledge creation and demonstrate the characterization of the SEW construct across nations. The validated cross-national SEW scale can be used to:

- Explore whether national culture influences how family owners prioritize different SEW dimensions (e.g., do Latin American family firms give more weight to family control than the US family firms?).
- Explore the antecedents of SEW across countries, especially those with divergent cultures (e.g., does the presence of the founder increase the level of identification with the family more in Arab countries than in Western cultures? Does fragmented ownership challenge the family's desire to maintain control differently in Anglo-Saxon and Latin countries? Is family ownership or management a better predictor of SEW in one country than in another?).
- Explore how SEW relates to firm strategic outcomes (i.e., governance, innovativeness, entrepreneurship, internationalization, diversification, or sustainability) across nations (e.g., does the level of family owners' identification with their firms influence the sustainability of Vietnamese and Spanish family firms differently?).
- Explore SEW-performance across countries and whether SEW impact performs differently across national boundaries (e.g., does the level of binding social ties influence the performance of Canadian and Mexican family firms differently?).

Comparative SEW studies help researchers unveil the specificities of the SEW approach across countries, creating comparative knowledge that would advance SEW research. Further, conducting context by comparing SEW research may help to understand the heterogeneity among family firms (Daspit et al., Chapter 5 in this book). However, comparative SEW studies do not help researchers address the manner in which context may alter the SEW approach. To do so, researchers should move forward to incorporate context into SEW studies and embrace a context-by-theorizing strategy.

**Context by Theorizing**

Bamberger (2008, p. 841) defines this approach as 'those theories that specify how surrounding phenomena or temporal conditions directly influence lower-level phenomena, condition relations between one or more variables at different levels of analysis, or are influenced by the phenomena nested within them'. This approach attempts to measure context and extends beyond contextualizing phenomena. Context-by-theorizing SEW research helps connect SEW variables and national culture variables at different levels to explain family firms' goals and outcomes. This line of research can challenge the current status quo of SEW knowledge as it may provide evidence on the relationship between different cultural settings and specific family firm behaviors caused by SEW heterogeneity. Hence, the context-by-theorizing approach in SEW research is challenging, as researchers should specify how, when, and where the instrument used to capture SEW (e.g., SEW measured through the FIBER scale or SEWi scale) is altered, modified, or constrained due to national culture. Inspired by studies from other research fields (e.g., Maloney et al., 2016), we recommend incorporating the national context into SEW research through any of the following mechanisms:

- *As a direct influence.* Future SEW studies should investigate how much of the heterogeneity among family owners results from the influence of national context on different SEW dimensions. For instance, research shows that family ownership concentration is common in higher power distance societies, where families with large shareholdings may exploit their dominant position in society (Dow & McGuire, 2016). Does this imply that family owners place more weight on the 'F' dimension in countries with high power distance?
- *As a moderator or mediator variable.* In addition researchers should theorize how the national context may shape the way SEW influences family firms' outcomes. For instance, research shows that differences in formal institutional and property rights affect family firms' development and exit (Carney et al., 2014). Furthermore, SEW research suggests that transgenerational intentions (a key SEW dimension) decrease family owners' willingness to sell their firm (Howorth et al., 2010). Hence, how do differences in institutional contexts across countries moderate SEW's influence on family firms' exit strategies? Moreover, future research should examine the moderating role of informal institutions. For instance, in regions, such as Latin America, characterized by strong religious influence (Gupta & Levenburg, 2010b), researchers should investigate how religion may shape the influence of SEW on firm outcomes, such as corporate social responsibility or firm performance.
- *Multilevel construct domain.* Major studies have explored SEW at the family firm level and recent family business research has investigated the impact of SEW at different levels, including how it affects non-family employees (Vandekerkhof et al., 2015) or how it influences family owners' activities beyond family firm boundaries (Nason et al., 2019). These studies acknowledge the complexity of the SEW construct, which operates

at multiple levels and includes the family, firm, and various stakeholders. Future research should incorporate the multilevel domain of the SEW construct into the context by theorizing SEW studies. For instance, SEW motives would drive family owners to engage in philanthropic activities not only through the firm (corporate philanthropy) but also beyond the firm boundaries (i.e., a family foundation). To what extent is this choice determined by the family firm's national culture?

- *As an outcome.* As mentioned earlier, if the SEW construct is inextricably intertwined with context, then not only does the context shape the SEW construct but the reverse should also hold. In other words, SEW may modify or shape aspects of the geographical area in which family firms operate. For instance, acknowledging the importance of transgenerational intentions for European family owners, the European Family Businesses association has consistently lobbied for tax and regulatory frameworks that do not disadvantage family businesses when a transfer occurs. This raises the question of whether the different evolutions of succession laws across countries could be partially explained by differences in family SEW.

Moreover, we encourage researchers to re-examine empirical family firms' studies, where the 'national context control variable' was reported to be statistically significant. This indicates that the national context may be a predictor variable in the study. A thorough review of the variance explained by the national context as a control variable in SEW research, especially in areas where no context theorizing has been conducted, may be an excellent place to start identifying potential research areas.

Future research could also look for mixed findings or inconsistencies that indicate possible contextual influences. As seen in the studies mentioned above, there are mixed findings regarding the relationship between SEW and the family firm's goals and outcomes. This calls for attention as divergent findings may be due to contextual influences. Hence, future research should investigate whether cultural or institutional differences exist among countries that shape how SEW influences family firm behavior. If these differences exist, then the SEW approach should be redefined by incorporating contextual elements that explain family firm heterogeneity across countries.

Lastly, we follow recent calls to further apply qualitative research methods (Trudell et al., Chapter 8 in this book; Kammerlander & Diaz-Moriana, Chapter 9 in this book) to advance knowledge in the family firm field and encourage researchers to conduct grounded or case-based qualitative research in the early stages of the context-by-theorizing SEW research. The insights from these studies could be used to better understand how specific aspects of context shape SEW and refine existing SEW models to include potential cross-country effects in large-scale SEW studies.

## CONCLUSION

Our work attempts to address the limitations of research without context in SEW studies by showing the existence of important differences across countries in family firms' behavior, which question the cross-national applicability of the SEW approach. Our proposed research agenda encourages SEW researchers to continue exploring their respective national contexts in specific SEW studies. We also encourage more SEW research that highlights the differences and similarities of family owners and family firms across countries and propose robust methodologies to conduct the SEW context by comparing research with rigor. Importantly, we urge SEW researchers to incorporate contextual measures into their studies and clarify the determinants of SEW differences among family owners, which can be explained by the national context in which the family firm operates.

By shifting the research effort from a context-less approach to context-sensitive investigation, we hope that this study encourages future researchers not only to account for contextual nuances of family firms in different countries, but also revisit the SEW approach based on how national context aspects may determine the SEW conceptualization and measurement.

## REFERENCES

Aguinis, H., & Edwards, J.R. (2014). Methodological wishes for the next decade and how to make wishes come true. *Journal of Management Studies* 51(1), 143–174.

Angulo, A., Villanueva, J., & Solís, E. (2016). The determinants of socioemotional wealth and the family firm's outcomes. *International Journal of Entrepreneurship* 20(1), 16–32.

Arijs, D., Botero, I., Michiels, A., & Molly, V. (2018). Family business employer brand: Understanding applicants' perceptions and their job pursuit intentions with samples from the US and Belgium. *Journal of Family Business Strategy* 9(3), 180–191.

Bamberger, P. (2008). From the editors beyond contextualization: Using context theories to narrow the micro–macro gap in management research. *Academy of Management Journal* 51(5), 839–846.

Basco, R., Calabrò, A., & Campopiano, G. (2018). Transgenerational entrepreneurship around the world: Implications for family business research and practice. *Journal of Family Business Strategy* 10(4), 100249.

Bennedsen, M., Tsoutsoura, M., & Wolfenzon, D. (2019). Drivers of effort: Evidence from employee absenteeism. *Journal of Financial Economics* 133(3), 658–684.

Berrone, P., Cruz, C., & Gómez-Mejía, L.R. (2012). Socioemotional wealth in family firms: Theoretical dimensions, assessment approaches, and agenda for future research. *Family Business Review* 25(3), 258–279.

Berrone, P., Cruz, C., Gómez-Mejía, L.R., & Larraza-Kintana, M. (2010). Socioemotional wealth and corporate responses to institutional pressures: Do family-controlled firms pollute less? *Administrative Science Quarterly* 55(1), 82–113.

Bertocchi, G. (2006). The law of primogeniture and the transition from landed aristocracy to industrial democracy. *Journal of Economic Growth* 11(1), 43–70.

Block, J.H., Fisch, C.O., Lau, J., Obschonka, M., & Presse, A. (2019). How do labor market institutions influence the preference to work in family firms? A multilevel analysis across 40 countries. *Entrepreneurship Theory and Practice* 43(6), 1067–1093.

Botero, I.C., Cruz, C., De Massis, A., & Nordqvist, M. (2015). Family business research in the European context. *European Journal of International Management* 9(2), 139–159.

Bratnicka-Myśliwiec, K., Wronka-Pośpiech, M., & Ingram, T. (2019). Does socioemotional wealth matter for competitive advantage? A case of Polish family businesses. *Journal of Entrepreneurship, Management and Innovation* 15(1), 123–146.

Briano-Turrent, G., Li, M., & Peng, H. (2020). The impact of family-CEOs and their demographic characteristics on dividend payouts: Evidence from Latin America. *Research in International Business and Finance* 51(1), 101086.

Brigham, K.H., & Payne, G.T. (2019). Socioemotional wealth (SEW): Questions on construct validity. *Family Business Review* 32(4), 326–329.

Calabrò, A., Minichilli, A., Amore, M.D., & Brogi, M. (2018). The courage to choose! Primogeniture and leadership succession in family firms. *Strategic Management Journal* 39(7), 2014–2035.

Carney, M., Gedajlovic, E., & Strike, V.M. (2014). Dead money: Inheritance law and the longevity of family firms. *Entrepreneurship Theory and Practice* 38(6), 1261–1283.

Carr, C., & Bateman, S. (2010). Does culture count? Comparative performances of top family and non-family firms. *International Journal of Cross-Cultural Management* 10(2), 241–262.

Chua, J.H., Chrisman, J.J., & De Massis, A. (2015). A closer look at socioemotional wealth: Its flows, stocks, and prospects for moving forward. *Entrepreneurship Theory and Practice* 39(2), 173–182.

Coli, A., & Rose, M.B. (1999). Families and firms: The culture and evolution of family firms in Britain and Italy in the nineteenth and twentieth centuries. *Scandinavian Economic History Review* 47(1), 24–47.

Coli, A., Fernandez-Perez, P., & Rose, M.B. (2003). National determinants of family firm development? Family firms in Britain, Spain and Italy in the nineteenth and twentieth centuries. *Enterprise and Society* 4(1), 28–64.

Corbetta, G., & Montemerlo, D. (1999). Ownership, governance, and management issues in small and medium-size family businesses: A comparison of Italy and the United States. *Family Business Review* 12(4), 361–374.

Davidov, E., Meuleman, B., Billiet, J., & Schmidt, P. (2008). Values and support for immigration: A cross-country comparison. *European Sociological Review* 24(5), 583–599.

Dayan, M., Ng, P.Y., & Ndubisi, N.O. (2019). Mindfulness, socioemotional wealth, and environmental strategy of family businesses. *Business Strategy and the Environment* 28(3), 466–481.

Dow, S., & McGuire, J. (2016). Family matters? A cross-national analysis of the performance implications of family ownership. *Corporate Governance: An International Review* 24(6), 584–598.

Ellul, A., Pagano, M., & Schivardi, F. (2018). Employment and wage insurance within firms: Worldwide evidence. *The Review of Financial Studies* 31(4), 1298–1340.

Galve-Górriz, C., & Hernandez-Trasobares, A. (2015). Institutional framework, concentration of ownership and results of large family corporations in Latin America and Spain. *Corporate Governance* 15(4), 409–426.

Gómez-Mejía, L.R., Basco, R., Gonzalez, A.C., & Muller, C.G. (2020). Family business and local development in Iberoamerica. *Cross Cultural & Strategic Management* 27(2), 121–136.

Gómez-Mejía, L.R., Cruz, C., Berrone, P., & De Castro, J. (2011). The bind that ties: Socioemotional wealth preservation in family firms. *The Academy of Management Annals* 5(1), 653–707.

Gómez-Mejía, L.R., Haynes, K., Nuñez-Nickel, M., Jacobson, K., & Moyano-Fuentes, J. (2007). Socioemotional wealth and business risks in family-controlled firms: Evidence from Spanish olive oil mills. *Administrative Science Quarterly* 52(1), 106–137.

Gundry, L.K., & Ben-Yoseph, M. (1998). Women entrepreneurs in Romania, Poland, and the United States: Cultural and family influences on strategy and growth. *Family Business Review* 11(4), 61–75.

Gupta, V., & Levenburg, N. (2010a). A thematic analysis of cultural variations in family businesses: The CASE Project. *Family Business Review* 23(2), 155–169.

Gupta, V., & Levenburg, N. (2010b). The catholic spirit and family business: Contrasting Latin America, Eastern Europe, and Southern Europe. *Advances in Entrepreneurship, Firm Emergence and Growth* 12(1), 185–228.

Gupta, V., Levenburg, N., Moore, L., Motwani, J., & Schwarz, T. (2011). The spirit of family business: A comparative analysis of Anglo, Germanic and Nordic nations. *International Journal of Cross-Cultural Management* 11(2), 133–151.

Hauck, J., Suess-Reyes, J., Beck, S., Prügl, R., & Frank, H. (2016). Measuring socioemotional wealth in family-owned and -managed firms: A validation and short form of the FIBER Scale. *Journal of Family Business Strategy* 7(3), 133–148.

Holt, D.T., Pearson, A.W., Payne, G.T., & Sharma, P. (2018). Family business research as a boundary spanning platform. *Family Business Review* 31(1), 14–31.

Howorth, C., Rose, M., Hamilton, E., & Westhead, P. (2010). Family firm diversity and development: An introduction. *International Small Business Journal* 28(5), 437–451.

Kellermanns, F.W., Eddleston, K., & Zellweger, T. (2012). Extending the socioemotional wealth perspective: A look at the dark side. *Entrepreneurship Theory and Practice* 36(6), 1175–1182.

Kline, R.B. (2005). *Principles and Practice of Structural Equation Modeling.* Guilford Press.

Kotlar, J., & De Massis, A. (2013). Goal setting in family firms: Goal diversity, social interactions, and collective commitment to family-centered goals. *Entrepreneurship Theory and Practice* 37(6), 1263–1288.

Krueger, N., Bogers, M., Labaki, R., & Basco, R. (2021). Advancing family business science through context theorizing: The case of the Arab world. *Journal of Family Business Strategy* 12(1), 100377.

Llanos-Contreras, O.A., & Jabri, M. (2019). Exploring family business decline with socioemotional wealth perspective. *Academia Revista Latinoamericana de Administracion* 32(1), 63–78.

Lussier, R.N., & Sonfield, M.C. (2012). Family businesses' succession planning: A seven-country comparison. *Journal of Small Business and Enterprise Development* 19(1), 7–19.

Maloney, M., Bresman, H., Zellmer-Bruhn, M., & Beaver, G. (2016). Contextualization and context theorizing in teams research: A look back and a path forward. *The Academy of Management Annals* 10(1), 891–942.

Mueller, H.M., & Philippon, T. (2011). Family firms and labor relations. *American Economic Journal: Macroeconomics* 3(2), 218–245.

Nason, R.S., Carney, M., Le Breton-Miller, I., & Miller, D. (2019). Who cares about socioemotional wealth? SEW and rentier perspectives on the one percent wealthiest business households. *Journal of Family Business Strategy* 10(2), 144–158.

Pittino, D., Visintin, F., Lenger, T., & Sternad, D. (2016). Are high performance work practices really necessary in family SMEs? An analysis of the impact on employee retention. *Journal of Family Business Strategy* 7(2), 75–89.

Porfírio, A., Carrilho, T., Hassid, J., & Rodrigues, R. (2019). Family business succession in different national contexts: A fuzzy-set QCA approach. *Sustainability* 11(22), 1–17.

Poza, E. (1995). Global competition and the family-owned business in Latin America. *Family Business Review* 8(4), 301–311.

Razzak, M.R., & Janssen, S. (2019). Socioemotional wealth and performance in private family firms: The mediation effect of family commitment. *Journal of Family Business Management* 9(4), 468–496.

Schulze, W.S., & Kellermanns, F.W. (2015). Reifying socioemotional wealth. *Entrepreneurship Theory and Practice*, 39(3), 447–459.

Steenkamp, J.B., & Baumgartner, H. (1998). Assessing measurement invariance in cross-national consumer research. *Journal of Consumer Research* 25(1), 78–90.

Swab, R.G., Sherlock, C., Markin, E., & Dibrell, C. (2020). 'SEW' what do we know and where do we go? A review of socioemotional wealth and a way forward. *Family Business Review* 33(4), 424–445.

Van Essen, M., Strike, V.M., Carney, M., & Sapp, S. (2015). The resilient family firm: Stakeholder outcomes and institutional effects. *Corporate Governance International Review* 23(3), 167–183.

Vandekerkhof, P., Steijvers, T., Hendriks, W., & Voordeckers, W. (2015). The effect of organizational characteristics on the appointment of nonfamily managers in private family firms: The moderating role of socioemotional wealth. *Family Business Review* 28(2), 104–122.

Verbeke, A., Yuan, W., & Kano, L.A. (2020). Values-based analysis of bifurcation bias and its impact on family firm internationalization. *Asia Pacific Journal of Management* 37(2), 449–477.

Welsh, D.H., & Raven, P. (2006). Family business in the Middle East: An exploratory study of retail management in Kuwait and Lebanon. *Family Business Review* 19(1), 29–48.

Welter, F. (2011). Contextualizing entrepreneurship: Conceptual challenges and ways forward. *Entrepreneurship Theory and Practice* 35(1), 165–184.

Wortman, M. (1995). Critical issues in family business: An international perspective of practice and research. In *Proceedings of the ICSB 40th World Conference* (pp. 53–76). Institute of Industrial Economics.

Wright, M., Chrisman, J.J., Chua, J.H., & Steier, L.P. (2014). Family enterprise and context. *Entrepreneurship Theory and Practice* 38(6), 1247–1260.

Zahra, S.A. (2016). Developing theory-grounded family business research: Some suggestions. *Journal of Family Business Strategy* 7(1), 3–7.

# 14. Nonresponse bias in family business research

## Matthew Rutherford and Duygu Phillips

Within family business, an important quality is the amorphous nature of the definition of family business. Since there is no agreed-upon population (Chua et al., 1999), the degree of nonresponse bias (NRB) present in any study (with regard to its external validity to that population) is challenging to ascertain. While this lack of definitional consensus exists in other fields, and in entrepreneurship in general, it is particularly acute in family business research (Brockhaus, 1994; Chua et al., 1999; Handler, 1994; Littunen & Hyrsky, 2000; Litz, 1995; Miller et al., 2007).

In addition to the overall population, the assessment of nonresponse bias also requires the consideration of response rates. In fact, the calculation of nonresponse bias includes response rate (Rogelberg & Stanton, 2007). Therefore, there is no doubt that response rates and nonresponse bias are closely related. On average, as the response rate of a given study declines, the concern about nonresponse bias rises. However, low response rates do not always induce nonresponse bias (Wright, 2015). Largely constrained to research employing field surveys, response rate is defined as the number of completed surveys with responding units divided by the number of eligible responding units in the sample (Wiseman & Billington, 1984); nonresponse bias occurs when samples of the population do not accurately reflect their populations because of under- (or over-) sampling of some types of respondents (Barclay et al., 2002; Berg, 2005; Boström et al., 1993; Siemiatycki & Campbell, 1984; Speklé & Widener, 2018).

Regardless, low response rates are an acute concern for family business research for a myriad of reasons. Two of the most important are (1) family businesses are known to be particularly difficult subjects to survey, because family members are more cautious than others about sharing information (e.g., Stamm & Lubinski, 2011; Wilson et al., 2014), and (2) family businesses are most likely over-surveyed (Baruch & Holtom, 2008). Interestingly, though this topic has been heavily discussed in the literature (e.g., Berg, 2005), the importance of low response rates to study quality remains poorly understood (e.g., Baruch, 1999)—particularly in the entrepreneurship and family business arenas (Pielsticker & Heibl, 2020; Rutherford et al., 2017).

In addition, since NRB depends upon both the response rate and the differences between the responders and nonresponders, the impact of a given response rate may depend heavily on the researcher's chosen definition of family firm. Herein, we suggest that nonresponse rate in family business studies should be considered alongside the definition of family business adopted in a given study as well as the role of the respondents within the family firm (family vs. nonfamily members).

## NONRESPONSE BIAS

From Rogelberg and Stanton (2007) we know that nonresponse bias can be specified with the formula nonresponse bias = $P_{NR}$ ($X_{Res} - X_{Pop}$), where $P_{NR}$ refers to the proportion of nonrespondents, $X_{Res}$ is the respondent mean on a survey relevant variable, and $X_{Pop}$ is the population mean on the corresponding survey-relevant variable. Obviously, this assumes that the actual population mean is known, which is seldom the case in family business research.

NRB, then, is 'the product of *both* the nonresponse rate *and* the distinctiveness of nonrespondents, relative to respondents, on a given variable of interest' (Wright, 2015, p. 305, emphasis in original). Notably, even with low response rates, when there is no significant difference between respondents and nonrespondents on the study variables, bias concern is allayed. However, though they are distinct constructs, response rate is a key contributor to NRB and since true population means are seldom known, low response rate is often equated with NRB. Scholars should be cautious in this regard, because while correlated, response rate is a substandard proxy for the presence of NRB (Nishimura et al., 2016).

NRB is known to have negative effects on statistical outcomes such as standardized differences, correlations, regression slopes, and model fit indices (Berk, 1983), and most importantly effect sizes (Rutherford et al., 2017). It has also been reported to generate range restriction and increase the likelihood of generating both Type I and Type II errors (Rogelberg & Stanton, 2007).

## RESPONSE RATES

Response rate is one of the key statistics used in assessing the credibility and the validity of survey-based research (Baruch & Holtom, 2008). Higher response rates often generate larger samples and greater statistical power (Baruch & Holtom, 2008), reduce the probability of sampling errors (Baruch & Holtom, 2008; Groves, 1989, 2006; Mitchell, 1985), and allow for increased statistical analysis options.

The issue of decreased sample size, caused by low response rates, is particularly acute. While the researcher can deal with this by surveying more respondents to reach the targeted sample size, the quality of the sample may be diminished. As a result of the decreased sample size, the type of statistical analysis should be reconsidered to ensure the validity and reliability of the findings. Another outcome of decreased sample size due to nonresponses is the reduced generalizability of the findings (Luong & Rogelberg, 1998; Rogelberg & Stanton, 2007). Each of these concerns and the potential negative effects of low response rates hamper the legitimacy of both a given study and its findings, as reviewers and readers become skeptical of the validity of the sample, and thus the results.

Other than collecting responses from 100 percent of the population, there is no way to guarantee that NRB is not present (Sheikh & Mattingly, 1981). While it has been suggested that high levels of nonresponse may lead to statistical biases (e.g., Greco et al., 2015), Rutherford et al.'s (2017) investigation of the meta-analyses of entrepreneurship studies revealed that, contrary to what is widely believed, response rate had no 'meaningful or consistent influence' (p. 93) on the relationships studied. Moreover, their study found that entrepreneurship researchers do not seem to be engaging in selective reporting when rates are nonideal. In spite of this finding, low response rates remain important in the peer review process.

A recent study on survey response rates in family business research published by Pielsticker and Hiebl (2020) analyzed family business studies in seven prominent journals, and reported the average response rate to be 21 percent, which is lower than management research (48%) and entrepreneurship research (30%; Baruch & Holtom, 2008; Dennis, 2003). These authors also found that the response rates have declined significantly over time. In light of this relatively low rate, a number of causes and associated remedies have been proposed that are particularly relevant to those studying family business.

## FACTORS INFLUENCING RESPONSE RATES AND NRB

With the foregoing in mind, all things equal higher response rates are preferred. Baruch and Holtom (2008) suggested two main reasons for nonresponses in survey studies: (1) failed delivery of the survey or unwillingness of survey addressees to participate in the study due to busy schedules or irrelevant content, and (2) survey fatigue.

Over-surveying—and the resultant survey fatigue—can lead to a low response rate, as respondents are overwhelmed by the increasing number of survey requests they receive (Baruch & Holtom, 2008). This issue has become even more common and increasing recently due to the rise of the social media and the spread of electronic surveys. This may be specifically true and more common for family businesses, as most family firms are privately owned, their secondary data is usually not available to researchers, and thus, they are more likely to be contacted to be surveyed and therefore fatigued (Wilson et al., 2014).

The overall population size naturally alters the response rates acquired, as well as their meaningfulness. Intuitively, large populations may seem to be more conducive to effective sampling. However, this may not always be the case. Response rate is often more related to the underlying fundamentals of the population and the resources possessed by the researchers (Pielsticker & Hiebl, 2020). In addition, surveying a family business can be more challenging depending on the target respondents (i.e., family members and/or nonfamily members) (Pielsticker & Hiebl, 2020). There are at least two reasons for this challenge: (1) family business surveys often target owner-managers, who are often more difficult to reach than others (Pielsticker & Hiebl, 2020; Armstrong & Hird, 2009) and (2) family businesses are purported to be more secretive than nonfamily businesses (Stamm & Lubinski, 2011). Therefore, the traditional techniques that are known to increase response rates in other populations may not be as efficient, or may have differential effects based on the role of the respondents within the family business (i.e., pre-contacts, reminders; Pielsticker & Hiebl, 2020).

## DIRECTED ADVICE FOR FAMILY BUSINESS RESEARCHERS

Since the true value of the population mean is seldom known, the case could be made that NRB can never be specified in a family business study. This property of the field should not be understated, since as researchers we are attempting to draw inferences about the population by drawing a sample of that population. But clearly, as family business researchers, we do not know the population, because there is no agreement on what exactly a family business is. So, exactly what population are we drawing inferences upon? The answer depends upon how the researcher defines a business as a family business. This dramatically expands the researcher's degrees of freedom (e.g., Anderson et al., 2019), as each researcher is, in essence, free to determine the population for a given study. This, though, does not render the assessment and diminution of NRB impossible, and here we focus upon both a priori approaches and post hoc analytical techniques that can be used to assess and reduce nonresponse bias.

# A PRIORI TECHNIQUES TO AVOID NONRESPONSE BIAS IN FAMILY BUSINESS RESEARCH

## Definitional Considerations

The issue here, in the context of NRB, is whether and to what degree the definition appropriately represents the population of family businesses. So, first and foremost, in choosing an appropriate definition, the onus falls upon the researcher to (1) fully understand the myriad conceptualizations of family business and the merits of each, and (2) choose a robust definition based upon family involvement and essence.

For the first challenge, unfortunately nothing can replace the time and effort dedicated to sincerely understanding the ontology of a family business via examination of the extant literature and theory. Therefore, the recommendation here is simply an intense examination of the phenomenon—ideally under the guidance of experienced family business researchers. In this regard, reviewing and constructing systematic reviews in family businesses can be helpful (Sherlock & Dibrell, Chapter 7 in this book).

The second issue—choosing a robust definition of family business—arguably can be summarized as choosing between two broad types of definitions: those tapping components of involvement versus those tapping essence. The former type (e.g., 10% family ownership) are generally more generous, in that they open the door to many collection possibilities (e.g., archival, public firm sampling); while the latter (e.g., power, experience, culture; Klein et al., 2005) limit these possibilities, on average.

This issue here is that while '[d]efinitions based on the components of family involvement—management, ownership, governance, and succession— are easy to operationalize, unfortunately, they cannot distinguish between two firms with the same level of family involvement when one considers itself a family business and the other does not' (Chua et al., 1999, pp. 19–20). Since Chua and colleagues extended the call for more investigation into the 'essence' of family business, some progress has been made, but the literature remains light and operationalizations have been inconsistent (Daspit et al., Chapter 5 in this book).

A more generous operationalization of family business will likely result in an elevated response rate and, ostensibly, alleviate nonresponse bias concerns. But since nonresponse bias and response rates are not identical constructs— nonresponse bias may still be present when response rate is high—this may not be the case. In this regard, Cook et al. (2020) cautioned researchers that the actual response representativeness is more important than the response rate itself.

## Research Design Considerations

An appropriate research design can help alleviate or reduce NRB in family business research. First, and most broadly, researchers must be sure that a field survey is the appropriate data collection methodology. Particularly in light of declining response rates and increased survey fatigue, collection via instrumentation may not be the best technique to address a given research question.

Instead, mixed-method studies can be valuable here.[1] These studies generally combine a quantitative data collection with a qualitative data collection to provide both rich and generalizable results. For example, an experiment combined with a field survey can triangulate findings so that response rates become far less of an issue. As an illustration, Craig et al. (2014) conducted a study that investigated the relationships between family business culture, innovation, and performance via a mail survey sent to 4,275 firms and reported a meager 9 percent response rate. However, before mailing the survey, the researchers interviewed members of 30 family businesses both to inform areas of weakness in the instrument and to establish ecological validity of the hypothesized relationships. This multimethod approach most assuredly allayed reviewer concerns regarding the low response rate, and the result is a rich study examining difficult-to-capture essence components of family businesses.

## Tactics to Increase Response Rates

Pielsticker and Hiebl (2020) investigated the family business literature to uncover tactics that might be useful for researchers conducting field surveys in this domain.[2] Their review of 126 family business studies, overall, confirms that family members who are also in charge of the family business (i.e., the top management team) are more challenging to convince to take surveys. However, they also make some broad suggestions to researchers that are likely to meaningfully increase response rates: (1) address smaller population sizes; (2) where appropriate, address only family members of family businesses; and (3) establish pre-contacts, specifically when targeting nonfamily members.

These findings are largely in line with findings from other fields of study (e.g., Hiebl & Richter, 2018; Shih & Fan, 2008), but it is interesting to note that many of the same tactics are ineffective in family business research (e.g., incentives, reminders). The authors caution that, even if all of these tactics are

---

[1]   For a complete review of mixed methods in family business, see Reilly and Jones (2017).
[2]   See Dillman et al. (2014) for best practices in optimizing response rates in other fields.

employed, low response rates are endemic in family business research and likely to persist in our field.

None of these, therefore, are foolproof and extant research suggests some nuances. For instance, while some studies hold that sending reminders can be effective to motivate target respondents to take the survey (e.g., Brennan, 1992; Kittleson, 1997), others have found that this technique actually has adverse effects. Baruch and Holtom (2008) found that reminders were associated with lower response rates. 'Hence, researchers must attain a higher level of trust when studying family businesses, which can potentially improve response rates and accuracy when eliciting information through direct means such as surveys (Schulze et al., 2001)' (Wilson et al., 2014, p. 8). In addition, the effectiveness of those techniques depends on the role of the respondent within the family business (Pielsticker & Hiebl, 2020). Pielsticker and Hiebl's (2020) results suggested that while reminders did not matter when both family and nonfamily respondents were targeted, when surveying only family members, it is more effective not to send reminders. They may perhaps utilize their personal relationships or networks to indirectly remind them to take the survey.

Further, there are also mixed findings about the effectiveness of incentives in reducing nonresponse rates in research. For instance, Rogelberg and Stanton (2007) suggested that incentives increased response rates, while Baruch and Holtom (2008) found that incentives were not effective in increasing response rates in organizational studies. Similarly, Pielsticker and Hiebl (2020) found that incentives did not encourage family business members to respond.

Following these findings, we suggest family business researchers implement different strategies based on the respondent's role in the family business. There seems to be no substitute for acquiring some level of trust with the targeted respondents. Specifically, researchers should establish relationships and trust through pre-contacts when surveying nonfamily members. However, they should be more cautious about the way they approach family business members before sending out the survey.

## POST HOC TECHNIQUES

To detect bias after the sample is acquired, nonresponse analyses can be conducted to determine the representativeness of the sample (Werner et al., 2007). To show evidence that the nonresponse rate did not lead to bias, statistical analyses must be conducted and presented in detail (e.g., wave analysis, passive nonresponse analysis, interest-level analysis; Rogelberg & Stanton, 2007). Rogelberg and Stanton (2007) presented a list of N-BIAS techniques to assess nonresponse bias. One of the most common nonresponse analyses is to compare respondents and nonrespondents on variables using an archival data-

*Table 14.1*     *A priori and post hoc techniques to increase response/assess and reduce NRB*

| Technique | Goal | To do | Representative citations |
|---|---|---|---|
| A priori techniques | Define family business | • An understanding and consideration of both components of involvement and essence when defining family businesses | Chua et al., 1999; Klein et al., 2005 |
| | Consider research design | • Consider designs such as field surveys, or mixed-methods designs | Craig et al., 2014; Reilly & Jones III, 2017; Harrison III, 2013 |
| | Increase response rates | • Sample smaller population<br>• Address only family members<br>• Select techniques based on the target respondent's role in the family business<br>• Establish trust and relationships, establish pre-contacts when surveying nonfamily members<br>• Do not send reminders surveying family members | Pielsticker & Hiebl, 2020; Dillman et al., 2014; Shih & Fan, 2008; Hiebl & Richter, 2018; Wilson et al., 2014; Baruch & Holtom, 2008 |
| Post hoc techniques | Assess NRB | • N-BIAS: Archival analysis, follow-up approach, wave analysis, passive nonresponse analysis, interest-level analysis, active nonresponse analysis, worst-case resistance, benchmarking analysis, demonstrate generalizability<br>• Time-trends approach | Rogelberg & Stanton, 2007; Werner et al., 2007; Armstrong & Overton, 1977; Wagner & Kemmerling, 2010 |
| | Reduce NRB | • Split samples<br>• Drop-and-collect-survey (DCS) method<br>• Dynamic web-based survey methods | Peytchev, 2020; Basly & Saunier, 2020; Ibeh et al., 2004; Bonometti & Tang, 2006 |
| | Corrections | • Direct range restriction<br>• Indirect range restriction | Thorndike, 1949; Hunter et al., 2006 |

base to show whether there are differences between the two sampling groups. This may be a particularly useful technique for family business researchers, but care must be taken to ensure that the comparison data are representative of the same subpopulations—that is, both sets use the same conceptualization of family business.

Resurveying nonrespondents is an alternative technique, though it may be challenging to motivate those in family businesses who did not take the survey. Another widely utilized technique is wave analysis, which compares late respondents to early ones. Passive nonresponse analysis and interest-level analysis focusing on the topic of the survey are among other techniques to detect nonresponse bias. Researchers can also conduct interviews with nonresponders to examine the reasons behind the nonresponses.

Robustness analyses also can be conducted, using simulated data. Benchmarking analysis and split samples (Peytchev, 2020) are also used to demonstrate the appropriateness of the obtained data. Finally, the replication of findings with a different research methodology may help with providing evidence for the generalizability of the findings.

In addition to these NRB assessment strategies, there are several techniques to detect and correct nonresponse bias (Rutherford et al., 2017). These techniques include direct range restriction corrections (Thorndike, 1949) and indirect range restriction (Hunter et al., 2006). Other techniques that have been suggested to reduce nonresponse bias include the drop-and-collect-survey method (Ibeh et al., 2004) and dynamic web-based survey methods (Bonometti & Tang, 2006; Baruch & Holtom, 2008).

Finally, and this is an area that often gets less attention when discussing the findings of the research, it is imperative—particularly in family business—to have an honest and robust discussion about external validity. That is, to which types of family firms these findings apply, and to which they may not apply. We encourage authors to be transparent and continue to report their response rate along with a detailed explanation of whom their target respondents were. While citing other research that has reported similar response rates is a common practice, it is important to select research with similar goals and sampling criteria (i.e., essence vs. components of involvement).

## CONCLUSION

The mismatch between the mean characteristics of respondents in a nonrandom sample and the mean characteristics of the population can lead to serious problems in uncovering and aggregating the antecedents and outcomes of family business phenomena (Berg, 2005). For all contributors to the field of family business, it is important to understand that—when employing field surveys—NRB will likely be present, so the tradeoff between the added value of the study versus the possibility of skewed results in the publication must be weighed. At least with regard to effect sizes, there is some evidence that low response rates do not introduce systematic bias.

Concerning a priori options, the only clear guidance that emerges from the literature is the establishing of some level of trust. This fact places the focus upon the post hoc techniques (outlined in Table 14.1), which can be particularly valuable to family business researchers.

As members of a relatively young field seeking to enter a 'normal science' phase of development (Kuhn, 1996), family business advocates need to assist in the legitimization of our field by discovering additional ways to advance robust research. We submit here that one way to accomplish this is to reflect upon the true role that nonresponse bias plays in hampering our development. While low nonresponse rate is never ideal, in fields such as ours, it may need to be tolerated so that researchers are freed to empirically investigate those relationships that remain the least understood.

## REFERENCES

Anderson, B. S., Wennberg, K., & McMullen, J. (2019). *2 Editorial: Enhancing Quantitative Theory-Testing Entrepreneurship Research* (No. 323). The Ratio Institute.

Armstrong, J. S., & Overton, T. S. (1977). Estimating nonresponse bias in mail surveys. *Journal of Marketing Research, 14*(3), 396–402.

Armstrong, S. J., & Hird, A. (2009). Cognitive style and entrepreneurial drive of new and mature business owner-managers. *Journal of Business and Psychology, 24*(4), 419–430.

Barclay, S., Todd, C., Finlay, I., Grande, G., & Wyatt, P. (2002). Not another questionnaire! Maximizing the response rate, predicting non-response and assessing non-response bias in postal questionnaire studies of GPs. *Family Practice, 19*(1), 105–111.

Baruch, Y. (1999). Response rate in academic studies: A comparative analysis. *Human Relations, 52*(4), 421–438.

Baruch, Y., & Holtom, B. C. (2008). Survey response rate levels and trends in organizational research. *Human Relations, 61*(8), 1139–1160.

Basly, S., & Saunier, P-L. (2020). Familiness, socio-emotional goals and the internationalization of French family SMEs. *Journal of International Entrepreneurship, 18*(3), 270–311.

Berg, N. (2005). Non-response bias. In Kempf-Leonard, K. (Ed.), *Encyclopedia of Social Measurement* (Vol. 2, pp. 865–873). London: Academic Press.

Berk, R. A. (1983). An introduction to sample selection bias in sociological data. *American Sociological Review, 48*(3), 386–398.

Bonometti, R. J., & Tang, J. (2006). A dynamic technique for conducting online survey-based research. *Competitiveness Review, 16*(2), 97–105.

Boström, G., Hallqvist, J., Haglund, B. J., Romelsjö, A., Svanström, L., & Diderichsen, F. (1993). Socioeconomic differences in smoking in an urban Swedish population: The bias introduced by non-participation in a mailed questionnaire. *Scandinavian Journal of Social Medicine, 21*(2), 77–82.

Brennan, M. (1992). Techniques for improving mail survey response rates. *Marketing Bulletin, 3*(4), 24–37.

Brockhaus Sr, R. H. (1994). Entrepreneurship and family business research: Comparisons, critique, and lessons. *Entrepreneurship Theory and Practice, 19*(1), 25–38.

Chua, J. H., Chrisman, J. J., & Sharma, P. (1999). Defining the family business by behavior. *Entrepreneurship Theory and Practice, 23*(4), 19–39.

Cook, C., Heath, F., & Thompson, R. L. (2000). A meta-analysis of response rates in web- or internet-based surveys. *Educational and Psychological Measurement, 60*(6), 821–836.

Craig, J. B., Dibrell, C., & Garrett, R. (2014). Examining relationships among family influence, family culture, flexible planning systems, innovativeness and firm performance. *Journal of Family Business Strategy, 5*(3), 229–238.

Dennis Jr, W. J. (2003). Raising response rates in mail surveys of small business owners: Results of an experiment. *Journal of Small Business Management, 41*(3), 278–295.

Dillman, D. A., Smyth, J. D., & Christian, L. M. (2014). *Internet, Phone, Mail, and Mixed-mode Surveys: The Tailored Design Method*. Hoboken, NJ: John Wiley & Sons.

Greco, L. M., O'Boyle, E. H., & Walter, S. L. (2015). Absence of malice: A meta-analysis of nonresponse bias in counterproductive work behavior research. *Journal of Applied Psychology, 100*(1), 75–97.

Groves, R. (1989). *Survey Errors and Survey Costs*. Hoboken, NJ: John Wiley & Sons.

Groves, R. M. (2006). Nonresponse rates and nonresponse bias in household surveys. *Public Opinion Quarterly, 70*(5), 646–675.

Handler, W. C. (1994). Succession in family business: A review of the research. *Family Business Review, 7*(2), 133–157.

Harrison III, R. L. (2013). Using mixed methods designs in the *Journal of Business Research*, 1990–2010. *Journal of Business Research, 66*(11), 2153–2162.

Hiebl, M. R., & Richter, J. F. (2018). Response rates in management accounting survey research. *Journal of Management Accounting Research, 30*(2), 59–79.

Hunter, J. E., Schmidt, F. L., & Le, H. (2006). Implications of direct and indirect range restriction for meta-analysis methods and findings. *Journal of Applied Psychology, 91*(3), 594–612.

Ibeh, K., Brock, J. K. U., & Zhou, Y. J. (2004). The drop and collect survey among industrial populations: Theory and empirical evidence. *Industrial Marketing Management, 33*(2), 155–165.

Kittleson, M. J. (1997). Determining effective follow-up of e-mail surveys. *American Journal of Health Behavior, 21*(3), 193–196.

Klein, S. B., Astrachan, J. H., & Smyrnios, K. X. (2005). The F-PEC scale of family influence: Construction, validation, and further implication for theory. *Entrepreneurship Theory and Practice, 29*, 321–339.

Kuhn, T. S. (1996). *The Structure of Scientific Revolutions* (3rd edition). Chicago, IL: University of Chicago Press.

Littunen, H., & Hyrsky, K. (2000). The early entrepreneurial stage in Finnish family and nonfamily firms. *Family Business Review, 13*(1), 41–53.

Litz, R. A. (1995). The family business: Toward definitional clarity. *Family Business Review, 8*(2), 71–81.

Luong, A., & Rogelberg, S. G. (1998). How to increase your survey response rate. *The Industrial-Organizational Psychologist, 36*(1), 61–65.

Miller, D., Le Breton-Miller, I., Lester, R. H., & Cannella Jr, A. A. (2007). Are family firms really superior performers? *Journal of Corporate Finance, 13*(5), 829–858.

Mitchell, T. R. (1985). An evaluation of the validity of correlational research conducted in organizations. *Academy of Management Review, 10*(2), 192–205.

Nishimura, R., Wagner, J., & Elliott, M. (2016). Alternative indicators for the risk of non-response bias: A simulation study. *International Statistical Review, 84*(1), 43–62.

Peytchev, A. (2020). Split-sample design with parallel protocols to reduce cost and nonresponse bias in surveys. *Journal of Survey Statistics and Methodology, 8*(4), 748–771.

Pielsticker, D. I., & Hiebl, M. R. (2020). Survey response rates in family business research. *European Management Review, 17*(1), 327–346.

Reilly, T. M., & Jones III, R. (2017). Mixed methodology in family business research: Past accomplishments and perspectives for the future. *Journal of Family Business Strategy, 8*(3), 185–195.

Rogelberg, S. G., & Stanton, J. M. (2007). Introduction: Understanding and dealing with organizational survey nonresponse. *Organizational Research Methods, 10*(2), 195–209.

Rutherford, M. W., O'Boyle, E. H., Miao, C., Goering, D., & Coombs, J. E. (2017). Do response rates matter in entrepreneurship research? *Journal of Business Venturing Insights, 8*, 93–98.

Schulze, W. S., Lubatkin, M. H., Dino, R. N., & Buchholtz, A. K. (2001). Agency relationships in family firms: Theory and evidence. *Organization Science, 12*(2), 99–116.

Sheikh, K., & Mattingly, S. (1981). Investigating non-response bias in mail surveys. *Journal of Epidemiology & Community Health, 35*(4), 293–296.

Shih, T. H., & Fan, X. (2008). Comparing response rates from web and mail surveys: A meta-analysis. *Field Methods, 20*(3), 249–271.

Siemiatycki, J., & Campbell, S. (1984). Nonresponse bias and early versus all responders in mail and telephone surveys. *American Journal of Epidemiology, 120*(2), 291–301.

Speklé, R. F., & Widener, S. K. (2018). Challenging issues in survey research: Discussion and suggestions. *Journal of Management Accounting Research, 30*(2), 3–21.

Stamm, I., & Lubinski, C. (2011). Crossroads of family business research and firm demography: A critical assessment of family business survival rates. *Journal of Family Business Strategy, 2*(3), 117–127.

Thorndike, R. L. (1949). *Personnel Selection: Test and Measurement Techniques.* Hoboken, NJ: John Wiley and Sons.

Wagner, S. M., & Kemmerling, R. (2010). Handling nonresponse in logistics research. *Journal of Business Logistics, 31*(2), 357–381.

Werner, S., Praxedes, M., & Kim, H. G. (2007). The reporting of nonresponse analyses in survey research. *Organizational Research Methods, 10*(2), 287–295.

Wilson, S. R., Whitmoyer, J. G., Pieper, T. M., Astrachan, J. H., Hair Jr, J. F., & Sarstedt, M. (2014). Method trends and method needs: Examining methods needed for accelerating the field. *Journal of Family Business Strategy, 5*(1), 4–14.

Wiseman, F., & Billington, M. (1984). Comment on a standard definition of response rates. *Journal of Marketing Research, 21*(3), 336–338.

Wright, G. (2015). An empirical examination of the relationship between nonresponse rate and nonresponse bias. *Statistical Journal of the IAOS, 31*(2), 305–315.

# 15. Latent profile analysis: a focus on applications for family firms

## Xin Gao, Laura Stanley, and Franz W. Kellermanns

The field of family firm research is continuously expanding (Debicki, Matherne, Kellermanns, & Chrisman, 2009; Rovelli, Ferasso, De Massis, & Kraus, 2021). While researchers struggled initially to define family firms consistently (Chrisman, Chua, & Sharma, 2005), the literature has made great advances in investigating family firms. Family firms are seen as inherently heterogenous (Chua, Chrisman, Steier, & Rau, 2012; Westhead & Howorth, 2007; Daspit, Chrisman, Skorodziyevskiy, Davis, & Ashton, Chapter 5 in this book), which poses challenges for family firm research. If one separates family firms into too many sub-groups (for an example, see Sharma, 2003), sampling, particularly *ex ante*, based on the overly detailed differentiation becomes unmanageable, if not impossible. At the same time, the mere distinction between family and non-family firms (e.g., Chrisman, Chua, & Kellermanns, 2009), while useful for many research questions, does not acknowledge differences among family firms. The differentiation between (lone) founder and family firms is coarse (Jaskiewicz, Combs, Block, & Miller, 2017; Miller, Le Breton-Miller, & Lester, 2010) and has the potential to confound non-family firms and family firms with the (lone) founder group.

The underlying heterogeneity of family firms calls for a methodological technique that distinguishes family firms in a meaningful way. While distinctions between family firms and non-family firms have been consistently made, finding differences among family firms on meaningful dimensions is a more difficult challenge. A variety of family firm-related variables vie for researchers' attention. For example, Combs, Shanine, Burrows, Allen, and Pounds (2020) point to factors such as family relationships, roles of family members, and family changes that shape different business families and affect the family businesses they control. Similarly, factors such as the F-PEC dimensions (Astrachan, Klein, & Smyrnios, 2002; Klein, Astrachan, & Smyrnios, 2005) and family climate (Björnberg & Nicholson, 2007) could be useful in distinguishing among family firms. Although regression analysis and other correlational methods can show the impact of these family-related variables on outcomes, they do not allow for grouping family firms in a meaningful way. Furthermore, regression analysis makes it difficult to examine and interpret three-way interactions, and virtually impossible to interpret interactions of four or more variables. Accordingly, researchers need a statistical tool that can separate family firms into groups based on family firm-related variables.

Configural analysis, which refers to any groupings of variables composed of common and conceptually distinguishable features (Meyer, Tsui, & Hinings, 1993), may be the best way to address this problem. The configural perspective argues that 'organizations are best understood as clusters of interrelated structures and practices rather than as subunits or loosely combined entities, and therefore cannot be understood in terms of analyzing components in isolation' (Fiss, 2007, p. 1180). Configural analysis takes a holistic and systematic approach, where multiple variables together, rather than a single variable, are used to establish relationships with a dependent variable (e.g., organizational performance). The configural perspective, which analyzes the relationship between factor configuration and outcome variables, emphasizes the complexity of causality (Delery, 1998; Ragin, 2014). Applied to family firms, the purpose of configural research is to examine the set of companies that share the same key characteristics and allow for comparison across groups (Short, Payne, & Ketchen, 2008).

In this chapter, we highlight the use of latent profile analysis (LPA) as a way to capture family business heterogeneity. We juxtapose LPA with regression analysis as the most commonly used statistical application in family firm research. LPA offers several advantages over regression in that it identifies profiles (i.e., groups) of firms using grouping variables and separates samples (i.e., family firms) into meaningful groups based on these variables. The established groups are homogeneous within each profile, but differ across profiles on the selected grouping criteria. The profile membership variable can be used in further analysis (e.g., ANCOVA) to infer differences between profiles in outcome variables (Stanley, Hernández-Linares, López-Fernández , & Kellermanns, 2019; Stanley, Kellermanns, & Zellweger, 2017). These groups can then be compared to facilitate insights beyond interactions or correlations between these variables. Indeed, interactions between four or more variables are difficult to interpret by regression, while the results from sub-groups gained via LPA that have different levels of the identified variables can be interpreted more easily. Therefore, LPA can produce theoretically meaningful groups (i.e., profiles) of firms using a wide range of classification criteria, enabling family firm researchers to hypothesize and test for the existence of typologies.

The remainder of this chapter is organized as follows. First, we briefly introduce the family firm heterogeneity literature. Second, we review configural approaches with a focus on LPA. We then highlight the advantages of LPA and compare them to other configural approaches. After providing the syntax and a brief example from the literature, we conclude with future research directions.

## FAMILY FIRM HETEROGENEITY

Family firm heterogeneity has been identified as an important aspect of family firm research (Chua et al., 2012; Westhead & Howorth, 2007). (In addition to our overview, please refer to Daspit et al., Chapter 5 in this book for a more detailed discussion.) This heterogeneity can stem from governance-related items (e.g., ownership structure, board), and can be informed by the family structure itself, as families are highly heterogeneous (Dyer Jr & Dyer, 2009) and the complexity of relationships increases over time (Gersick, Davis, Hampton, & Lansberg, 1997). Scholars have gradually realized the importance of the role of the family in analyzing the nature of the family business (e.g., Huang, Chen, Xu, Lu, & Tam, 2020; Morris & Kellermanns, 2013). As the relationships of family members can vary by generation (Gersick et al., 1997; Jaskiewicz, Combs, Shanine, & Kacmar, 2017), the roles of family members in the family system are determined based on social relations such as consan-guinity and marriage. These family roles affect not only family relationships, but also family members and their behavior within the organization. These family relationships are further complicated by taking the family life cycle stages into account.

These factors affect the goals and values of the family business (Chrisman, Chua, & Steier, 2005; Fiegener, 2010; Williams, Pieper, Kellermanns, & Astrachan, 2018, 2019). For example, socio-emotional wealth (SEW) (Gómez-Mejía, Haynes, Núñez-Nickel, Jacobson, & Moyano-Fuentes, 2007; Schulze & Kellermanns, 2015) distinguishes between economic and non-economic goals, with the latter divided into multiple sub-dimensions (Berrone, Cruz, & Gómez-Mejía, 2012; Debicki, Kellermanns, Chrisman, Pearson, & Spencer, 2016). This underlying goal heterogeneity represented by the varying strength of SEW's sub-dimensions can drive behavioral outcomes for the firm and capture essential differences between family and non-family businesses. (SEW is discussed more fully by Cruz, Batterjee, and Sanchez-Famoso, Chapter 13 in this book.)

Given that the complexities of family relationships lead not only to perfor-mance differences between non-family and family firms (Carney, van Essen, Gedajlovic, & Heugens, 2015; Hansen & Block, 2020; Lohwasser, Hoch, & Kellermanns, 2022; Wagner, Block, Miller, Schens, & Xi, 2015), but also among family firms (Gedajlovic, Carney, Chrisman, & Kellermanns, 2012), a tool that can meaningfully capture this heterogeneity in a statistical analysis is desirable. Although three-way interactions and even non-linear relationships have been discussed (Mazzola, Sciascia, & Kellermanns, 2013), complexities beyond three variables and their interactions are difficult to interpret with traditional regression analysis and similar techniques. While we touch upon various tools that make it possible to overcome these complexities, we focus on LPA, which we believe is a superior technique for capturing complex interactions (Stanley et al., 2019; Stanley et al., 2017).

## OVERVIEW OF CONFIGURAL APPROACHES

Configural approaches can be traced back to typology research in the social sciences (i.e., ideal classifications for comparisons) (Weber, 1978). Typologies, which are conceptual in nature, have long been a popular classification method in the study of organizational strategy and structure and are particularly useful for family firm research (Neubaum, Kammerlander, & Brigham, 2019). While the actual observed types derived from LPA may not fully map onto the ideal types a typology may suggest, abstracting from the ideal types can easily reveal and explain the reason for the deviation. However, earlier research has focused more on the description of types while ignoring the usefulness of typologies for theoretical construction. Therefore, typologies are often criticized as a classification system rather than as theoretically driven (Doty & Glick, 1994). When utilizing LPA, the chosen input variables should be theoretically driven. If the variables that are used as input are derived from a typology, the input should be theoretically sound.

Taxonomies, as another configural approach, are similar to typologies in that they are classification systems, but are empirical in nature. While typologies can be developed theoretically based on ideal types, taxonomies are developed by analyzing multiple variables, taking the relationships between those variables into account, and classifying them based on these relationships. These classifications can be applied to individuals or firms. LPA can be applied to both taxonomies and typologies. One of the benefits of LPA is that it can be used to empirically test for the existence of different groups of firms that share similar characteristics (i.e., patterns of classification variables). LPA is flexible in its application, as the characteristics (i.e., variables to describe the phenomenon) can be taken from theory (in the case of typologies) or based on prior empirical observations (in the case of taxonomies).

Configural approaches represent methods that can identify multiple sub-groups in a given sample. They use combinations of variables (e.g., organizational attributes that are interrelated), which should be theoretically chosen, in a complex and integrated way. The difference between configural approaches and the more traditional approach lies in the use of the variables. With traditional methods that are correlation-based (i.e., regression), independent variables are assumed to act independently; the relationships between variables are not investigated. Even if relationships are investigated (i.e., moderation analysis), this analysis can be usefully interpreted only for three variables (three-way interactions), and not for four or more. Correlation-based analyses show the effect of a variable in isolation on the dependent variable (or with very limited interactions in the case of moderation analysis in a regression).

Because social phenomena are often characterized by a larger number of variables of interest, which can interact and have complex cause and effect relationships, a more holistic analysis is warranted. LPA, as a configural approach, can provide such an analysis. A configural approach sorts cases into groups based on the interplay of three or more variables, thus establishing patterns among variables of interest. The resulting groups can then be used in further analysis to show differences between them (e.g., ANOVAS, ANCOVAS, regression analysis).

The heterogeneity of different family businesses is often caused by multiple variables. Therefore, configural approaches can be used to complement traditional methods. In the family firm literature, where there are often three or more family firm-related variables of interest, the application of LPA seems most useful.

## LPA VERSUS ALTERNATIVE CONFIGURAL APPROACHES

While we focus on LPA, we still need to briefly discuss some alternative configuration analyses; specifically, median splits, cluster analysis, and qualitative comparative analysis (QCA). Median splits determine the median according to the ungrouped data. Each unit is arranged in order of size and the position of the midpoint is determined. Based on the midpoint, the sample is then divided into two sets of data (e.g., Gellatly, Hunter, Curriea, & Irving, 2009). Median splits, while having the advantages of simplicity and easy communicability, have at least three disadvantages. First, if the data are distributed unevenly, the resulting split groups may be distorted. Second, two groupings cannot capture the finer nuances between sub-groups (Rucker, McShane, & Preacher, 2015). Third, complexities among multiple variables cannot be sufficiently captured (DeCoster, Gallucci, & Iselin, 2011). Accordingly, median splits can be regarded only as a rudimentary tool and should not be used in isolation.

In cluster analysis, individuals (samples) or objects (variables) are classified according to the degree of similarity (distance), so that cases in the same class are more like each other than cases in other classes (Sinclair, Tucker, Wright, & Cullen, 2005). The aim is to maximize the homogeneity of cases within classes and the heterogeneity of cases between classes (Cunningham & Maloney, 2001). Cluster analysis is a more user-friendly application than LPA; however, the disadvantage lies in its strong subjectivity because fit statistics are not used. While some newer approaches exist (see Almeida, Barbosa, Pais, & Formosinho, 2007), at least in traditional methods, researchers' intentions can affect the number of clusters and the corresponding results.

QCA is mainly used in social sciences such as sociology and political science to carry out cross-case comparative analysis with small samples (Ragin, 2014). QCA, a relatively new method, has attracted the interest of scholars interested in analyzing complex configurations (Fiss, 2007; Misangyi et al., 2017). While following the normative analysis procedures and methods of quantitative research, QCA tries to avoid the criticism of the subjectivity of qualitative research. Yet, it is still a somewhat qualitative (and subjective) approach. There are challenges associated with QCA. First, the ratio of independent variables to sample size must be low because the number of possible combinations increases exponentially with each added independent variable (Hsiao, Chen, Chang, & Chiu, 2016). Second, QCA is not suitable for large data sets (Hino, 2009). Last, because QCA dichotomizes the independent variables, fine-grained differences may be lost (De Meur, Rihoux, & Yamasaki, 2009).

While each of these approaches may be valuable and useful, the limitations of each contrast with the advantages of LPA. LPA can process large data sets in a more objective and probability-based way (Meyer, Stanley, & Vandenberg, 2013), by using objective fit statistics, rather than subjective distance measures or 'eyeballing' the data, to determine the optimal number of profiles. In addition, LPA can provide a set of variables to support further studies on the relationships between independent and dependent variables (i.e., the classification variable; Meyer, Stanley, & Parfyonova, 2012; Meyer et al., 2013). For example, Meyer et al. (2012) used profiles of organizational commitment to predict turnover intention. However, LPA has some limitations such as the selection of variables for the profiles and the naming of profiles, which may involve some subjectivity. Due to the large number of possible classification variables and the need for a method that allows for the objective testing and identification of a taxonomy of family firms based on these classification variables, we believe that LPA is the best choice due to its ability to capture complex patterns of four or more variables and its reliance on probability-based fit indices. As large data sets are necessary to establish the generalizability of these taxonomies, LPA is the method of choice.

## HOW TO CONDUCT A LATENT PROFILE ANALYSIS

When conducting an LPA, the first step is to select input variables. While we provide a detailed example for family firm research, we also need to briefly mention one of the currently most prominent applications of the configural approach, which is related to the commitment literature. There are four targets of commitment (affective, normative, high sacrifice, and lack of alternatives); the combination of these variables has a differential influence on outcome variables (Meyer, Morin, & Vandenberghe, 2015; Meyer et al., 2012; Meyer et al., 2013). The same logic can be applied to the family firm literature, where three or more variables are chosen to generate homogenous groups with the help of LPA and then link those groups to outcome variables.

The selection of these grouping variables should be theoretically driven. An application for family firm research has been made in two initial studies, where family firm-specific variables were selected (Stanley et al., 2019; Stanley et al., 2017). In their study, Stanley et al. (2017) provided a syntax and detailed instructions regarding how to conduct the analysis. We use their study to illustrate and explain the syntax for a four-variable LPA application; that is, how four variables are used as inputs to generate homogenous classes:

## BOX 15.1  EXAMPLE OF SYNTAX

Data: File is C:/Projects/Example/ForMplus.txt;
VARIABLE: Names are Variable1 Variable2 Variable3 Variable4;
missing are all (999);
classes = c (4);
ANALYSIS: TYPE = MIXTURE;
LRTBOOT=100;
LRTSTARTS 2 1 100 50;
MODEL:
%OVERALL%
Variable1;
Variable2;
Variable3;
Variable4;
SAVEDATA: SAVE=CPROBABILITIES;
FILE IS 5Prof.txt;
OUTPUT: sampstat tech14;

The analysis begins by examining a 1-profile model and recording the fit indices. Another profile is then added to examine a 2-profile model and record the fit indices. This continues in an iterative process. The models are evaluated by comparing the fit indices to one another to identify the best fitting model. A variety of maximum-likelihood fit indices are examined, as well as the number of cases in each profile and the posterior probabilities associated with each profile. The best fitting model will show optimal fit indices, high posterior probabilities (i.e., at least a 70% probability that a firm belongs to the assigned profile and not the remaining profiles), and a representative number of cases (>5% of the sample) (Stanley et al., 2017). These results indicate clearly defined profiles (Nylund, Asparouhov, & Muthén, 2007).

Once the profiles are established, the patterns within the profiles need to be interpreted and the profiles need to be named. This step, by itself, can provide valuable insights about the population of firms that is represented in the sample. The resulting profiles can then be used in further analysis. For example, an ANCOVA with control variables can be conducted to investigate differences between the profiles for any given outcome variable. Alternatively, these profiles can be dummy-coded and then entered into a regression analysis as predictors (please also refer to Stanley et al., 2017, for a more detailed explanation of the analysis).

## DISCUSSION

Our discussion and example revealed that LPA can be a useful tool to capture heterogeneity among family firms and to show the differential impact of different homogenous groups of family firms on an outcome variable. Accordingly, we suggest that LPA should be more commonly applied to family firm research. Figure 15.1 shows the outcome of an LPA application to the family firm literature based on the syntax introduced by Stanley et al. (2017). The analysis for their data based on common family firm-related variables (five input variables) yielded five meaningfully different profiles. As Figure 15.1 shows, the five input variables differ from the five identified profiles yet are homogenous within each identified profile. This approach provides three advantages. First, the differences can be visually portrayed (e.g., in bar charts), which allows for easy interpretation of visual differences. Second, the established profiles can be further analyzed and linked to outcome variables (e.g., via ANCOVA or as input in a regression analysis). Third, the data can be collected first and meaningful profiles, if present, can then be derived from the available data. This greater flexibility in data collection allows researchers to collect more general data as opposed to data with prior identified characteristics.

We briefly want to highlight a few areas of research where LPA can be applied to the family firm literature. As has been stressed, the choice of variables utilized in LPA should be theoretically driven. A good starting point is a robust literature analysis (Sherlock & Dibrell, Chapter 7 in this book) in the area of interest to identify both theoretically sound choices and operationalizations of the input variables.

More performance-related studies are needed that capture performance differences among family firms. While differences between family firms and non-family firms have been studied and performance advantages have been

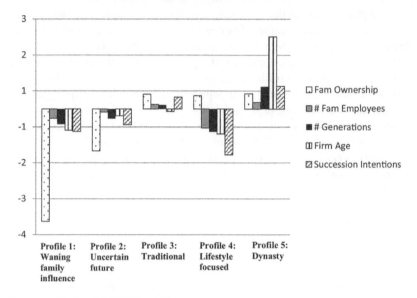

*Source*:    Stanley et al. (2017), p. 102.

*Figure 15.1    Family firm profiles*

consistently found (Lohwasser et al., 2022), little is known about performance differences among family firms. To address this gap and to contribute to the growing body of family firm heterogeneity concerns, common family firm-related variables (e.g., generation, age, succession intentions, ownership, F-PEC, SEW) can be chosen to establish profiles and then link the established profiles to performance.

In addition to performance, other important outcomes should be investigated. For example, Stanley et al. (2019) compared difference in entrepreneurial orientation across family firm profiles. Other outcome variables may also provide fruitful insights (Yu, Lumpkin, Brigham, & Sorenson, 2012). As family dynamics are likely driven by a variety of family firm-specific variables, LPA allows researchers to identify patterns of these variables and how they affect outcomes such as good and bad conflict in family firms, family firm commitment, satisfaction, and so on.

Another important application could be to family firm succession, where heterogeneity among family firms may be particularly pronounced. Variables such as CEO tenure, CEO age, family status of the CEO, age of family successor, and family ownership (among others) can be used to generate family firm profiles and to investigate the degree of succession planning or successful succession events. Researchers could then identify those conditions that would likely facilitate family firm succession and those that would likely hinder it (De Massis, Chua, & Chrisman, 2008). The combination of variables whose effect can be shown through LPA will likely be far more insightful than the main effects and single interactions that are normally investigated via regression analysis.

Many of the initial applications are more micro-oriented in the general management literature, while family firm research is often macro- (i.e., performance) oriented. This, however, does not mean that micro-related variables should not be utilized in family firm research to establish profiles. For example, the multi-dimensional family firm climate scale (Björnberg & Nicholson, 2007) could be used to establish profiles based on family firm dynamics. Similarly, profiles related to conflict (Eddleston, Otondo, & Kellermanns, 2008; Kellermanns & Eddleston, 2007; Qui & Freel, 2020) and/ or conflict management (De Dreu & Van Vianen, 2001; McKee, Madden, Kellermanns, & Eddleston, 2014; Sorenson, 1999) could be investigated.

Many examples of qualitative approaches are provided here (e.g., Salvato & Corbetta, Chapter 10 in this book; Kammerlander & Diaz-Moriana, Chapter 9 in this book), indicating that data generated from a more qualitative approach could be utilized. For example, Bement and Short (Chapter 11 in this book) describe text analysis as a useful tool in family firm research. Such an approach could yield a large enough sample size to utilize the identified dimensions (as input in an LPA) and thus establish homogeneous sub-groups in the sample, which can then be linked to outcome variables.

Last, research on SEW-related outcomes (Gómez-Mejía et al., 2007) is desirable. Not only could family firm profiles be linked to different SEW dimensions (Berrone et al., 2012; Debicki et al., 2016; Hauck, Suess-Reyes, Beck, Prügl, & Frank, 2016; Cruz et al., Chapter 13 in this book), but the opposite approach could be possible; that is, establishing distinct SEW profiles and linking these to outcomes and/or family firm-related characteristics.

In conclusion, this chapter provides an overview of LPA and a syntax template for the application of LPA in the family firm literature. This novel and useful approach to family firm heterogeneity (on this topic in this book see Daspit et al., Chapter 5) allows for flexible data collection and a theoretically driven selection of input variables that can provide meaningful different profiles of family firms. We hope that this approach will generate a plethora of future research that can better explain differences among family firms.

## REFERENCES

Almeida, J. A. S., Barbosa, L. M. S., Pais, A. A. C. C., & Formosinho, S. J. 2007. Improving hierarchical cluster analysis: A new method with outlier detection and automatic clustering. *Chemometrics and Intelligent Laboratory Systems, 87*(2): 208–217.

Astrachan, J. H., Klein, S. B., & Smyrnios, K. X. 2002. The F-Pec scale of family influence: A proposal for solving the family business definition problem. *Family Business Review, 15*(1): 45–58.

Berrone, P., Cruz, C., & Gómez-Mejía, L. R. 2012. Socioemotional wealth in family firms: Theoretical dimensions, assessment approaches, and agenda for future research. *Family Business Review, 25*(3): 258–279.

Björnberg, Å., & Nicholson, N. 2007. The family climate scales: Development of a new measure for use in family business research. *Family Business Review, 20*(3): 229–246.

Carney, M., van Essen, M., Gedajlovic, E. R., & Heugens, P. P. M. A. R. 2015. What do we know about private family firms? A meta-analytical review. *Entrepreneurship Theory & Practice, 39*(3): 513–544.

Chrisman, J. J., Chua, J. H., & Kellermanns, F. W. 2009. Priorities, resource stocks, and performance in family and non-family firms. *Entrepreneurship Theory and Practice, 33*(3): 739–760.

Chrisman, J. J., Chua, J. H., & Sharma, P. 2005. Trends and directions in the development of a strategic management theory of the family firm. *Entrepreneurship Theory and Practice, 29*(5): 555–576.

Chrisman, J. J., Chua, J. H., & Steier, L. P. 2005. Sources and consequences of distinctive familiness: An introduction. *Entrepreneurship Theory and Practice, 29*(3): 237–248.

Chua, J. H., Chrisman, J. J., Steier, L. P., & Rau, S. B. 2012. Sources of heterogeneity in family firms: An introduction. *Entrepreneurship and Theory and Practice, 36*(6): 1103–1113.

Combs, J. G., Shanine, K. K., Burrows, S., Allen, J. S., & Pounds, T. W. 2020. What do we know about business families? Setting the stage for leveraging family science theories. *Family Business Review, 33*(1): 38–63.

Cunningham, W. V., & Maloney, W. F. 2001. Heterogeneity among Mexico's microenterprises: An application of factor and cluster analysis. *Economic Development and Cultural Change, 50*(1): 131–156.

De Dreu, C. K. W., & Van Vianen, A. E. M. 2001. Managing relationship conflict and the effectiveness of organizational teams. *Journal of Organizational Behavior, 22*: 309–328.

De Massis, A., Chua, J. H., & Chrisman, J. J. 2008. Factors preventing intra-family succession. *Family Business Review, 21*(2): 183–199.

De Meur, G., Rihoux, B., & Yamasaki, S. 2009. Addressing the critiques of QCA. In B. Rihoux, & C. C. Ragin (Eds.), *Configurational Comparative Methods*: 147–165. Los Angeles: Sage.

Debicki, B., Kellermanns, F. W., Chrisman, J., Pearson, A. W., & Spencer, B. 2016. Development of a socioemotional wealth importance (SEWi) scale for family firm research. *Journal of Family Business Strategy, 7*(1): 47–57.

Debicki, B. J., Matherne, C. F., Kellermanns, F. W., & Chrisman, J. J. 2009. Family business research in the new millennium: An overview of the who, the where, the what, and the why. *Family Business Review, 22*(2): 151–166.

DeCoster, J., Gallucci, M., & Iselin, A. M. R. 2011. Best practices for using median splits, artificial categorization, and their continuous alternatives. *Journal of Experimental Psychopathology, 2*(2): 197–209.

Delery, J. E. 1998. Issues of fit in strategic human resource management: Implications for research. *Human Resource Management Review*, 8(3): 289–331.

Doty, D. H., & Glick, W. H. 1994. Typologies as a unique form of theory building: Toward improved understanding and modeling. *Academy of Management Review*, 19(2): 230–251.

Dyer Jr, W. G., & Dyer, W. J. 2009. Putting the family into family business research. *Family Business Review*, 22(3): 216–219.

Eddleston, K., Otondo, R., & Kellermanns, F. W. 2008. Conflict, participative decision-making, and generational ownership dispersion: A multilevel analysis. *Journal of Small Business Management*, 47(1): 456–484.

Fiegener, M. K. 2010. Locus of ownership and family involvement in small private firms. *Journal of Management Studies*, 47(2): 296–321.

Fiss, P. C. 2007. A set-theoretic approach to organizational configurations. *Academy of Management Review*, 32(4): 1180–1198.

Gedajlovic, E., Carney, M., Chrisman, J. J., & Kellermanns, F. W. 2012. The adolescence of family firm research: Taking stock and planning for the future. *Journal of Management*, 38(4): 1010–1037.

Gellatly, I. R., Hunter, K. H., Curriea, L. G., & Irving, P. G. 2009. HRM practices and organizational commitment profiles. *International Journal of Human Resource Management*, 20(4): 869–884.

Gersick, K. E., Davis, J. A., Hampton, M. M., & Lansberg, I. 1997. *Generation to Generation: Life Cycles of the Family Business*. Boston, MA: Harvard Business School Press.

Gómez-Mejía, L. R., Haynes, K. T., Núñez-Nickel, M., Jacobson, K. J. L., & Moyano-Fuentes, H. 2007. Socioemotional wealth and business risk in family-controlled firms: Evidence from Spanish olive oil mills. *Administrative Science Quarterly*, 52(1): 106–137.

Hansen, C., & Block, J. 2020. Exploring the relation between family involvement and firms' financial performance: A replication and extension meta-analysis. *Journal of Business Venturing Insights*, 13: e00158.

Hauck, J., Suess-Reyes, J., Beck, S., Prügl, R., & Frank, H. 2016. Measuring socioemotional wealth in family-owned and -managed firms: A validation and short form of the FIBER Scale. *Journal of Family Business Strategy*, 7(3): 133–148.

Hino, A. 2009. Time-series QCA: Studying temporal change through Boolean analysis. *Sociological Theory and Methods*, 24(2): 247–265.

Hsiao, Y. H., Chen, L. F., Chang, C. C., & Chiu, F. H. 2016. Configurational path to customer satisfaction and stickiness for a restaurant chain using fuzzy set qualitative comparative analysis. *Journal of Business Research*, 69(8): 2939–2949.

Huang, X., Chen, L., Xu, E., Lu, F., & Tam, K. C. 2020. Shadow of the prince: Parent-incumbents' coercive control over child-successors in family organizations. *Administrative Science Quarterly*, 65(3): 710–750.

Jaskiewicz, P., Combs, J. G., Block, J. H., & Miller, D. 2017. Founder versus family owners' impact on pay dispersion among non-CEO top managers: Implications for firm performance. *Journal of Management*, 43(5): 1524–1552.

Jaskiewicz, P., Combs, J. G., Shanine, K. K., & Kacmar, K. M. 2017. Introducing the family: A review of family science with implications for management research. *Academy of Management Annals*, 11(1): 309–341.

Kellermanns, F. W., & Eddleston, K. 2007. Family perspective on when conflict benefits family firm performance. *Journal of Business Research*, 60(10): 1048–1057.

Klein, S. B., Astrachan, J. H., & Smyrnios, K. X. 2005. The F-PEC scale of family influence: Construction, validation, and further implication for theory. *Entrepreneurship: Theory & Practice, 29*(3): 321–339.

Lohwasser, T. S., Hoch, F., & Kellermanns, F. W. 2022. Strength in stability: A meta-analysis of family firm performance moderated by institutional stability and regime type. *Entrepreneurship Theory and Practice, 46*(1): 117–158.

Mazzola, P., Sciascia, S., & Kellermanns, F. W. 2013. Non-linear effects of family sources of power on performance. *Journal of Business Research, 66*(4): 568–574.

McKee, D., Madden, T. M., Kellermanns, F. W., & Eddleston, K. A. 2014. Conflicts in family firms: The good and the bad. In L. Melin, M. Nordqvist, & P. Sharma (Eds.), *SAGE Handbook of Family Business*: 514–528. London: Sage.

Meyer, A. D., Tsui, A. S., & Hinings, C. R. 1993. Configurational approaches to organizational analysis. *Academy of Management Journal, 36*(6): 1175–1195.

Meyer, J. P., Morin, A. J., & Vandenberghe, C. 2015. Dual commitment to organization and supervisor: A person-centered approach. *Journal of Vocational Behavior, 88*: 56–72.

Meyer, J. P., Stanley, L. J., & Parfyonova, N. M. 2012. Employee commitment in context: The nature and implications of commitment profiles. *Journal of Vocational Behavior, 80*(1): 1–16.

Meyer, J. P., Stanley, L. J., & Vandenberg, R. J. 2013. A person-centered approach to the study of commitment. *Human Resource Management Review, 23*(2): 190–202.

Miller, D., Le Breton-Miller, I., & Lester, R. H. 2010. Family ownership and acquisition behavior in publicly traded companies. *Strategic Management Journal, 31*(2): 201–223.

Misangyi, V. F., Greckhamer, T., Furnari, S., Fiss, P. C., Crilly, D., & Aguilera, R. 2017. Embracing causal complexity: The emergence of a neo-configurational perspective. *Journal of Management, 43*(1): 255–282.

Morris, L., & Kellermanns, F. W. 2013. Family relations and family businesses: A note from the guest editors. *Family Relations, 62*: 379–383.

Neubaum, D. O., Kammerlander, N., & Brigham, K. H. 2019. Capturing family firm heterogeneity: How taxonomies and typologies can help the field move forward. *Family Business Review, 32*(2): 106–130.

Nylund, K. L., Asparouhov, T., & Muthén, B. O. 2007. Deciding on the number of profiles in latent profile analysis and growth mixture modeling: A Monte Carlo simulation study. *Structural Equation Modeling: A Multidisciplinary Journal, 14*(4): 535–569.

Qui, H., & Freel, M. 2020. Managing family-related conflicts in family businesses: A review and research agenda. *Family Business Review, 33*(1): 90–113.

Ragin, C. C. 2014. *The Comparative Method: Moving Beyond Qualitative and Quantitative Strategies*. Oakland, CA: University of California Press.

Rovelli, P., Ferasso, M., De Massis, A., & Kraus, S. 2021. Thirty years of research in family business journals: Status quo and future directions. *Journal of Family Business Strategy, 13*(3): 100422.

Rucker, D. D., McShane, B. B., & Preacher, K. J. 2015. A researcher's guide to regression, discretization, and median splits of continuous variables. *Journal of Consumer Psychology, 25*(4): 666–678.

Schulze, W. S., & Kellermanns, F. W. 2015. Reifying socioemotional wealth. *Entrepreneurship Theory & Practice, 39*(3): 447–459.

Sharma, P. 2003. *A Typology of Family Firms using Internal Stakeholders*. Paper presented at the Proceedings of the Administrative Sciences Association of Canada's annual conference in Halifax.

Short, J. C., Payne, G. T., & Ketchen, D. J. 2008. Research on organizational configurations: Past accomplishments and future challenges. *Journal of Management, 34*(6): 1053–1079.

Sinclair, R. R., Tucker, J. S., Wright, C., & Cullen, J. C. 2005. Performance differences among four organizational commitment profiles. *Journal of Applied Psychology, 90*: 1280–1287.

Sorenson, R. L. 1999. Conflict management strategies used in successful family businesses. *Family Business Review, 12*(4): 325–339.

Stanley, L., Hernández-Linares, R., López-Fernández, M. C., & Kellermanns, F. W. 2019. A taxonomy of family firms and entrepreneurial orientation. *Family Business Review, 32*(2): 174–194.

Stanley, L. J., Kellermanns, F. W., & Zellweger, T. 2017. Latent profile analysis: Understanding family firm profiles. *Family Business Review, 30*(1): 84–102.

Wagner, D., Block, J. H., Miller, D., Schens, C., & Xi, G. 2015. A meta-analysis of the financial performance of family firms: Another attempt. *Journal of Family Business Strategy, 6*(1): 3–13.

Weber, M. 1978. *Economy and society: An outline of interpretive sociology*. Oakland, CA: University of California Press.

Westhead, P., & Howorth, C. 2007. 'Types' of private family firm: An exploratory conceptual and empirical analysis. *Entrepreneurship and Regional Development, 19*(5): 405–431.

Williams, R., Pieper, T., Kellermanns, F. W., & Astrachan, J. 2018. Family business goals and their effect on strategy, family and organizational behavior: A review and research agenda. *International Journal of Management Reviews, 20*(S1): S63–S82.

Williams, R. I., Pieper, T. M., Kellermanns, F. W., & Astrachan, J. H. 2019. Family business goal formation: A literature review and discussion of alternative algorithms. *Management Review Quarterly, 69*: 329–349.

Yu, A., Lumpkin, G. T., Brigham, K. H., & Sorenson, R. L. 2012. The landscape of family business outcomes: A summary and numerical taxonomy of dependent variables. *Family Business Review, 25*(1): 33–57.

# 16. An introduction to the use of social network analysis in family business research

## Curt B. Moore and Karen Nicholas

## INTRODUCTION

Social structure is the persistent pattern of social ties among actors in a system (Berkowitz, 1982). Common social structures examined in family business research are the family (i.e., the business family) and the family business (i.e., the family business organization). Conceptually, scholars suggest familial and organizational social structures are interdependent, nested systems (Chirico & Salvato, 2016; Distelberg & Blow, 2011); enmeshed collectives that are non-distinct from one another (Carr et al., 2011; Pearson et al., 2008); or in terms of a distinct, dominant family group with concentrated ownership and management within the business (Arregle et al., 2007). Despite somewhat different conceptualizations of a family's embeddedness in a family business, scholars share the view that this embeddedness differentiates family businesses from other organizations (Craig & Lumpkin, Chapter 3 in this book; Sharma, 2008; Zellweger et al., 2019). For example, research suggests family businesses share distinct communication patterns, relational norms, and social goals (Aldrich & Cliff, 2003; Zellweger, 2017). Additionally, social structure has also been used to advance explanations of the family firm's internal and external social capital (e.g., Arregle et al., 2007; Sirmon & Hitt, 2003), resilience (e.g., Chrisman et al., 2011), and survival (e.g., Dyer & Mortensen, 2005).

Herein, we present a practical, introductory guide on the use of social network analysis to examine relational patterns (i.e., social structures) that are paramount to understanding family businesses, such as ties among family members, familial and non-familial ties within a family business, or between a family business and its external partners (Zellweger et al., 2019). Social network analysis is designed to model social structure and analyze one set of relations (e.g., among family members) in the context of one or more other sets of relations (e.g., among members of a family business) (Marin & Wellman, 2011) across multiple levels of analysis (Gedajlovic et al., 2013; Payne et al., 2011). Therefore, social network analysis is especially suited to contribute to family business research given familial social structure (i.e., network of relations among family members) influences both the internal social structure of the family business and external relationships with stakeholders (e.g., Pearson et al., 2008; Sharma, 2008; Sorenson et al., 2009; Steier et al., 2009, 2015).

In the following, we present an overview of basic social network concepts and terminology. We then discuss research design and data collection. Finally, we conclude with a discussion of data management and software.

## OVERVIEW OF SOCIAL NETWORKS

Social network data consist of a set of nodes (i.e., actors) and edges (i.e., relations among nodes). Contrary to conventional data that consists of a set of actors and their attributes, social network data is constructed as a set of actors and their relations. While nodes could conceivably be almost anything, nodes in business research are typically individuals or collectives (e.g., groups or teams, business units, organizations, or communities) (Borgatti & Foster, 2003). In addition, a variety of relations (e.g., friendship, communication, resource exchange, ownership, etc.) among actors can be analyzed. However, each relation constitutes a particular social network. For example, if one analyzes friendship ties among a set of actors, he or she is studying a friendship network. If one analyzes communication between a set of actors, then a communication network is being studied.

### Types of Ties

Researchers tend to analyze two basic types of ties (see Table 16.1): relational states (i.e., continuous relationships between nodes that exist over some period of time) and relational events (e.g., discrete incidents or occurrences) (Borgatti & Halgin, 2011). Types of relational states include similarities (e.g., location, membership, attributes, etc.) and social relations (e.g., kinship and other roles, thoughts or feelings that individuals have about one another, etc.). Types of relational events include interactions (e.g., advising, communication, etc.) and flows (e.g., information, resources, etc.).

In family business research, scholars have examined a variety of relational states and events between individuals and collectives (see Table 16.1). In terms of individual similarities, scholars have examined differences between female and male founders' use of family support (e.g., Powell & Eddleston, 2013) and ties among family business leaders that are members of the same professional or civic associations (e.g., Caspersz & Thomas, 2015). Other relational roles

*Table 16.1*　　*Types of ties*

| | Relational States | | Relational Events | |
| --- | --- | --- | --- | --- |
| | Similarities | Social Relations | Interactions | Flows |
| | Location (e.g., same spatial or temporal space) Membership (e.g., same club, event, etc.) Attribute (e.g., same gender, attitude, etc.) | Kinship or Other Roles (e.g., mother of; friend of; competitor of, etc.) Affective or Cognitive (e.g., trust; acquaintance, aware of, etc.) | e.g., seeks advice from; communicates with, etc. | e.g., information, resources, etc. |
| Individual-level Relations | Female vs. male founders; Members of a managerial roundtable | Kinship networks; Trust between family and non-family members | Frequency of interactions between family members; Feedback or advice from family members | Intergenerational knowledge transfer between family business leaders; Financial support from family members |
| Collective-level Relations | Family Businesses co-located in the same community or region; Members of Small Business Development Centers | Supplier or marketing partnerships; Strategic alliances and joint ventures; Competitors | Frequency of interaction between alliance partners; Repeated transactions between a family firm and its business partners (e.g., supplier or customer organizations) | Family firm's equity investments in new ventures; Information sharing between a firm and its business partners |

*Source:*　　Adapted from Borgatti et al. (2018).

include cooperative and competitive ties between organizations (e.g., Moore et al., 2019; Sorenson et al., 2009). In addition to family and kinship roles (e.g., Daspit & Long, 2014), examples of individual social relations include inter-personal trust and support among family members and other individuals in the family business, such as top management team members or other employees in the family business (e.g., Chang et al., 2009; Salvato & Melin, 2008).

In terms of individual relational events, family business research includes frequency of interaction and advising among family members (e.g., Chang et al., 2009; Mustakallio et al., 2002), between family members and other family business leaders (e.g., Caspersz & Thomas, 2015), and resource flows (e.g., information sharing, knowledge sharing, and financial capital) between family members (e.g., Edelman et al., 2016; Steier, 2001). Examples of collective-level relational states in family business research include family businesses that are members of economic development centers (e.g., Mustakallio et al., 2002; Werbel & Danes, 2010) and family businesses in the same region or country (e.g., Salvato & Melin, 2008; Su & Carney, 2013). Social relations among family businesses and other organizations include inter-organizational ties with customers, government agencies, financial organizations, and other businesses (e.g., Sorenson et al., 2009; Zahra, 2010). Finally, examples of collective-level flows include information sharing and equity investments between family firms and other businesses or organizations (e.g., Wu, 2008; Zahra, 2010).

Despite some exceptions, social network analysis generally treats different relations as separate social structures. For example, communication ties are conceptually distinct from trust ties, as repeated communications between employees and a manager do not necessarily equate to trust. Further, trust ties may be characterized by frequent or infrequent communication – e.g., a person may have relatively few or frequent interactions with someone she or he trusts (Levin et al., 2011). In another example, contractual marketing or supply agreements between organizations are logically distinct from joint venture relations that require substantially more commitment and equity investments between firms (Cross et al., 2009), unless one were simply ana-lyzing 'inter-organizational' ties without respect to the level of investment or commitment between firms. Thus, scholars employing social network analyses must make deliberate choices when defining a particular relation and nodes based on the research question and explanatory theory (Borgatti & Halgin, 2011).

## RESEARCH DESIGN

A social network is a social structure, within which actors are embedded, defined by a relation. Instead of selecting a random sample of actors, network studies usually include all of the actors within some kind of *boundary defined by a relation* (Borgatti & Halgin, 2011). Consequently, it is the researcher that defines a network by choosing a type of tie and set of nodes based on the study's research question and theoretical framing. Below, we discuss approaches to designing social network research and related levels of analysis.

Broadly speaking, there are two basic approaches used in social network analysis. On one hand, an ego-centric approach is focused on each actor's local social environment and network position at the node-level (Scott, 1991). In social network analysis, the term 'ego' refers to a focal actor, such as an individual or firm, and the actors connected to a particular ego are referred to as 'alters'. From an ego-centric perspective, the influence of networks on a node is mediated by direct links to its alters (Scott, 1991). For example, a research question regarding how well an employee is connected within an organization (e.g., the number of direct friendship ties to other nodes in the network) is related to his or her leadership ability would be consistent with an ego-centric approach. As another example in a family business context, we might define the focal relation in terms of advice ties and be particularly interested in nodes from whom family members seek advice.

On the other hand, a socio-centric approach focuses on the pattern or structure of connections at the network-level, including the composition of the network in terms of cohesive sub-group structures (e.g., cliques). From a socio-centric perspective, the influence of the network on its members is not only mediated through their direct links, but also by the group- or network-level structure (Scott, 1991). For example, a research question regarding how cohesion within a family business is related to firm-level outcomes is consistent with a socio-centric approach.

Socio-centric approaches include analysis of the composition of sub-groups within a network. Analyzing cohesive sub-groups may uncover unique socio-structural aspects of family businesses. For example, family business scholars have conceptualized the family as a distinct, dominant coalition within the family business who have concentrated ownership and management (Arregle et al., 2007). Social network analysis could be utilized to examine the social structure of the family business in terms of the family sub-group and other cohesive sub-groups to uncover the costs or benefits of the family occupying a dominant coalition (e.g., Gentry et al., 2016). In addition, research questions may relate to how stratification within the family business's social network influences differences in group- or network-level properties (e.g., diffusion, shared values, information exchange, etc.). In social network analyses, sub-groups are also identified by the terms: cluster, community (Borgatti et al., 2018), sub-graphs (Scott, 2017), and cliques (Luke, 2015).

In addition to node- and network-levels of analysis, dyadic-level analyses focus on relations between pairs of actors, examining the nature of relationships between actors and 'how these relational characteristics affect the likelihood of the relationship's renewal, continuation, dissolution, or other outcomes' (Zaheer et al., 2010, p. 66). Since the dyadic level of analysis focuses on pairwise relations, these analyses usually examine how one type of relation (e.g., friendship ties) is related to another kind of relation (e.g., advice ties) among the same set of actors (cf., Mizruchi & Marquis, 2006). For example, assume a researcher is interested in how a family business's strategic alliance ties are predictive of the firm's mergers and acquisitions. A dyadic analysis would assess the degree to which pairs of firms with strategic alliance relationships develop into merger/acquisition ties.

As discussed in the 'Types of Ties' section, social network methods require the researcher to clearly define network boundaries based on the research question and explanatory theory. For example, Brass (1984) examined how an organization's social structure influences perceptions of power and promotions. In this study, he modeled an organization's social structure in terms of multiple intra-organizational networks, defined in terms of formal reporting, communication, and friendship ties. His findings indicated that occupying a local, central position within a department's communication network was positively related to power and promotions, while occupying a central position within the entire organization's communication network was not.

## DATA COLLECTION

In this section, we discuss survey and archival methods to collect relationship data for (1) directed or undirected ties, (2) valued or binary ties, and (3) one- or two-mode data. We follow this overview with a discussion of survey and archival data collection.

Directed ties are used to represent a relationship from one actor to another. For example, a researcher studying advice ties may be interested in actors who seek or receive advice. Alternatively, the researcher may be interested in actors who tend to provide advice. A third alternative would be reciprocated ties – i.e., individuals who seek and provide advice to one another. For relations where direction is of no import or direction is not available, undirected ties are used. For example, if one was collecting data on actors who sit on a board of a professional organization together, then simply coding an undirected tie between all members is logical. However, if one were collecting data on communication patterns, advice seeking, etc., then directed ties might be more useful.

In addition to directed or undirected ties, relationships may be measured as binary or valued. On one hand, binary ties simply indicate the presence of a relationship between two nodes. On the other hand, valued ties are used to measure the strength of a relationship. Granovetter (1973, p. 1361) suggested tie strength to be multidimensional when stating, 'the strength of a tie is a (probably linear) combination of the amount of time, the emotional intensity, the intimacy (mutual confiding) and the reciprocal services which characterize the tie.' Subsequent research by Marsden and Campbell (1984) suggests time spent in the relationship (e.g., relationship duration and frequency of contact) and depth of the relationship (e.g., closeness or intensity) are distinct aspects of tie strength between individuals (Marsden & Campbell, 1984). Other scholars drawing on social psychology have suggested the provision of emotional support and reciprocity serve as important measures of tie strength (Friedkin, 1990; Wellman, 1982). In terms of inter-organizational relationships, tie strength measures include transaction frequency between organizations and the degree to which a firm's transactions are concentrated in a set of partners (Moore et al., 2018). In addition, inter-organizational tie strength has been conceptualized as varying from information-sharing agreements to integrated decision making (Cross et al., 2009). In sum, there are a variety of ways to conceptualize tie strength. Like any research, the ultimate decision regarding how best to measure a construct (e.g., tie strength) begins with theoretical conceptualization (e.g., Marsden & Campbell, 2012). For example, Shi et al. (2009) suggest tie strength in a marketing context be conceptualized in terms of (1) emotional attachment, (2) expectations that a relationship will be rewarding, and (3) long-term commitment.

The preceding discussion of directed and valued ties was oriented to collecting data on relational ties between a single set of actors, which is referred to as one-mode data. However, relationship data may also be in the form of actors that are members of the same group or attend the same events. Since these data consist of two types of nodes – one type consisting of the actors and another type consisting of groups or events – it is referred to as two-mode data. For example, data on interlocking directorates is often in the form of individual company directors (first mode) and the companies on whom each individual is a board member (second mode).

## Survey Data Collection

Data collected for social network research generally utilizes observational/ field designs to collect survey or archival data. Depending on the number of nodes in a social network, surveys[1] that collect social network data typically include a full roster of all nodes included in the network or, in the case of large networks, utilize name generator instruments. Figure 16.1 is an example of

---

[1]    *Organizational Network Analysis Surveys* (www.onasurveys.com) provides a set of tools for collecting social network data via surveys.

| | Q1. Related to by blood or marriage | Q2. Consider a friend | Q3. Go to for professional advice | Q4. Go to for personal advice | Q5. Prefer to avoid | Q6. Usually communicate with | | | | |
|---|---|---|---|---|---|---|---|---|---|---|
| | | | | | | Seldom (less than once weekly) | | | | Often (several times daily) |
| Jae Johannes | ☐ | ☐ | ☐ | ☐ | ☐ | 1 | 2 | 3 | 4 | 5 |
| Elsa Edge | ☐ | ☐ | ☐ | ☐ | ☐ | 1 | 2 | 3 | 4 | 5 |
| Fredericka Fogarty | ☐ | ☐ | ☐ | ☐ | ☐ | 1 | 2 | 3 | 4 | 5 |
| Jaye Jonas | ☐ | ☐ | ☐ | ☐ | ☐ | 1 | 2 | 3 | 4 | 5 |
| Serita Schoening | ☐ | ☐ | ☐ | ☐ | ☐ | 1 | 2 | 3 | 4 | 5 |
| Claretta Crouch | ☐ | ☐ | ☐ | ☐ | ☐ | 1 | 2 | 3 | 4 | 5 |
| Patria Pinkard | ☐ | ☐ | ☐ | ☐ | ☐ | 1 | 2 | 3 | 4 | 5 |
| Latarsha Leone | ☐ | ☐ | ☐ | ☐ | ☐ | 1 | 2 | 3 | 4 | 5 |
| Debby Darville | ☐ | ☐ | ☐ | ☐ | ☐ | 1 | 2 | 3 | 4 | 5 |
| Mohammad Meserve | ☐ | ☐ | ☐ | ☐ | ☐ | 1 | 2 | 3 | 4 | 5 |
| Arden Ambrose | ☐ | ☐ | ☐ | ☐ | ☐ | 1 | 2 | 3 | 4 | 5 |
| Robbin Ridlon | ☐ | ☐ | ☐ | ☐ | ☐ | 1 | 2 | 3 | 4 | 5 |
| Nakia Nailor | ☐ | ☐ | ☐ | ☐ | ☐ | 1 | 2 | 3 | 4 | 5 |
| Dorian Dustin | ☐ | ☐ | ☐ | ☐ | ☐ | 1 | 2 | 3 | 4 | 5 |
| Queen Quijas | ☐ | ☐ | ☐ | ☐ | ☐ | 1 | 2 | 3 | 4 | 5 |
| Maddie Mainor | ☐ | ☐ | ☐ | ☐ | ☐ | 1 | 2 | 3 | 4 | 5 |
| Erich Escareno | ☐ | ☐ | ☐ | ☐ | ☐ | 1 | 2 | 3 | 4 | 5 |

*Source*:    Adapted from Borgatti et al. (2018) and Brass (1984).

*Figure 16.1    Example of social network data collection via a survey*

using a roster to collect one-mode, survey data. All of the questions (Q1–6) collect directed ties, any of which could be converted to undirected ties by symmetrizing the relationships (symmetrizing is discussed in the next section). Questions 1–5 ask respondents to simply indicate if a tie is present to capture the presence of various ties including family, friendship, and advice ties. Since questions 1–5 do not assess the frequency or strength of a tie, these are examples of binary ties. Question 6, however, asks the respondent how frequently she or he communicates with another actor, which is an example of a valued tie. Additional questions could be included to capture the strength of one or more ties by asking questions such as 'How much do you trust ____?', or 'How much does this person help you beyond that required by their job?', or 'How much influence does this person have on the organization?'

For surveys with many nodes, data collection using a full roster can be burdensome for the respondent and lead to non-responses (Borgatti et al., 2018). In these situations, name generator instruments may be used to ask a respondent to name a specified number of people with whom they have a particular type of relationship (e.g., list five people whom you seek advice from).

**Archival Data Collection**

Archival data on social networks is frequently two-mode. At the organizational level, an example of archival data is the Securities Data Company (SDC)

Platinum™ Joint Ventures and Alliance Database which provides data on the joint ventures and strategic alliances of public companies. These data include an alliance ID number that indicates group membership by a particular set of alliance partners. Analyses based on two-mode data typically assume that membership in the same group or event indicates interactions among actors and, therefore, a social relationship. Also, this type of data is typically treated as undirected. A common approach to analyzing this data is to convert two-mode data to one-mode using social network analytical software, which is discussed in the following Data Management and Software section of this chapter.

A consistent challenge with network research is ensuring the research question and the network measures are aligned. For example, research focusing on the benefits of association networks may attempt to use association membership as an indication of a tie. If that tie only indicates the payment of an annual membership fee, then it may not be a valid measure of an actual engagement or social relationship. Thus, measuring meeting attendance or actual engagement may be necessary to produce a reliable and valid measure of the construct. The link between the theoretical argument and the network measure should be explicit.

## DATA MANAGEMENT AND SOFTWARE

Ultimately, network analyses will require the data to be structured into an affiliation or adjacency matrix. An adjacency matrix is used for one-mode data and constructed as a square, actor-by-actor matrix. An affiliation matrix is used for two-mode data constructed as an actor-by-groups or events matrix. This data can be imported into social network analysis software in three primary formats: a matrix or as an edgelist, one-mode or two-mode, and directed or undirected. In the following, we provide examples of each.

Figure 16.2 illustrates one-mode, directed data depicted in graphical, matrix, and edgelist formats. All three formats provide the same information, but in different formats. For example, the graph in Figure 16.2 indicates a directed tie from actor 0 to both actor 1 and actor 2, while actor 1 only has a directed tie to actor 3. This information is depicted in the matrix format as an actor-by-actor matrix, where rows represent the source of a tie and columns represent the recipient of the tie. For actor 0, a value of 1 is entered in cells (row 0, column 1) and (row 0, column 2). For actor 1, a value of 1 is entered in cell (row 1, column 3). The edgelist in Figure 16.2 depicts this same information organized as the source of tie in the first column and recipient in the second column. Social network analysis software will also enable the user to import edgelist data, then convert the data to a square, actor-by-actor, adjacency matrix.

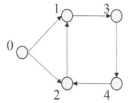

| | Matrix | | | | | Edgelist | |
|---|---|---|---|---|---|---|---|
| | **0** | **1** | **2** | **3** | **4** | **0** | **1** |
| **0** | 0 | 1 | 1 | 0 | 0 | 0 | 2 |
| **1** | 0 | 0 | 0 | 1 | 0 | 1 | 3 |
| **2** | 0 | 1 | 0 | 0 | 0 | 2 | 1 |
| **3** | 0 | 0 | 0 | 0 | 1 | 3 | 4 |
| **4** | 0 | 0 | 1 | 0 | 0 | 4 | 2 |

*Figure 16.2*     *Example directed graph and one-mode network data formatted as an adjacency matrix and edgelist*

This example uses binary ties to indicate the presence (value = 1) or lack (value = 0) of tie between two actors. If a strength of tie measure was used, then values other than 1 would be entered. Further, the software can also 'dichoto-mize' valued ties – i.e., convert valued ties to binary ties. Furthermore, social network analysis software can easily 'symmetrize' directed ties – i.e., convert directed ties to undirected ties. Symmetrizing involves making the top right half of the matrix the mirror image of the bottom half (Borgatti et al, 2018).

Figure 16.3 illustrates two-mode, undirected data depicted in graphical, matrix, and edgelist formats. Two-mode data illustrate connections between actors and their membership (e.g., between people and events or organizations and alliance membership). All three formats provide the same information, albeit in different formats. A two-mode matrix typically has actors in rows (e.g., actors 0–4) and group membership or events in columns (e.g., group or event A–E), while the edgelist will have actors listed in the first column and events or groupings in the second column. Although a variety of advanced analytical procedures are available for two-mode affiliation data, many researchers use the software to easily convert two-mode data to one-mode data. The final edgelist in Figure 16.3 has transformed the two-mode dataset into a one-mode dataset, removing the grouping structure and indicating the direct relationships between actors.

While there are multiple software options available for analyzing networks (see Huisman & van Duijn, 2011 for a review of social network analysis soft-ware), we wish to highlight three core tools: UCINET, R, and Stata. UCINET (Borgatti et al., 2002) was developed for the analysis of social network data and comes with NetDraw, which is a visualization tool. A free trial version of the software is available and a license is reasonably priced. The book *Analyzing Social Networks* (Borgatti et al., 2018), while an excellent text on the topic, also provides examples of how to analyze network data with UCINET. The main drawback in using UCINET is its challenges when dealing with large datasets (> 5000 nodes) as is noted in its documentation.

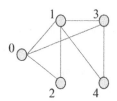

| | A | B | C | D | E | Two-mode Edgelist | | One-mode Edgelist | |
|---|---|---|---|---|---|---|---|---|---|
| | | | Matrix | | | 0 | A | 0 | 1 |
| 0 | 1 | 1 | 1 | 0 | 0 | 0 | B | 0 | 2 |
| 1 | 1 | 0 | 0 | 1 | 1 | 0 | C | 0 | 3 |
| 2 | 0 | 1 | 0 | 1 | 0 | 1 | A | 1 | 2 |
| 3 | 0 | 0 | 1 | 0 | 1 | 1 | D | 1 | 3 |
| 4 | 0 | 0 | 0 | 0 | 1 | 1 | E | 1 | 4 |
| | | | | | | 2 | B | 3 | 4 |
| | | | | | | 2 | D | | |
| | | | | | | 3 | C | | |
| | | | | | | 3 | E | | |
| | | | | | | 4 | A | | |
| | | | | | | 4 | E | | |

*Figure 16.3    Example of undirected graph and network data formatted as a one-mode affiliation matrix, two-mode edgelist, and one-mode edgelist*

In most cases, network analysis will be utilized to create one or more variables that are subsequently used in other analyses (e.g., OLS regression). For example, if a researcher is interested in how individual-level outcomes (e.g., promotion, job satisfaction, etc.) are predicted by how well connected an actor is to others, then social network software (e.g., UCINET) could be used to generate a centrality measure. Then, this centrality could be used as an independent variable in another statistical software package (e.g., SPSS, SAS, Stata) to model its effect on one or more dependent variables. While UCINET can also conduct other statistical analyses, it is likely that users will create network measures within UCINET and then import the measures into the statistical software package of their choice for more traditional analysis (e.g., OLS regression).

R is a free, open-source software program, providing 'an integrated suite of software facilities for data manipulation, calculation and graphical display' ('The R Environment', www.r-project.org/about.html). For those not willing to spend the time to get acquainted with some of the idiosyncrasies of the R workspace and syntax, downloading RStudio (a friendly, free user interface) will ease the process tremendously. The pros and cons of R tend to be two sides of the same coin. On the positive side, the R system contains thousands of packages that support statistical analyses. On the not-so-positive side, with this expansive list of capabilities there are commensurate challenges with knowing which package to use and when to use them. Luke's (2015) text *A User's*

*Guide to Network Analysis in R* takes the reader through multiple packages to support the analysis and visualization of social networks.

Stata can be used for social network analysis by installing the *nwcommands* package developed by Thomas Grund. The *nwcommands* package provides extensive capabilities for analyzing and visualizing social networks within Stata (https://nwcommands.wordpress.com). This package needs to be installed separately from the core Stata product. While a much-anticipated book *Social Network Analysis Using Stata* is not in press at the time of writing this chapter, Grund has provided extensive help and support materials on the website www.nwcommands.org. Note that the process to create network variables in Stata requires similar efforts (importing matrix or edgelist, denoting directed or undirected, etc.) as it does in UCINET or R.

## CONCLUSION

We see substantial promise in the use of social networks to model prominent social structures of interest to family business researchers. We hope that this brief chapter provides interested scholars with a practical introduction to the use of social network analysis in family business research.

## REFERENCES

Aldrich, H. E. & Cliff, J. E. (2003). The pervasive effects of family on entrepreneurship: Toward a family embeddedness perspective. *Journal of Business Venturing, 18*(5), 573–596.

Arregle, J-L., Hitt, M. A., Sirmon, D. G., & Very, P. (2007). The development of organizational social capital: Attributes of family firms. *Journal of Management Studies, 44*, 73–95.

Berkowitz, S. D. (1982). *An Introduction to Structural Analysis: The Network Approach to Social Research.* Butterworth & Co.: Toronto.

Borgatti, S. P. & Foster, P. C. (2003). The network paradigm in organizational research: A review and typology. *Journal of Management, 29*(6), 991–1013.

Borgatti, S. P. & Halgin, D. (2011). On network theory. *Organization Science, 22*(5), 1168–1181.

Borgatti, S. P., Everett, M. G., & Freeman, L. C. (2002). *UCINET for Windows: Software for Social Network Analysis.* Analytic Technologies: Harvard, MA.

Borgatti, S. P., Everett, M. G., & Johnson, J. C. (2018). *Analyzing Social Networks*, 2nd edition. Sage: London.

Brass, D. J. (1984). Being in the right place: A structural analysis of individual influence in an organization. *Administrative Science Quarterly, 29*, 518–539.

Carr, J. C., Cole, M. S., Ring, J. K., & Blettner, D. P. (2011). A measure of variations in internal social capital among family firms. *Entrepreneurship Theory and Practice, 35*(6), 1207–1227.

Caspersz, D. & Thomas, J. (2015). Developing positivity in family business leaders. *Family Business Review, 28*(1), 60–75.

Chang, E. P. C., Memili, E., Chrisman, J. J., Kellermanns, F. W., & Chua, J. H. (2009). Family social capital, venture preparedness, and start-up decisions: A study of Hispanic entrepreneurs in New England. *Family Business Review, 22*(3), 279–292.

Chirico, F. & Salvato, C. (2016). Knowledge internalization and product development in family firms: When relational and affective factors matter. *Entrepreneurship Theory and Practice, 40*(1), 201–229.

Chrisman, J. J., Chua, J. H., & Steier, L. P. (2011). Resilience of family firms: An introduction. *Entrepreneurship Theory and Practice, 35*(6), 1107–1119.

Cross, J. E., Dickmann, E., Newman-Gonchar, R., & Fagan, J. M. (2009). Using mixed-method design and network analysis to measure development of interagency collaboration. *American Journal of Evaluation, 30*(3), 310–329.

Daspit, J. J. & Long, R. G. (2014). Mitigating moral hazard in entrepreneurial networks: Examining structural and relational social capital in East Africa. *Entrepreneurship Theory and Practice, 38*(6), 1343–1350.

Distelberg, B. J. & Blow, A. (2011). Variations in family system boundaries. *Family Business Review, 24*(1), 28–46.

Dyer, W. G. & Mortensen, P. S. (2005). Entrepreneurship and family business in a hostile environment: The case of Lithuania. *Family Business Review, 18*(3), 247–258.

Edelman, L. F., Manolova, T., Shirokova, G., & Tsukanova, T. (2016). The impact of family support on young entrepreneurs' start-up activities. *Journal of Business Venturing, 31*(4), 428–448.

Friedkin, N. E. (1990). A Guttman Scale for the strength of an interpersonal tie. *Social Networks, 12*(3), 239–252.

Gedajlovic, E., Honig, B., Moore, C. B., Payne, G. T., & Wright, M. (2013). Social capital and entrepreneurship: A schema and research agenda. *Entrepreneurship Theory and Practice, 37*(3), 455–478.

Gentry, R., Dibrell, C., & Kim, J. (2016). Long-term orientation in publicly traded family businesses: Evidence of a dominant logic. *Entrepreneurship Theory and Practice, 40*(4), 733–757.

Granovetter, M. S. (1973). The strength of weak ties. *American Journal of Sociology, 78*, 1360–1380.

Huisman, M. & van Duijn, M. A. J. (2011). A reader's guide to SNA software. In J. Scott & P. J. Carrington (Eds.), *The SAGE Handbook of Social Network Analysis* (pp. 578–600). Sage: Thousand Oaks, CA.

Levin, D. Z., Walter, J., & Murnighan, J. K. (2011). Dormant ties: The value of reconnecting. *Organization Science, 22*(4), 923–939.

Luke, D. A. (2015). *A User's Guide to Network Analysis in R.* Springer: London.

Marin, A. & Wellman, B. (2011). Social network analysis: An introduction. In J. Scott & P. Carrington (Eds.), *The SAGE Handbook of Social Network Analysis* (pp. 11–25). Sage: London.

Marsden, P. V. & Campbell, K. E. (1984). Measuring tie strength. *Social Forces, 63*(2), 482–501.

Marsden, P. V. & Campbell, K. E. (2012). Reflections on conceptualizing and measuring tie strength. *Social Forces, 91*(1), 17–23.

Mizruchi, M. S. & Marquis, C. (2006). Egocentric, sociocentric, or dyadic? Identifying the appropriate level of analysis in the study of organizational networks. *Social Networks, 28*(3), 187–208.

Moore, C. B., Payne, G. T., Autry, C. W., & Griffis, S. E. (2018). Project complexity and bonding social capital in network organizations. *Group and Organization Management, 43*(6), 936–970.

Moore, C. B., Payne, G. T., Filatotchev, I., & Zajac, E. J. (2019). The cost of status: When social and economic interests collide. *Organization Science, 30*(5), 869–884.

Mustakallio, M., Autio, E., & Zahra, S. A. (2002). Relational and contractual governance in family firms: Effects on strategic decision making. *Family Business Review, 15*(3), 205–222.

Payne, G. T., Moore, C. B., Griffis, S. E., & Autry, C. W. (2011). Multilevel challenges and opportunities in social capital research. *Journal of Management, 37*(2), 491–520.

Pearson, A. W., Carr, J. C., & Shaw, J. C. (2008). Toward a theory of familiness: A social capital perspective. *Entrepreneurship Theory and Practice, 32*(6), 949–969.

Powell, G. N. & Eddleston, K. A. (2013). Linking family-to-business enrichment and support to entrepreneurial success: Do female and male entrepreneurs experience different outcomes? *Journal of Business Venturing, 28*(2), 261–280.

Salvato, C. & Melin, L. (2008). Creating value across generations in family-controlled businesses: The role of family social capital. *Family Business Review, 21*(3), 259–276.

Scott, J. (1991). *Social Network Analysis*. Sage: London.

Scott, J. (2017). *Social Network Analysis* (4th edition). Sage: London.

Sharma, P. (2008). Familiness: Capital stocks and flows between family and business. *Entrepreneurship Theory and Practice, 32*(6), 971–977.

Shi, G., Yi-zheng, S., Allan, K. K. C., and Wang, Y. (2009). Relationship strength in service industries. *International Journal of Market Research, 51*(5), 659–685.

Sirmon, D. G. & Hitt, M. A. (2003). Managing resources: Linking unique resources, management, and wealth creation in family firms. *Entrepreneurship Theory and Practice, 27*(4), 339–358.

Sorenson, R. L., Goodpaster, K. E., Hedberg, P. R., & Yu, A. (2009). The family point of view, family social capital, and firm performance: An exploratory test. *Family Business Review, 22*, 239–253.

Steier, L. (2001). Next-Generation entrepreneurs and succession: An exploratory study of modes and means of managing social capital. *Family Business Review, 14*, 259–276.

Steier, L. P., Chrisman, J. J., & Chua, J. H. (2015). Governance challenges in family businesses and business families. *Entrepreneurship Theory and Practice, 39*(6), 1265–1280.

Steier, L. P., Chua, J. H., & Chrisman, J. J. (2009). Embeddedness perspectives of economic action within family firms. *Entrepreneurship Theory and Practice, 33*(6), 1157–1167.

Su, E. & Carney, M. (2013). Can China's family firms create intellectual capital? *Asia Pacific Journal of Management, 30*(3), 657–675.

Wellman, B. (1982). Studying personal communities. In P. V. Marsden & N. Lin (Eds.), *Social Structure and Network Analysis* (pp. 61–80). Sage: Thousand Oaks, CA.

Werbel, J. D. & Danes, S. M. (2010). Work family conflict in new business ventures: The moderating effects of spousal commitment to the new business venture. *Journal of Small Business Management, 48*(3), 421–440.

Wu, W. (2008). Dimensions of social capital and firm competitiveness improvement: The mediating role of information sharing. *Journal of Management Studies, 45*, 122–146.

Zaheer, A., Gözübüyük, R., & Milanov, H. (2010). It's the connections: The network per-spective in interorganizational research. *Academy of Management Perspectives, 24*(1), 62–77.

Zahra, S. A. (2010). Harvesting family firms' organizational social capital: A relational perspective. *Journal of Management Studies, 47*(2), 345–366.

Zellweger, T. M. (2017). *Managing the Family Business: Theory and Practice.* Edward Elgar Publishing: Cheltenham, UK and Northampton, MA, USA.

Zellweger, T. M., Chrisman, J. J., Chua, J. H., & Steier, L. P. (2019). Social structures, social relationships, and family firms. *Entrepreneurship Theory and Practice, 43*(2), 207–223.

# 17. Endogeneity and the family involvement–firm performance relationship: on the daunting search for instrumental variables

## Wim Voordeckers, Alana Vandebeek, and Ludo Peeters

Since Berle and Means (1932) started the academic conversation about the relationship between ownership structure and performance, many authors have investigated the effects of ownership dispersion or concentration on financial firm performance. During the last two decades, the increasing awareness of the predominance of family ownership around the world has directed this research stream toward the impact of family ownership on firm performance (e.g., Anderson & Reeb, 2003; Maury, 2006; Villalonga & Amit, 2006; Barontini & Caprio, 2006). Although the empirical evidence is not conclusive, several of these studies found that family ownership in general and under specific circumstances can be considered an effective organizational structure. These insights triggered a further investigation of the performance impact of family involvement in governance (e.g., board chair, proportion of family directors) or management (e.g., the family CEO vs. nonfamily CEO distinction) (Bennedsen et al., 2007; Bohren et al., 2019; Daspit et al., Chapter 5 in this book).

An important statistical challenge faced by this ever-growing research stream is the identification of the relationship between family participation in ownership, governance and management and firm performance (Bohren et al., 2019). Indeed, previous studies investigating the relationship between ownership dispersion and performance have pointed to the possibility that the direction of the relationship between ownership and performance may be reversed from firm performance to ownership dispersion (reverse causality) or that both ownership and performance are affected by variables excluded (omitted) from the regression model (representing unobserved heterogeneity), which may introduce an endogeneity problem. Endogeneity is a serious concern as it violates the Ordinary Least Squares (OLS) assumption that the regressor is uncorrelated with the error term, which will lead to inconsistent and biased coefficients (Bascle, 2008). Similar concerns about causal interpretations may apply to the relationship between the CEO or board chair position (Bennedsen et al., 2007; Bohren et al., 2019) and firm performance.

Among the palette of potential solutions, instrumental variables methods rank ahead as the most popular route to address the problem. The standard textbook solution proposes to look for a set of variables – instrumental variables (IVs) – that are significantly 'correlated with the endogenous regressor but uncorrelated with the error in the structural equation' (Larcker & Rusticus, 2010, p. 186). However, the more simple textbook solutions can look, the more daunting the practical challenges can be. Family business scholars face the difficult struggle to find valid ('uncorrelated with the unobserved error term' or 'full exogeneity', which is also referred to as 'exclusion restriction')[1] and strong instruments ('significantly correlated with the regressor' or 'relevance'). This challenging search journey often ends with IVs that do not fully conform to these central statistical requirements. Providing incontestable evidence that the IVs satisfy the exclusion restriction seems to be impossible as the available tests like the Sargan and Hansen J-tests are only partial tests and depend on the assumption that at least one of the chosen instruments is exogenous (Clarke & Matta, 2018). Furthermore, an important practical problem is that the strength and the validity of an instrument seem to be at odds with each other, i.e., finding a stronger instrument entails that it may be related to the error term, violating the exclusion restriction condition (Semadeni et al., 2014). Finally, using IV methods when the exclusion restriction condition is not fulfilled may even produce more biased estimates than OLS, which is sometimes used as an easy argument for not making any attempt to address the endogeneity problem. Of course, this kind of reasoning does not make the endogeneity problem disappear (Larcker & Rusticus, 2010; Semadeni et al., 2014).

The objective of this chapter is to revisit the endogeneity problem creeping into the relationship between *family involvement* (through ownership, management and governance) and *firm performance*, based on new insights regarding the statistical implications of 'less-than-perfect' instrumental variables and the development of a number of workable solutions (Conley et al., 2012; Nevo & Rosen, 2012; Kiviet, 2020). Building on these innovative econometric developments, we aim to contribute to the empirical family involvement–performance

---

[1]    In the wording of Wooldridge (2016, p. 463): 'In the context of omitted variables, instrument exogeneity means that [the IV] should have no partial effect on y (after x and omitted variables have been controlled for), and [the IV] should be uncorrelated with the omitted variables.' Stated differently, the IV should not itself appear in (to be excluded from) the structural equation.

debate by providing family business scholars with a useful hands-on guide to possible ways for addressing the endogeneity problem.

In the remainder of this chapter, we first discuss the theoretical arguments for a potential endogeneity problem behind the family involvement–performance relationship. Indeed, endogeneity is not only a statistical problem but also a problem of theory (Gippel et al., 2015). Next, we provide an overview of the instrumental variables proposed in prior family business research, followed by a discussion of the theoretical arguments behind them. Finally, we discuss how the recent advances in the econometric literature on *imperfect instruments* can help family business researchers to mitigate any potential endogeneity concerns.

## IS ENDOGENEITY A REAL CONCERN IN THE FAMILY INVOLVEMENT–FIRM PERFORMANCE RELATIONSHIP?

The first step when discussing a potential endogeneity problem is asking the question whether there are theoretical reasons to assume that endogeneity is a concern in a specific sample (Bascle, 2008). A first argument that can help us in answering this question is that in samples in which ownership is not optimally chosen, i.e., when the costs of adjusting ownership are high so that owners are hesitant to change their ownership stake, reversed causality is less of a problem[2] (Nagar et al., 2011). Consequently, ownership turns out to be exogenously predetermined in such a sample. This condition applies very well in the context of privately held firms because there is no liquid market for the shares of private firms which makes it difficult and costly for share-holders to change their holdings (Nagar et al., 2011). Moreover, an additional argument could be made when considering the context of private family firms. Shareholders in private family firms generally have long time horizons, result-ing in patient financial capital (Daspit et al., Chapter 5 in this book), which is a different situation compared to the usual shorter-term investment strategy of investors in public companies. As such, private family firm owners usually

---

[2]    For example, an investor of a listed firm will be inclined to sell his shares (the optimal choice) when a firm is underperforming because of this weak performance. Such an investor can sell his shares easily without bearing much (transaction) costs. Thus, a researcher investigating the ownership–performance relationship faces the problem that performance may also determine ownership structure. However, this reversed relationship will be less of a problem in the case of family shareholders in private family firms who are not inclined to sell their shares because of weak perfor-mance as selling will entail substantial financial as well as emotional costs (the subop-timal choice).

do not have the willingness or ability to change their holdings, even when the family firm performs lower during a specific year or even a much longer time period. In addition, a similar argument applies to the position of the CEO or the board chair. Family owners in private family firms are less likely to replace the CEO when firm performance is bad. Furthermore, replacing a family CEO with a nonfamily CEO may also create high adjustment costs in terms of the loss of socioemotional wealth ('nonfinancial aspects of the firm that meet the family's affective needs') (Gomez-Mejia et al., 2007; Cruz et al., Chapter 13 in this book). Theoretical arguments alone can seldom be a convincing reason to assume that endogeneity is not a problem. Therefore, some preliminary empirical testing is warranted in helping to judge the merit of the theoretical arguments cited above. For example, researchers could test the ownership turnover or the family firms that raised new equity in the near past from existing or new owners (Nagar et al., 2011). For private family firms, it could be expected that this figure is very low, which can be interpreted as reverse causality is not a big problem.

## INSTRUMENTAL VARIABLE METHODS IN FAMILY BUSINESS RESEARCH

Even in the case that the theoretical arguments and preliminary testing suggest that reverse causality is not a problem, it cannot be taken as proof that the endogeneity problem is non-existent. Indeed, reverse causality can still be present in these databases. Moreover, there are also other situations in which the exogeneity requirement is violated such as omitted variable bias – e.g., due to unobserved *self-selection* processes – and measurement errors[3] (Bascle, 2008). Therefore, the logical next step to address the problem, as suggested in the econometric literature, is the use of IV methods of which Two-Stage Least Squares (2SLS) is most frequently used (Murray, 2006). In contrast to conventional OLS methods, IV estimation methods yield consistent estimates under endogeneity. In other words, the IV estimator converges in probability to the true value of the parameter when the sample is sufficiently large.

Ideally, IVs should fulfill three essential conditions: (1) they are excluded from the original (structural) equation, (2) they are correlated with the suspicious (endogenous) explanatory X-variable, and (3) they are uncorrelated with the error term in the structural equation (Murray, 2006). The 'ideal instrument' is said to be 'the result of a "natural experiment" event that changes the

---

[3]    In this chapter, our focus is on endogeneity resulting from reserve causality and omitted variable bias in family business research. For a further discussion on endogeneity resulting from measurement error, we refer to the discussion in Bascle (2008).

endogenous regressors, but leaves the other aspects of the economic system unaffected' (Larcker & Rusticus, 2010, p. 197) or a biological event (Roberts & Whited, 2013). When the researcher has found IVs that fulfill the three conditions, a first stage (reduced-form) regression can be estimated with OLS in which the IVs together with the non-suspect X-variables from the original equation are used as explanatory variables for the troublesome endogenous X-variable. Armed with the fitted values of the endogenous X-variable obtained from the first stage regression, the researcher can estimate a second stage regression, which is similar to the original equation with one crucial difference. Restated, the actual values of the endogenous variable will be replaced by the fitted values from the first stage regression. An important point of attention when looking for instruments is the identification of the equation, i.e., the number of instruments needs to be at least the same as the number of endogenous explanatory variables (Murray, 2006). Note that although IVs that are truly exogenous can deliver consistent estimates, they are not efficient (i.e., larger standard errors than OLS). Therefore, a note of caution is warranted. Trying to remedy endogeneity with IV methods when it is not present will lead to less efficient estimates (Semadeni et al., 2014). Therefore, it is important to test whether the suspicious independent variable is indeed endogenous. Commonly used tests are the Hausman or Durbin–Wu–Hausman tests. These tests will identify the existence of an endogeneity problem and the appropriateness of OLS versus IV under the assumption that at least one of the instruments is valid. Testing the appropriateness of instruments is thus a first essential step before executing the Hausman test (Larcker & Rusticus, 2010).

**The Exclusion Restriction: on the Validity of Instrumental Variables**

When an IV is correlated with the error term, it does not pass the exclusion restriction requirement and the IV method will deliver inconsistent and biased estimators (Larcker & Rusticus, 2010). The econometric literature recommends researchers to perform two steps to establish an instrument's validity: (1) developing a theoretical argument in support of the validity and (2) executing formal validity tests.

Building an argument supporting an instrument's validity should ideally rely on economic theory (Larcker & Rusticus, 2010). An intuitive argument can be very helpful, however, as long as it is supplemented with checks on the available data (Murray, 2006). For instance, researchers could utilize a number of falsification tests to see whether alternative hypotheses regarding the endogeneity problem can be excluded (Roberts & Whited, 2013) or whether potential reasons of endogeneity of the instrument can be anticipated (Larcker & Rusticus, 2010). To get a better insight into the theoretical arguments in support of the instruments' validity in the family business field, we executed a literature review on influential papers investigating the relationship between family involvement in management, ownership and governance and firm performance that addressed the endogeneity problem with IV techniques.[4] We selected 15 relevant papers, which are listed in Table 17.1, and added some methodological key characteristics. The last two columns of Table 17.1 show the instruments that were used and indicate whether a theoretical argument was developed for an instrument's validity or not. Curiously, from the 15 papers included in Table 17.1, only six provide a well-developed argument for their instruments' validity. The other papers focused more on the execution of formal testing of the validity, which we will discuss later in this section.

Of all the papers included in Table 17.1, the paper of Bennedsen et al. (2007) can be considered an exemplary illustration of an intuitive argument concerning the validity of an IV in the family business literature. In their seminal paper on the performance consequences of a family firm succession by a nonfamily versus family CEO, Bennedsen et al. (2007) face the difficult challenge of finding an appropriate IV, which should be a randomly assigned family trait that is related to the CEO succession decision but not with firm performance. Indeed, the choice between a family CEO and a nonfamily CEO as successor may be endogenous to firm performance. Kahn and Whited (2018, p. 5) describe this identification problem as follows: 'poor performance may force the family to choose an outside CEO instead of a relative, and good performance may make a family insouciant about the specter of an incompetent family CEO'. Consequently, the beta coefficient of the suspicious succession variable in the model is a function of agency costs as well as unobserved economic variables (Kahn & Whited, 2018); this raises the issue of endogeneity in the model. To address the problem, Bennedsen et al. (2007) considered family size, marital history, death of departing CEOs around succession and the gender of the first-born child of the departing CEO as potential instruments for the CEO succession decision. The first three candidate IVs seem to be related with the CEO succession decision but unfortunately, also with economic incentives; this violates the exclusion restriction condition. Nonetheless, Bennedsen et al. (2007) use the third variable as an alternative IV to establish robustness of their results. The fourth candidate IV, gender of the first-born child, is a type of biological event that is likely to be randomly assigned and thus intuitively not related with firm performance (Bennedsen et al., 2007; Roberts & Whited, 2013). As an informal check, they found out that 'profitability, age, and size do not differ statistically as a function of the gender

---

[4] We do not attempt to provide a comprehensive overview of studies in this field. Our focus is restricted to the (in our opinion) most prominent seminal and exemplary studies.

*Table 17.1* Overview of former empirical analyses of the relationship between family firm ownership, management and governance and firm performance

| Paper | Sample | Performance measure | Methodology | Key results | Instruments | Theoretical justification of instruments |
|-------|--------|--------------------|-------------|-------------|-------------|------------------------------------------|
| Panel A: Papers examining relationship between family ownership and firm performance | | | | | | |
| Anderson and Reeb (2003) | S&P 500 nonfinancial firms (2,713 firm-year observations), 1992 to 1999 | Tobin's Q, ROA | IV-2SLS | Family firms perform better than nonfamily firms. The relation between family holdings and firm performance is nonlinear and that when family members serve as CEO, performance is better than with outside CEOs | (a) Natural log of total assets (b) Square of the natural log of total assets (c) Monthly stock return volatility | No |
| Andres (2008) | 275 German listed companies (1,701 firm-year observations), 1998 to 2004 | Tobin's Q, ROA | Linear IV regressions | Family ownership is related to superior firm performance only under certain conditions | Ownership variables are instrumented by their lagged values | No |
| Barontini and Caprio (2006) | 675 publicly listed firms in 11 continental European countries, 1999 to 2001 | Tobin's Q, ROA | Linear IV regressions | Valuation and operating performance are significantly higher in founder-controlled corporations and in corporations controlled by descendants who sit on the board as non-executive directors | (a) Alpha of the ordinary share (b) Share volatility (i.e., stock return variance) (c) Log of the age of the corporation | No |

| Paper | Sample | Performance measure | Methodology | Key results | Instruments | Theoretical justification of instruments |
|-------|--------|---------------------|-------------|-------------|-------------|------------------------------------------|
| Block et al. (2011) | Standard & Poor's 500 firms (3,058 firm-year observations), 1994 to 2003 | Market-to-book-value | Bayesian | Family ownership has a positive effect on performance whereas family management has a neutral effect on performance | An instrument using log assets, market risk, debt/equity and industry variables to predict the family and founder variables | No |
| Chu (2009) | 639 nonfinancial firms in Taiwan, 2002 to 2006 | Tobin's Q, ROA | IV-2SLS | Founding-family ownership is positively associated with firm performance | (a) Natural log of total sales (b) 2-year lagged values of family ownership | No |
| Maury (2006) | 1,675 nonfinancial Western European firms, 1996 to 1999 | Tobin's Q, ROA, ROE | Heckman's (1979) two-step procedure | Active family control is associated with higher profitability compared to nonfamily firms, whereas passive family control does not affect profitability | The instruments for the family firm dummy are: Log of equity, the logarithm of market value of equity (USD); $STD_a$, the standard deviation of the 5-year net income / total assets (or available years); $STD_a$ dummy variable equal to 1 if data were missing to compute the risk measure; the relevant performance variable (Tobin's Q or ROA); and all other control variables that enter the second stage, excluding industry dummies that perfectly predict family firms | No |
| Villalonga and Amit (2006) | 508 Fortune 500 listed firms (2,808 firm-year observations), 1994 to 2000 | Tobin's Q | Heckman's (1979) two-step procedure | Family ownership creates value only when the founder serves as CEO of the family firm or as Chairman with a hired CEO | (a) Idiosyncratic risk (b) Lagged Tobin's Q | Yes |

Panel B: Papers examining relationship between family management and governance and firm performance

| Paper | Sample | Performance measure | Methodology | Key results | Instruments | Theoretical justification of instruments |
|---|---|---|---|---|---|---|
| Adams et al. (2009) | 321 Fortune 500 firms (2,128 firm-year observations), 1992 to 1999 | Tobin's Q, ROA | IV-2SLS | After instrumenting for founder-CEO status, they identify a positive causal effect of founder-CEOs on firm performance which is quantitatively larger than the effect estimated through standard OLS regressions | (a) Dummy variable that takes the value of 1 if the founder died before the start of our sample period and zero otherwise (b) Number of founders of each firm | Yes |
| Amore et al. (2014) | 2,400 Italian firms per year (10,154 firm-year observations), 2000 to 2010 | ROA | Propensity score matching and 2SLS | Female interactions improve the profitability of family firms | (a) Gender composition of the pool of potential family heirs (dummy equal to 1 if the CEO has a female child) (b) Geographic variations in gender roles (dummy equal to 1 if the firm is located in northern Italy) | Yes |
| Anderson and Reeb (2004) | 403 Standard & Poor's 500 firms (2,686 firm-year observations), 1992 to 1999 | Tobin's Q | Simultaneous equation model | The most valuable public firms are those in which independent directors balance family board representation. In contrast, in firms with continued founding-family ownership and relatively few independent directors, firm performance is significantly worse than in nonfamily firms | Board independence is modeled as a function of firm age, officer and director ownership (minus family ownership), institutional investors, firm size, prior period performance, growth opportunities, and industry affiliation | No |

| Paper | Sample | Performance measure | Methodology | Key results | Instruments | Theoretical justification of instruments |
|---|---|---|---|---|---|---|
| Bennedsen et al. (2007) | 5,334 successions in Denmark, 1994 to 2002 | Industry-adjusted Operating ROA | IV-2SLS | Family successions are negatively correlated with firm performance around CEO successions | (a) Gender of the first-born child of a departing CEO<br>(b) Death of departing chief executive around succession | Yes |
| Bennedsen et al. (2008) | 7,496 Danish closely held firms, 1990 | ROA | IV-2SLS | Board size negatively impacts firm performance | (a) Family size: number of children of the CEO<br>(b) Number of founders' children | Yes |
| Bohren et al. (2019) | About 70,000 private Norwegian family firms (410,000 firm-year observations), 2000 to 2013 | Average return on assets over the past 3 years | IV-2SLS | The positive effect of performance on (family) participation is twice as strong as the positive effect of participation on performance. The endogeneity of participation should therefore be carefully accounted for when analyzing the effect of family governance on the family firm's behavior | Instruments for performance:<br>(a) Lagged growth in value added<br>(b) Employment in the county where the firm is headquartered<br>Instrument for participation:<br>Size of the controlling family | Yes |

| Paper | Sample | Performance measure | Methodology | Key results | Instruments | Theoretical justification of instruments |
|---|---|---|---|---|---|---|
| Miller et al. (2007) | 896 Fortune 1000 firms, 1996 to 2000 | Tobin's Q | Heckman's (1979) two-step procedure | Fortune 1000 firms that include relatives as owners or managers never outperform in market valuation, even during the first generation. Only businesses with a lone founder outperform | First stage model includes variables which instrument for family or lone founder status: cash holdings; sales growth; director tenure; and unsystematic risk, plus all control variables of the second stage | No |
| Miller and Le Breton-Miller (2011) | 263 Fortune 1000 family firms, 1996 to 2000 | Tobin's Q, total shareholder returns | IV-2SLS | Firms with lone founder owners and CEO will outperform post-founder family owner and CEO's and family firm founders | Estimated predicted values by regressing Entrepreneurial Orientation onto lagged values for sales growth, firm age, firm size, industry and beta. Then used these predicted values in a second stage predicting performance | No |

of the first child' (Bennedsen et al., 2007, p. 650). Although these kinds of informal checks cannot be considered as a formal validity test, the combination of the argument (biological event) and informal checks provide a strong case for the plausibility of 'gender of first-born child' as IV for CEO succession decisions (Roberts & Whited, 2013). Nevertheless, even in this exemplary case, it can be argued that the biological event is not fully exogenous as it builds on the assumption that female CEOs do not differ from male CEOs (Kahn & Whited, 2018) which can be questioned in some circumstances. Suppose that families with a very talented eldest daughter will still choose the daughter as the successor, then family CEO succession may enhance firm performance while in boy-first families CEO succession may deteriorate firm performance which may cause the IV estimator to overstate the negative effect (Roberts & Whited, 2013). In addition, Kahn and Whited (2018, p. 6) make the important observation that the validity of the gender variable as an instrument depends on the assumption that family firms 'are somewhat sexist' and that 'sexism affects firm performance only through the choice of a family CEO'. Again, the validity of the instrument can be questioned when boys and girls are raised differently with a different career perspective in mind (e.g., boys as next leaders of the family firm, girls for other careers outside the family firm). These additional theoretical reflections show that it is almost impossible to find 100 percent exogenous instruments; this highlights again the importance of additional checks on the data to address these kinds of theoretical counter-arguments (Roberts & Whited, 2013). The paper by Bennedsen et al. (2007) provides several interesting examples of such additional checks.

In their search for instruments, researchers are often inclined to use lagged endogenous variables as instruments as they are easily available and have a strong relation with the endogenous variable; this makes them potential IV candidates to consider. However, there is much controversy over this type of instrument choice in the econometric literature. An implicit assumption underlying such a choice is that the lagged endogenous variable only affects the dependent variable through its effect on the endogenous regressor. Accordingly, the lagged endogenous variable is assumed to comprise both an *exogenous* part that persists over time and an *endogenous* part that will disappear over time (Larcker & Rusticus, 2010). This assumption is hard to justify, however, since it still cannot eliminate the possibility that the instrument is at least partly endogenous (Roberts & Whited, 2013). Moreover, Reed (2015) shows that the use of lagged endogenous variables is an effective strategy only when the lagged values do not belong to the structural equation and have a sufficiently high correlation with the suspect endogenous independent variable.

Besides the development of a sound theoretical argument, formal validity tests play an essential role in establishing an instrument's validity and accordingly, the credibility of a study's findings. Several formal tests on the exogeneity condition (also called the 'orthogonality condition') are available of which the Sargan, Hansen's J-statistic and Basman are the most commonly used (Kiviet, 2020). These tests require that more instrumental variables are available than endogenous regressors and are often labeled as tests of 'over-identifying restrictions'. A crucial assumption of these tests is that at least one instrument is exogenous from a theoretical point of view, which again points to the importance of the development of a theoretical argument that the IV is exogenous (Bascle, 2008). Therefore, researchers should avoid that the instruments share a common theoretical rationale because it will make *all* instruments questionable when one instrument is invalid (Murray, 2006). Accordingly, the results of exogeneity tests like the Sargan test will be invalid when this happens. A potential solution for this problem is the difference-in-Sargan test which builds further on the Sargan and Hansen J-statistic. This test can be used when the researcher has at least two more IVs than endogenous regressors available (Bascle, 2008). The difference-in-Sargan test examines the exogeneity of instruments building on the other instruments under the assumption that the other instruments are exogenous. Nevertheless, this test is still no waterproof solution for identifying exclusion restrictions. Therefore, Murray (2006) suggests to test different *alternative* instruments in different IV estimations instead of putting all IVs in one single test. When all the exogeneity tests with different IVs show similar estimates, it will increase the credibility of the estimates. This advice has been echoed by Semadeni et al. (2014) who suggest to identify multiple instruments as they give the researcher more flexibility to test and address the endogeneity problem. When there is only one instrument, the validity of the instrument will depend on the strength of the theoretical argument.

**On the Implications of Semi-endogenous Instruments and New Solutions**

The discussion above has clearly demonstrated that finding and defending a zero-correlation *'perfectly exogenous'* IV with the unobserved error term in the structural equation ('validity') is far from straightforward. On top of that, the strong assumption of validity in an IV setting is untestable. This raises the obvious question of what the implications are of using so-called *'semi-endogenous'* (Larcker & Rusticus, 2010), *'partly exogenous'* (Bennedsen et al., 2007) or *'imperfect'* (Nevo & Rosen, 2012) instruments.

The idea of allowing for some degree of invalidity of the IVs for identification is not a new one, though. Two methodologies have been developed already quite a few years ago – one by Conley et al. (2012) and another by Nevo and Rosen (2012) – for inference with IVs that (potentially) violate the typical IV validity condition. Both methods are designed to estimate bounds for the coefficient on the endogenous regressor of interest with instruments that do not necessarily have zero correlation with the unobserved error term (thus, allowing for violations of the exogeneity restriction).

The inference procedure introduced by Conley et al. (2012) – under the heading '*relaxing the exclusion restriction*' – involves using some sort of information about the extent of deviations from the exact exclusion restriction, where the IVs need only be *plausibly exogenous*. More precisely, assumptions can be made regarding the range of the non-zero (positive or negative) values that the coefficient on the instrument ($\gamma$) in the structural equation can take. Although this method provides set identification rather than point identification, it allows researchers to make inferences 'within-constraints' robust to the violation of exogeneity and, hence, to enhance the credibility of their IV-based results. Conversely, the inference method developed by Nevo and Rosen (2012) – under the heading '*relaxing IV correlation*' – is based on the use of *imperfect IVs*, which is capable of providing bounds on the possible values of the coefficient on the endogenous regressor under two weaker-than-traditional assumptions. The first assumption (Assumption 3 in their paper) asserts that the (potentially) endogenous variable $X$ and the instrument $Z$ are *correlated in the same direction* with the unobserved error term $u$ in the structural equation ($\rho_{Xu}\rho_{Zu} \geq 0$), while the second (Assumption 4 in their paper) adds the condition that the instrument $Z$ is *less endogenous* than $X$ ($|\rho_{Zu}| \leq |\rho_{Xu}|$). The syntaxes of the corresponding Stata commands, *plausexog* and *imperfectiv*, respectively, have been described in Clarke and Matta (2018).

In closing, we should also mention the method developed by Kiviet (2020) – under the heading '*instrument-free kinky least-squares inference*', which provides an attractive alternative to the identification approaches that may cause imprecise inference due to possibly weak or invalid instruments. The purpose of this new procedure is to construct *kinky* least-squares (KLS) confidence bands – by confining the admissible correlation of the endogenous regressor with the error term within plausible bounds – which are expected to be more informative (providing us with narrower confidence intervals) than those obtained from IV estimation, especially in the case of weak instruments. Moreover, KLS inference avoids the problems associated with the precarious search for strong and valid instruments. Finally, the KLS method facilitates a sensitivity analysis for standard IV inference, as it enables the testing of any potential exclusion restrictions. In effect, it is sensible to consider the instrument-free KLS approach as a complement (rather than a substitute) to the procedures proposed by Conley et al. (2012) and Nevo and Rosen (2012), which both rely on loosening the (often incredible) full exogeneity assumption underlying traditional IV estimations. The syntax of the corresponding Stata command *kinkyreg* has been described in Kripfganz and Kiviet (2021).

### The Need for Strong Instruments: on the Relevant Condition of Instrumental Variables

IV estimators such as 2SLS can be seriously biased in finite samples (even in large samples) when the instruments are weak. In addition, (extremely) weak instruments may yield large standard errors. These two problems can make standard inference instruments such as t-statistics misleading (Larcker & Rusticus, 2010). In practice, researchers often are confronted with the weak instrument problem as instruments that fulfill the exclusion restriction ('valid') condition are usually found to be weak.

Therefore, it is recommended to calculate diagnostics on the strength of the instruments (i.e., the 'relevance' condition) using an F-test on the joint signifi-cance of the instruments in the first stage regression. Several thresholds for the required size of the F-statistic have been developed by Stock and Yogo (2005). What is important to note is that the critical threshold increases by the number of instruments. Adding more low-quality instruments will thus increase the likelihood that the null hypotheses of weak instruments cannot be rejected and that inference is potentially problematic (Larcker & Rusticus, 2010).

Several alternative IV methods have been proposed to cope with the weak instruments problem. For example, Moreira's Conditional Likelihood Ratio (CLR) and Wald have been recommended as good choices to tackle the weak instruments problem as it allows to draw correct inference based on the con-ditional distribution of nonpivotal statistics which make them independent of the instruments' strength (Bascle, 2008; Larcker & Rusticus, 2010). The Stata syntax for this method is available (*'condivreg'*, Moreira & Poi, 2001).

Another useful estimation strategy is Limited Information Maximum Likelihood (LIML). The weak instrument bias of LIML will be less than 2SLS but at the cost of larger variance (Bascle, 2008). An alternative to this method is a modified LIML version, known as Fuller's LIML. This estimation method is more robust to weak instrument bias than 2SLS and performs better when the researcher has many weak instruments (Bascle, 2008). These LIML methods are standard available in Stata.

## CONCLUSIONS

One of the predominant themes in the family business literature is the relation-ship between family involvement in ownership management and governance and firm performance. Empirical research in this field is typically plagued by tricky endogeneity problems. From a statistical point of view, endogeneity is a major concern as it violates the central Ordinary Least Squares assumption that the regressor is uncorrelated with the error term, giving rise to inconsistent and biased estimates (Bascle, 2008).

A common remedy for this problem is the use of IV techniques. In the past, several papers discussed this problem and provided interesting and practical usable roadmaps for an IV approach (see, for example, Table 1 in Bascle, 2008, as well as Table 4 in Larcker & Rusticus, 2010). However, finding suitable IVs that satisfy the conditions of 'validity' and 'relevance' is a real challenge. Therefore, the aim of this study was to provide family business scholars with a structured discussion of the problem and to provide several useful ways for identification based on state-of-the-art econometric research dealing with 'imperfect' and/or 'weak' instruments. Our discussion constitutes an important complement to the existing roadmaps for addressing endogeneity problems. First, we surveyed common IVs used in the 'family involvement–performance' literature, which can be viewed as interesting IV candidates for future studies, even when they do not always fulfill strict exogeneity conditions. Next, we discussed several potential econometric remedies for partially valid – i.e., 'imperfect' – and weak instruments. Based on this review, our main conclusion is that – in spite of the lack of perfect ways of solving endogeneity problems in practice – recently developed tools in applied econometrics for dealing with 'imperfect' and 'weak' instruments can assist family-business researchers in underscoring the reliability of their empirical findings.

## REFERENCES

Adams, R., Almeida, H., & Ferreira, D. (2009). Understanding the relationship between founder-CEOs and firm performance. *Journal of Empirical Finance, 16*(1), 136–150.

Amore, M.D., Garofalo, O., & Minichilli, A. (2014). Gender interactions within the family firm. *Management Science, 60*(5), 1083–1097.

Anderson, R.C., & Reeb, D.M. (2003). Founding-family ownership and firm performance: Evidence from the S&P 500. *The Journal of Finance, 58*(3), 1301–1328.

Anderson, R.C., & Reeb, D.M. (2004). Board composition: Balancing family influence in S&P 500 firms. *Administrative Science Quarterly, 49*(2), 209–237.

Andres, C. (2008). Large shareholders and firm performance: An empirical examination of founding-family ownership. *Journal of Corporate Finance, 14*(4), 431–445.

Barontini, R., & Caprio, L. (2006). The effect of family control on firm value and performance: Evidence from continental Europe. *European Financial Management, 12*(5), 689–723.

Bascle, G. (2008). Controlling for endogeneity with instrumental variables in strategic management research. *Strategic Organization, 6*(3), 285–327.

Bennedsen, M., Kongsted, H.C., & Nielsen, K.M. (2008). The causal effect of board size in the performance of small and medium-sized firms. *Journal of Banking & Finance, 32*(6), 1098–1109.

Bennedsen, M., Nielsen, K.M., Pérez-González, F., & Wolfenzon, D. (2007). Inside the family firm: The role of families in succession decisions and performance. *The Quarterly Journal of Economics, 122*(2), 647–691.

Berle, A., & Means, G. (1932). *The Modern Corporation and Private Property*. New York: Macmillan.

Block, J.H., Jaskiewicz, P., & Miller, D. (2011). Ownership versus management effects on performance in family and founder companies: A Bayesian reconciliation. *Journal of Family Business Strategy*, *2*(4), 232–245.

Bohren, O., Stacescu, B., Almli, L., & Sondergaard, K.L. (2019). When does the family govern the family firm? *Journal of Financial and Quantitative Analysis*, *54*(5), 2085–2117.

Chu, W. (2009). The influence of family ownership on SME performance: Evidence from public firms in Taiwan. *Small Business Economics*, *33*(3), 353–373.

Clarke, D., & Matta, B. (2018). Practical considerations for questionable IVs. *The Stata Journal*, *18*(3), 663–691.

Conley, T.G., Hansen, C.B., & Rossi, P.E. (2012). Plausibly exogenous. *The Review of Economics and Statistics*, *94*(1), 260–272.

Gippel, J., Smith, T., & Zhu, Y. (2015). Endogeneity in accounting and finance research: Natural experiments as a state-of-the-art solution. *ABACUS*, *51*(2), 143–168.

Gomez-Mejia, L.R., Haynes, K.T., Nuñez-Nickel, M., Jacobson, K.J.L., & Moyano-Fuentes, J. (2007). Socioemotional wealth and business risks in family-controlled firms: Evidence from Spanish olive oil mills, *Administrative Science Quarterly*, *52*(1), 106–137.

Heckman, J.J. (1979). Sample selection bias as a specification error. *Econometrica: Journal of the Econometric Society*, *47*(1), 153–161.

Kahn, R., & Whited, T. (2018), Identification is not causality, and vice versa. *Review of Corporate Finance Studies*, *7*(1), 1–21.

Kiviet, J.F. (2020). Testing the impossible: Identifying exclusion restrictions. *Journal of Econometrics*, *218*(2), 294–316.

Kripfganz, S., & Kiviet, J. (2021). kinkyreg: Instrument-free inference for linear regression models with endogenous regressors. *The Stata Journal*, *21*(3), 772–813.

Larcker, D., & Rusticus, T. (2010). On the use of instrumental variables in accounting research. *Journal of Accounting and Economics*, *49*, 186–205.

Maury, B. (2006). Family ownership and firm performance: Empirical evidence from Western European corporations. *Journal of Corporate Finance*, *12*(2), 321–341.

Miller, D., & Le Breton-Miller, I. (2011). Governance, social identity, and entrepreneurial orientation in closely held public companies. *Entrepreneurship Theory and Practice*, *35*(5), 1051–1076.

Miller, D., Le Breton-Miller, I., Lester, R.H., & Cannella Jr, A.A. (2007). Are family firms really superior performers? *Journal of Corporate Finance*, *13*(5), 829–858.

Moreira, M., & Poi, B. (2001). Implementing conditional tests with correct size in the simultaneous equations model. *The Stata Journal*, *1*(1), 1–15.

Murray, M. (2006). Avoiding invalid instruments and coping with weak instruments. *Journal of Economic Perspectives*, *20*(4), 111–132.

Nagar, V., Petroni, K., & Wolfenzon, D. (2011). Governance problems in close corporations. *Journal of Financial and Quantitative Analysis*, *46*(4), 943–966.

Nevo, A., & Rosen, A. (2012). Identification with imperfect instruments. *The Review of Economics and Statistics*, *94*(3), 659–671.

Reed, W. (2015). On the practice of lagging variables to avoid simultaneity. *Oxford Bulletin of Economics and Statistics*, *77*(6), 897–905.

Roberts, M., & Whited, T. (2013). Endogeneity in empirical corporate finance. In Constantinides, G.M., Harris, M., & Stulz, R.M. (Eds.), *Handbook of the Economics of Finance* (Vol. 2, pp. 493–572). Amsterdam: North Holland.

Semadeni, M., Withers, M., & Certo, T. (2014). The perils of endogeneity and instrumental variables in strategy research: Understanding through simulations. *Strategic Management Journal, 35,* 1070–1079.

Stock, J. & Yogo, M. (2005). Testing for weak instruments in linear IV regression. In: Andrews, D.W.K., & Stock, J. (Eds.), *Identification and Inference for Econometric Models* (pp. 80–108). New York: Cambridge University Press.

Villalonga, B., & Amit, R. (2006). How do family ownership, control and management affect firm value? *Journal of Financial Economics, 80*(2), 385–417.

Wooldridge, J.M. (2016). *Introductory Econometrics: A Modern Approach* (6th edn). Boston, MA: Cengage Learning.

# Index

Printed and bound by CPI Group (UK) Ltd, Croydon, CR0 4YY

16/04/2025

14658491-0003